Corporate Trust

A Partner in Finance

Update

Jeff
I wish you every success
in Corporate Trust

Jeff Powell

Corporate Trust

A Partner in Finance

Update

Jeffrey J. Powell

HudsonRiver**Publishing**.com

ISBN 10: 0-9791273-4-3

ISBN 13: 978-0-9791273-4-2

Printed in the United States of America

10 9 8 7 6 5 4 3 2 1

~ Table of Contents ~

Exhibits:

~ Introduction~

This book is for all the misunderstood Corporate Trustees (also referred to as indenture Trustees or Trustees) and those who seek to understand and appreciate us. My forty-two years in the business of being a Corporate Trustee have shown me both the critical importance we play in the securities markets as well as how little is truly known about our role and responsibilities. I have spent my life educating Corporate Trust professionals, bank managers, underwriters, issuers, regulators, and anyone who would listen about what we really do. This book is my attempt to achieve that goal of helping everyone to understand us as true partners in the securities markets. As such, this book represents only my opinions and not those of any organization or individual.

I have written this book in a more informal, conversational style from my personal perspective. My purpose is to make the chapters more real and easily readable by avoiding the temptation to write in a more technical, legal manner. This is in spite of the fact that the Corporate Trust business is very much a technical, legal business. I leave that treatise to others. My objective is to talk to you as I have always done in training thousands of professionals over the course of my career. My purpose is to bring this meaningful business to life in an understandable way. I want you to leave this book with a true understanding of the roles, responsibilities, and risks that challenge Corporate Trustees, all the while remembering the key principle that we Trustees are there to facilitate the working of the bond issue to a successful conclusion—as a true partner in finance.

The book includes fourteen chapters. Each chapter deals with a specific aspect of the Corporate Trustee's responsibilities. I begin each chapter with a brief story from my personal experience to focus attention on the contents of the chapter. Examples and illustrations will be used throughout. The simple, no-frills artwork and illustrations embedded within the book are included to convey a point for further understanding of a particular concept. A brief summary of the key points of the chapter will appear at the chapter's end to reinforce learning. I also include one real-life case study to make you think. The exhibits (A-G) are at the end of the book and include:

A. Trust Indenture Act of 1939: Summary of Key Sections
B. Corporate Trust: A Brief Description
C. How to Successfully Manage Risk in Corporate Trust: Best Practices
D. Products and Bond Issue Descriptions for Municipal Bonds
E. SEC Transfer Agent Rules
F. Types of Asset-backed Securities
G. Typical Asset-backed Bond Issue

The Trust Indenture Act of 1939 as Amended is the cornerstone legislative act defining what the Corporate Trustee is required to do and is *the* standard. I have provided a brief summary of the more critical sections of this standard. I have also included a brief description of Corporate Trust, distilled down to a few short phrases for anyone to understand. The other exhibits are self-explanatory.

My hope is that my readers will become educated, informed, and engaged with regard to this fascinating business that has been the life's work of many Corporate Trust professionals all over the world. For many Corporate Trust professionals, including myself, it is a business we become drawn to. We do not want to leave this unique business of service as a Corporate Trustee. The main reason I have stayed is because of the exciting challenge of learning new aspects of the business. Corporate Trust follows the developments in the securities markets, which means constant change with new securities structures and market demands. Trustees are facilitators of the financings and work as partners with a variety of other securities professionals. I also believe we help produce tangible benefits for the business and government entities that are raising capital to build or produce products and services. It is a business that constantly keeps your interest, one in which you never stop learning. It truly grows on you.

I must express my sincere appreciation to many people I have known in this business. The list is too long to recount of colleagues, coworkers, and students I have known, but here are a few I want to mention: Bill Barett, Harold Kaplan, Mark Hebbeln, Steve Wagner, Kristin Going, Marla Cohen, Brian Calder, Terry McRoberts, Dennis Egan, Karen Atkinson, Missy Jennings, Nancy Duke, Molly Carlson, Tony Guthrie, Agatha Wade, David Leverich, Gordon Glaza, Ann Friedman, Brian Hunter, Dorothy Friedlander, Dave Butler, Leland Hansen, Jack Kruger, Donald Alvin, John Mull, Dennis McDonald, Troy Kilpatrick, Carmela Ehret, Jenni Minardi, Doc Walter, Sheri Gillund, Susan Danner, Bruce Wandersee, Cris Naser, Sally Miller, David Ursa, Kathleen Ursa, Jane Pope, Holly Pattison, Lori Donahue, George Kubin, Damien Sauter, Elisa Monk, Martin Reeves, Sally Gilding, Angeline Garvey, Lynne Malina, Lee Cobb, Debbie Schwaub, Tracy Montone, Cris Hilcoat, James Spiotto, Bob Landau, Gary Vaughn, David Co, Rick Schall, Todd Duncan, Connie Marmet, Rafaat Sarkis, John Finley, Larry Kusch, Tabor Ban, Janet Choi, Bill Ekey, Brian Mabuse, Mike Gorlicki, Jack Beeson, Jim DellaSalla, Kevin Kirby, Kevin Dobrava, Brent Varzaly, Kris Johnson, Kimberlee Wilson, Linda Wilder, Stephanie Wickouski, and many others.

Thank you all for your support and friendship over the years. I'd also like to extend a special thanks to Daniel Northrop of Drinker Biddle for his editorial support.

And to my wife, Judy, and daughters, Kristen and Denise, and son-in-laws, Ryan and Uriah, who finally know what I do for a living. Without their help and support, this book would not be possible.

~ Chapter 1 ~

The Role of the Trustee

Paris, France—1989

It's evening after a long day of client calls. I am sitting in a hotel room in Paris, the City of Light, where I have come to prospect for new business for Corporate Trust. We called on several major French companies today, where I learned that arguing with your clients is the way to do business (they appear to like it!). In the various countries where I have done business, cultural differences have certainly kept me on my toes. And while what goes on during my interactions with people of these eclectic cities is often most notable, I notice the effects of what I do in Corporate Trust everywhere—even in a hotel room that could be anywhere.

I turn on the television, and after flipping through several channels in French, I finally settle on CNN, the only channel in English. I take interest in a news story that is just unfolding about an elderly couple. They are in a modestly furnished home, and their clothing and surroundings indicate they are not rich. They appear to be ordinary people who have worked hard all their lives and are living out their retirement in a quiet, unassuming fashion.

They are handed a check representing recovery of their investment in the infamous Lincoln Savings and Loan debacle, which was one of the thousand financial institutions that collapsed in an implosion of reckless investments during the 1980s and '90s. As the smiling couple looks at the check, there is an expression of both joy and relief. The newscaster is explaining that these two people are bondholders in Lincoln Savings and Loan. The check represents a good part of their retirement savings they had worked so hard for. As they hold up the check to the camera, I notice in large print the words "Bank of America as Trustee."

That is when it really hits me. I sit frozen in place. After seventeen years in the Corporate Trust business, I truly understand for the first time the real purpose of the Trustee. Trustees are here to bring a smile of relief to those investors who count on them to maximize their recovery in troubled times. It suddenly becomes personal to me. No matter where I go in this business, or whom I work for, I will never forget the picture of this elderly couple smiling for the camera and holding the check with the words "as Trustee" on it. . .

Chapter Objective

This introductory chapter will discuss the duties and responsibilities of the Corporate Trustee, which I will refer to throughout the book as "Trustee." Topics include:

    I.   The Role of the Trustee: A Brief History and Evolution

    II.   What Is a Trustee, and What Does a Trustee Do?

    III.   The Misunderstood Role of the Trustee

The case study at the end of the chapter will provide a scenario related to a municipal bond issue and give readers an opportunity to determine the Trustee's role within that particular bond issue.

I. The Role of the Trustee: A Brief History and Evolution

When the first Trustee crawled out of the primeval swamp and looked around, life in the financial services industry was very different. In truth, the first Trustees were individuals, appointed to oversee the workings of railroad bond issues in the early 1800s. The railroads required large amounts of capital for expansion and turned to issuing bonds. Investors became more comfortable having a professional, impartial third party to monitor the provisions of the bond issue contracts and look after their interests. Since this was long before the formal development of corporations, the Trustee was usually a well-respected individual.

There were four problems with this relationship:

- The Trustee had very limited powers to act and limited responsibilities.
- Individuals died leaving no one to assume the role of the Trustee.
- There were no formal standards of conduct for Trustees to follow either by law or by custom and practice.

- Since there were no requirements to appoint a Trustee on a bond issue, it was common for the bond issues most in need of a Trustee to not have one.

The result was that there was really no one to provide the service needed for issuers and the protection for the bondholders.

This unsatisfactory situation persisted until the crisis of the Great Depression, which began in 1929. By then, municipalities and corporations commonly used bond issues to finance their capital needs. Many corporate issues went into default during the economic disaster that followed. To rescue the financial system in the United States, Congress enacted the basic securities laws—the Securities Act of 1933 and the Securities Exchange Act of 1934.

To address the need for bondholder protection, Congress enacted the Trust Indenture Act of 1939 (TIA) as an amendment to the Securities Act of 1933. The TIA established the formal role of the Trustee covering public, corporate debt. Now there was a federal law that established definitive standards for a Trustee. This law required the appointment of a Trustee for public, corporate debt, which were the issues most at risk of default during the Great Depression. Now the duties and responsibilities of Trustees were clearly defined for both pre-default and post-default roles. Equally important, the TIA created the authority for the Trustee to carry out his/her duties. As defined by the TIA, the Trustee had to be a bank—a professional organization—to provide ongoing continuity of service for the life of the bond issue.

From that time forward to the present day, the concept of the Trustee for bond financings has evolved and strengthened. Many different bond issues, which were not required to have a Trustee under the TIA, such as municipal bonds and privately placed bonds, have commonly appointed Trustees. The expansion of the role of the Trustee to cover other bond issues not mandated by the TIA demonstrates the value the financial markets place on the services of Trustees. That value can be summarized as follows:

- Bondholders value the presence and services of a Trustee when they make their investment decision because they know there is a professional, independent third party who is dedicated to protecting their interests.

- The appointment of a Trustee lowers the cost of capital because, when Trustees perform their role, they have brought stability and confidence to the securities markets—the exact intent of the TIA.

- There is no one else to provide all the ongoing services of paying, monitoring, processing, and protecting that the Trustee accomplishes for both issuers and bondholders.

When I testified before a congressional committee in the mid-1990s on the importance of the role of the Trustee as envisioned in the TIA, I was proud to say that Trustees have proved their value in functioning to facilitate the workings of the securities markets. The role of the Trustee has grown to become a critical part of the process by which issuers finance their capital requirements. Trustees have done their job well.

II. What Is a Trustee, and What Does a Trustee Do?

I have often been asked to define just what a Trustee is. The short answer is: a Trustee is a bank, financial services company, or trust company that provides Trustee services for a bond issue. A bond issue is originated by an issuer and bought by bondholders (investors). The purpose of the bond issue is to raise capital for an issuer to build or buy something.

The issuer could be a municipal issuer, such as a city, county, state, or even a conduit entity created by the state (e.g., a housing authority). These are municipal bonds. either tax-exempt or taxable, and are normally used to finance infrastructure building.

A second issuer could be a corporation that issues corporate bonds, both secured and unsecured. A third issuer could be an entity that creates a structured finance bond identified in the following categories:

- Asset-Backed Securities (ABS)
- Mortgage-Backed Securities (MBS)
- Collateralized Debt Obligations (CDOS)

The Trustee is hired by the issuer to provide services on behalf of the issuer in administering the terms and conditions of the bonds. The issuer will appoint the Trustee based upon experience, relationship, and fees, in many cases not in that order. Unfortunately, issuers often appoint Trustees solely based upon the lowest fee, not experience, service quality, or expertise. The reality is that Trustees are paid minimal fees in relation to the true nature of their services and risks. Here is why. As I have stated previously, the Trustee is hired by the issuer to provide services. Those services are provided during the life of the bond issue, which can last for up to thirty years or more. Since the majority of bonds do not go into "default," a scary word filled with risk, the Trustee lives in a nondiscretionary agent role for which it receives minimal compensation. This pre-default role is where the Trustee has very limited responsibilities and, as such, as long as it performs those functions, is not rewarded with high fees, especially when compared to the amount of the bonds. An example is a $10 million bond issue that may bring the Trustee $1,500 in annual fees—hardly big money. I have often heard it said that "the best Trustee is the one you never hear from." We Trustees are expected to do our job behind the scenes, with quiet efficiency and little fanfare.

Thus, the reality is that the Trustee in his/her usual pre-default role is not paid what he/she is really worth because of this perceived limited role. I say *perceived* because there are many responsibilities Trustees assume during this time and because more is being demanded of Trustees in our increasingly complex and litigious financial world.

All of that changes suddenly, and sometimes without warning, when a default occurs. When an issuer defaults in its obligations to the bondholders, the Trustee must spring into action, change into a superhero costume, and leap tall buildings on behalf of those bondholders. The Trustee must dramatically change from an agent role to a "prudent man/person" role, as stated in the governing Trust documents. The Trustee is responsible for protecting the interests of the bondholders, who rely on the Trustee to pursue their claims for recovery. This is the true essence of what the Trustee is hired to do. In other words, the Trustee is hired to both "*serve* the issuer and *protect* the bondholders":

- Serve the issuer by performing all pre-default duties as described in the indenture, which is the governing Trust agreement between the issuer and bondholders.
- Protect the bondholders in a default to maximize their recovery.

To "serve and protect" should be a familiar motto to all. It is the motto of the police. To me, it embodies the true nature of what a Trustee is: the policeman of the indenture. Our job is to monitor and enforce provisions of the indenture as specifically described pre-default. This is certainly not a trivial job. It requires well-trained staff, systems, and operations-processing capabilities. This is all in keeping with understanding and working with one of the most complicated financial contracts existing—the indenture—plus other Trust documents.

Once trouble occurs in the nature of a default, such as a bankruptcy or nonpayment of principal, the Trustee's duty shifts from serving the issuer to protecting the bondholders. Our job post-default is to maximize bondholder recovery. Again, our role is to *maximize*, not guarantee, that the bondholders will recover their investment. We can only pursue their claims as a prudent man/person given the circumstances at the time. This is the standard under which the Trustee operates. It is our challenge and our ultimate purpose for being appointed as Trustee in a bond issue.

Over the years, Trustees have performed extremely well in fulfilling our obligations to bondholders as was originally envisioned by issuers, bondholders, regulators, and the drafters of the securities laws—namely the Trust Indenture Act of 1939. This act formally established the role of the Trustee. The intent of the act was to provide a professional, independent, conflict-free third party to both serve the issuer and protect the bondholders.

The purpose of the Trustee is to facilitate the workings of the bond issue so that both issuers and bondholders receive the benefit of their bargain. That bargain is for the issuer to raise capital through a bond issue and the bondholders to receive a rate of return and the repayment of their principal investment. In addition, the capital markets process works best if all parties have confidence that they will achieve their objectives. The existence of a Trustee provides that confidence.

The Unique Role of the Trustee: The Party in the Middle

The key to really understanding the role of the Trustee is envisioning the Trustee in the middle of the bond issue:

| ISSUER | ⟷ | TRUSTEE | ⟷ | BONDHOLDERS |

The role of Trustee is a unique role not duplicated in any other banking service, which is why it is so little understood or appreciated. The Trustee is truly in the middle of the bond transaction. The issuer pays us, but we are ultimately responsible to the bondholders. It is interesting to note that while the issuer appoints us and pays our fees, we really work for the bondholders—the parties we have not met or, in most cases, do not even know. The reason we do not know the bondholders is that most bond issues are held in book entry form on the records of the depository: the Depository Trust Company (DTC), which is part of the Depository Trust Clearing Corporation (DTCC). The Trustee cannot gain access to the real identities of bondholders; they are referred to as beneficial owners. So strange as it may seem, Trustees ultimately work for parties they do not know and who do not pay their fees or appoint them. This is a unique relationship, to say the least, and one that is unparalleled in the financial services industry.

The Primary Parties to a Bond Issue

To be clear, let's further define these parties:

- **Issuer**: This is the party who issues the bonds. Examples include: City of Chicago, Cook County, Illinois Housing Development Authority, and State of Illinois. These are examples of municipal issuers.

- **Obligor:** This is a term that applies to a party who is "obligated" to pay the bonds. This may be the issuer or a third party. An example would be an industrial revenue bond issue. Here the obligor and issuer are two separate parties. The issuer is a city or municipal authority that sponsors the issuance of the bonds. The obligor is a private corporation that wants to construct a plant with tax-exempt bond proceeds and the eventual owner of the plant after the bonds are paid off. In this example, consider the Dow Chemical Corporation, which wants to build a chemical plant in Chicago. The City wants to sponsor the bond issue that will fund the building of the plant for the tax revenue and job creation. The City is the issuer, but the City will not be responsible for paying off the bonds. It is "nonrecourse" to the City. Instead, Dow Chemical Corporation is the party obligated to pay the principal and interest on the bonds. Dow Chemical Corporation is the obligor.

- **Bondholders**: The investors who purchase the bonds are the bondholders. There are two general classes of bondholders:
  - **Retail Bondholders**: These are individual public investors who are also referred to as "mom and pop" bondholders.
  - **Institutional Bondholders**: These are institutions such as corporations, banks, insurance companies, pension funds, mutual funds, hedge funds, and private equity funds, to name a few. They are sophisticated investors with financial knowledge and resources.

All bondholders have one common objective: to be paid back their investment. This basic objective of bondholders is the key reason for the existence of Trustees. Bonds are a promise to pay the bondholders back their principal and interest. A bondholder is a "creditor" of the issuer/obligor who is the "debtor." A bondholder's expectation of being paid back after buying a bond is why the role of the Trustee is so important. This is not the case for stock. A stock issue is an equity issue. There is no promise to pay back the shareholders because they are owners of the company—not creditors. Shareholders are paid by the profits or take the losses of the company. There is no third party to protect the interests of shareholders because there is no promise to pay. With a bond, there is the obligation to pay. This is why the role of the Trustee was created for bond issues.

The bondholders are the real bosses of the Trustee. They are the five-hundred-pound gorilla in the room that the Trustee ultimately answers to.

500 LB GORILLA

The Trustee Role Illustrated

To further understand the role of the Trustee, let me illustrate it in two parts.

1. Pre-default: Agent Role

INDENTURE

TRUSTEE

So long as the Trustee stays within the four corners of the indenture and performs the responsibilities as specifically described, this is the extent of the Trustee's responsibilities. There is little or no discretion for the Trustee to venture outside the confines of the indenture without the authority to do so, authority which is itself also very limited.

14

2. Post-default: Prudent Man/Person Role

The leap of the Trustee from agent to prudent man/person is pictured in the diagram that follows in the next two pages. The Trustee spends most of his/her life on the majority of bond issues as an agent. But when an Event of Default occurs, as defined in the indenture, then the Trustee "steps up" immediately into a higher standard of care as a prudent man/person. As stated in Section 315(c) of the Trust Indenture Act of 1939, the Trustee's standard of care post-default is:

> The indenture Trustee shall exercise in case of default (as such term is defined in such indenture) such as the rights and powers vested in it by such indenture, and to use the same degree of care and skill in their exercise, as a prudent man would exercise or use under the circumstances in the conduct of his/her own affairs.

> The "prudent man" standard, also referred to as the "prudent person" standard, means that the Trustee will follow the prudent course of action that seems right given the circumstances at the time.

> This is the gold standard of Trustee conduct. It also means that the Trustee must treat the bondholders' money as if it were his/her own.

> In that role, the Trustee must follow several guiding principles:

- Pursue the bondholders' claims proactively on behalf of *all* the bondholders—not just a few
- Communicate early and often with the bondholders
- Rely on counsel and other experts to achieve the best results

I have learned these principles firsthand in my experience in default situations. As I stated at the beginning of this chapter, we Trustees are responsible for fighting for bondholder recovery in a default. It is real money that impacts real people. I could not help but be deeply moved in my many conversations with bondholders as I learned how much it means to them to achieve a recovery of their hard-earned money—for both individuals and institutional investors, who are responsible for their constituents. It is why Trustees are here.

The following illustration gives a true picture of the dual role of the Trustee.

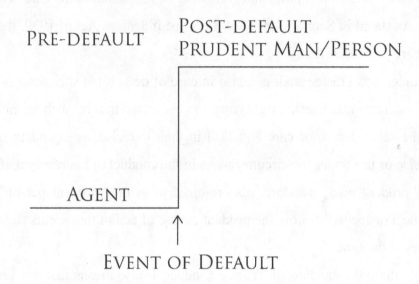

PRE-DEFAULT   POST-DEFAULT
PRUDENT MAN/PERSON

AGENT

↑

EVENT OF DEFAULT

The Many Supporting Roles the Trustee Plays

The Trustee has many supporting roles to perform in a bond issue. I like to illustrate this using an umbrella diagram:

TRUSTEE

REGISTRAR PAYING
AGENT

TRANSFER
AGENT

OTHER
TENDER AGENT
ESCROW AGENT
COLLATERAL AGENT
CALCULATION AGENT

The Trustee role can include a number of individual agent roles as demonstrated above. It is common practice to bundle these separate duties under the control of the Trustee as added responsibilities. Yet each role can be separated from the Trustee and performed by a different party. A brief description of each role follows:

- **Registrar**: Holding the records of the bondholders' names and addresses, plus monitoring the outstanding amount of bonds that were issued

- **Paying Agent**: Receiving funds and paying bondholders

- **Transfer Agent**: Transferring bonds from the selling bondholder to the buying bondholder

- **Tender Agent**: Processing bonds tendered or put by a bondholder to the trust for full payment

- **Collateral Agent**: Holding collateral for the trust

- **Calculation Agent**: Performing a calculation of principal or interest payments

- **Disclosure Agent**: On municipal issues, receiving and forwarding information from municipal issues to the secondary market disclosure system, called the Electronic

Municipal Market Access System (EMMA®) and administered by the Municipal Securities Rulemaking Board (MSRB)

There are other agency roles to be sure, but this is the most common list. Escrows are a separate agency product that will be discussed later.

III. The Misunderstood Role of the Trustee

There are many misconceptions made by participants in the marketplace concerning the true role of the Trustee. Here is my more realistic list of what the Trustee does and does not do:

- The Trustee is not a guarantor of the financing but a facilitator in achieving a positive outcome for the bondholders.
- The Trustee makes no representation as to how bond proceeds will be used nor is he/she responsible for any fraud or misuse of bond proceeds by issuers or third parties.
- The Trustee is not responsible for the accuracy or content of public disclosures of information in a prospectus or official statement created by the underwriters.
- The Trustee does not structure or draft the documents in a financing but can make comments concerning the duties and responsibilities placed on the Trustee.
- The Trustee has the right to seek advice of counsel or experts at the issuer's expense if the Trustee deems it appropriate.
- The Trustee can rely on opinions and information he/she receives under the indenture as true without having a duty to look behind or investigate those statements to verify their accuracy.
- The bondholders holding 25 percent of the principal amount of bonds outstanding have the *right* to direct the Trustee's actions. However, this is only a right of the bondholders,

and the Trustee is not obligated to follow that direction if the Trustee deems it harmful to the other bondholders.

- Unless specifically required in the indenture, the Trustee has no responsibility to monitor any covenant in the indenture. The Trustee has no duty to receive reports, financial statements, insurance forms, or other evidence of issuer covenant compliance unless the indenture has language saying the Trustee *shall* receive such evidence. If the indenture is silent, then the Trustee has no duty to request it or receive it.

The Trustee Is Not a Fiduciary

I am compelled to address one of the most common misconceptions about the role of the Trustee in Corporate Trust. It is important to understand that the Trustee in the Corporate Trust role is *not* a fiduciary. First, this is substantiated by federal law. The Trust Indenture Act of 1939 clearly states that the Trustee is a "Prudent Man/Person" post-default. A fiduciary is a well-established legal concept requiring broad discretionary responsibility and increased liability for the party that acts under that standard. An example is the Wealth Management Trust business where the Trustee is a fiduciary. A fiduciary must act as a professional who has the knowledge and skills to oversee the interests of his/her clients. As such, a fiduciary is held to a much higher standard of care in performing his/her responsibilities for the clients and is held to the standard that he/she must make the decisions for clients that are right at all times. This is different from the prudent man/person standard for Corporate Trustees, who must take the appropriate action in a default *given the circumstances at the time*. This means the Trustee is acting prudently if the Trustee is taking action as he/she sees the current circumstances require at the time of action. If later events prove that action was not the best, then the Trustee is not liable and has acted as required under this standard of care. A fiduciary would still have liability.

Second, the many years of custom and practice in the Corporate Trust industry support the non-fiduciary standard in court cases and bankruptcies.

Third, the indenture under which the Trustee performs does not impose a fiduciary standard on Trustees.

Finally, the reality is that Trustees are not paid to act as fiduciaries. Our fees are low because of our agent and prudent man/person standards, which are not fiduciary. I have always taught my students in Corporate Trust under penalty of death (or default) to never refer to the role of the Trustee in Corporate Trust as a fiduciary. It is simply not correct.

Conclusion

The role of the Trustee is a unique and important part of the capital markets. Trustees are true partners to the other participants in the process of bringing a successful bond issue to conclusion. That role will continue to evolve over time as the needs of the financial markets change.

Chapter Summary

- The role of the Trustee is one of serving the issuer of a bond financing and protecting the bondholders in a default. *Serve* and *protect.*
- The dual standard for Trustees is to act as an agent pre-default and as a prudent man/person post-default. *Act as agent* and *prudent man/person.*
- Trustees have little discretion pre-default and must adhere to the provisions of the indenture in performing their duties and responsibilities. *The indenture governs.*
- The long history of Trustees began in the early 1800s for railroad bonds and was formalized by the securities laws as a result of the Great Depression. *Protect investors.*
- The key federal law that established the formal role of the Trustee was the Trust Indenture Act of 1939 (TIA).

- The Trustee is not a fiduciary but a prudent man/person post-default. *Is not a fiduciary.*
- The Trustee must act proactively to protect the interests of all the bondholders and not just the few. *Protect all the bondholders equally.*

~ Case Study ~

You are serving as the Trustee on a municipal bond issue to finance the building of an entertainment center in a local community. Unfortunately, the initial revenue projections for the project were wildly overstated. The predictable result was that the project went into default. Bondholders sued the Trustee, alleging: 1) there was a breach of fiduciary duty, 2) the Trustee was directly responsible for the collapse of the project since the Trustee actively participated in the drafting and contents of the official statement, and 3) the Trustee was negligent in performing his/her duties and failed to monitor the project to assure that the bondholders would be paid. Answer the following question:

What would you say in defense of your actions in your role as the Trustee?

Answer

First, while it is unfortunate that the project failed and resulted in a loss for the bondholders, the Trustee cannot prevent nor is he/she responsible for such an economic failure. Our job is to enforce the terms and conditions of the indenture as an agent with limited discretion pre-default. We have no authority to step in or interfere with the workings of the project prior to a default. As long as we act prudently and proactively post-default, we have done our job. We are not a fiduciary, and it is wrong to charge us with that standard of care.

Second, we do not draft or participate in drafting the official statement. We are not a party to it and bear no responsibility for its content. Simply put, we do not structure the deal and have no responsibility for the economics of the project.

Third, the Trustee is not liable for negligence as long as he/she fulfills the pre-default duties in keeping with the specific responsibilities described in the indenture. If that is the case, then the Trustee cannot be charged with negligence. The Trustee cannot be held accountable for a "bad deal" that was improperly structured or mismanaged.

Therefore, understanding the role of the Trustee both pre- and post-default and performing as required in that role will be the standard of care under which Trustees must operate. The Trustee cannot be held liable for a bad deal and should not be a target for litigation as a deep pocket just because the bondholders lose money.

~ Chapter 2 ~

The Indenture and Agency Documents

Chicago, Illinois—1990

Today we are closing a bond issue, which represents the first of many with a new client. Bond counsel has been dealing with another Trustee bank because of previous issues. Upon receiving drafts of the indenture, we proceed to make comments. There are several provisions we feel are important to change, such as involving indemnification language for the Trustee from the issuer. We are surprised to notice that what is considered standard indemnity language is not present. That language would normally state that the issuer or bondholders will indemnify the Trustee at the Trustee's request.

When we present our comments to bond counsel, we receive the following response, "The other Trustee never questioned the documents or insisted upon their provisions." Bond counsel was reluctant to make the changes we asked for—comments we considered crucial to our ongoing role as Trustee.

We hold our ground. Finally, after intense negotiation, we have our comments incorporated into the indenture.

After the closing, I talk to a lawyer for bond counsel, and he says something to me I will never forget. He says, "You really were a tough negotiator on this deal, but you did get what you needed. We were looking for a dumb Trustee." After a moment of silence on my part, I reply, "I am happy to disappoint you."

I never forgot that lesson. Trustees must have courage in reviewing the governing documents and never be afraid to state their position—even if it may cause some discomfort. In the end, the Trustees are the ones who must live with the documents for the next ten to thirty years. Trustees should never forget that.

Chapter Objective

Understanding the Trustee's role must include a discussion of the basic legal documents impacting the Trustee. While there are a number of different legal documents defining the roles and responsibilities of the Trustee, the key document is the indenture. This chapter will explore the indenture as it shapes the Trustee's duties from the following perspectives:

I.   History of the Indenture and Evolution of the Modern Indenture
II. What the Trustee Should Know about Indenture Structure and Requirements
III. The Main Provisions of a Trust Indenture That Concern a Trustee: Key Questions
IV. Tips on How the Trustee Should Review and Comment on the Indenture
V.   Other Trust Documents Impacting Trustees

I. History of the Indenture and Evolution of the Modern Indenture

The word *indenture* means, in law, a deed or written agreement between two or more parties. In a bond financing, it is the governing legal document that details the terms and conditions necessary for the operation of the bond financing from closing to final maturity.

The indenture first appeared in 1830 but did not become widely used until the rise of corporate business in the late 1800s. As America grew in economic power, the corporation was created as a means of raising the needed capital to produce goods and services on a massive scale necessary to meet increasing demands. Corporations increasingly turned from the issuance of stock to the issuance of bonds to raise capital they needed to expand their business. The indenture became the vehicle of choice by which the bonds were issued.

As the different types of bond issues expanded from the first days of the first mortgage railroad bonds in the early 1800s to an ever-growing number of diverse and complex bond structures, the indenture became the mechanism to facilitate the bond issuances. It developed into a hybrid legal document serving as (in order):

1. A contract
2. A Trust
3. An establishment of a security interest

The indenture is, first and foremost, a contract. As such, it is subject to contract law in all its aspects. It is a legal, binding agreement establishing contractual rights and responsibilities among three parties:

1. Issuer/obligor who issues the bonds and agrees to pay principal and interest
2. Trustee who serves as agent for the issuer but fulfills a prudent man/person role to the bondholders in a default
3. Bondholders/investors who purchase the bonds

The indenture establishes a number of contractual rights between these three parties. These rights are specified in the indenture sections as a course of conduct for the issuer, Trustee, and bondholders. In keeping up with these responsibilities, the indenture prescribes proper authority for monitoring and remedying those duties or covenants. It is a complex web of interrelationships that is in place to achieve one objective: to allow for the money to be borrowed by the issuer from the bondholders with the promise to pay it back. The indenture is there to set the terms and conditions under which the dual objectives of borrowing money and paying it back are achieved.

As such, the indenture stands at the center of the bond financing. Other documents, agreements, and guaranties exist around it, depending upon the nature of the transaction.

Existing laws and court procedures that impact how the indenture operates surround it all. Therefore, the indenture has evolved into one of the most complex financial documents in existence today. The indenture remains the definitive document that forms the core of the financing.

To meet the demands of a changing securities market and the increasing need of issuers to find new ways to raise capital, the indenture must be flexible, adaptive, and structurally sound in dictating literally the rules by which the bonds operate for their life. Not an easy task. Yet the indenture, as a contract, must meet all these requirements. Breach of the contract provisions by any of the parties through negligence, gross negligence, or willful misconduct will result in liability and damages under the law.

The indenture is also considered a Trust but only in a more limited sense from other Trust relationships. Under an indenture, the Trustee does not have direct management responsibilities for the assets of the Trust and is in a more passive role prior to a default. The real Trust aspects of the indenture emerge post-default when the Trustee assumes the prudent man/person standard of care and now has real power and authority to manage and secure Trust assets for the benefit of the bondholders.

The indenture may also establish a security interest to support the bondholder's claim for repayment. This is true for a variety of bond structures. For example, first mortgage bonds are backed by the physical plant, land, and equipment of the issuer such as an elective utility company. Revenue bonds are backed by a security interest in the source of revenue payments, which could be supported by property or equipment. Collateral trusts are supported by the actual equipment financed, such as the case is with equipment trust or leverage lease bond issues. I refer to these security issues as "planes, trains, and automobiles." Asset-backed securities also are currently a well-known security structure whereby specific assets are separated from the issuer/originator and pledged solely to the repayment of the bondholders. There are a vast number of bond structures today with some form of security interest supporting repayment, as defined by the indenture and other Trust documents.

II. What the Trustee Should Know about Indenture Structure and Requirements

The structure of the indenture as a legal contract, a Trust, and security agreement has evolved to accommodate a wide variety of bond financings. Whether the bonds are secured or unsecured, public or private, corporate or municipal, the indenture can create an effective framework for the workings of a bond issue from start to finish (from closing, when the bonds are initially issued, to the final maturity).

Because the period of time for which the indenture must operate can be lengthy, ten, twenty, or thirty years or longer, it must be able to be flexible enough to survive changing conditions. Inevitably, there will be changes in laws and economic conditions that can dramatically affect the indenture and the bonds. I liken the indenture to a living, breathing document. It is like the US Constitution. It must survive the test of time, meet unforeseeable developments, and remain flexible enough to allow for amendments. In other words, it must provide a solid framework to effectively govern the financing and the parties involved yet allow for changes in order to remain effective.

The indenture is an amazing creation that has delivered on all these objectives. It has remained current and has evolved to address the needs of new security structures in a changing legal and economic climate. It will continue to do so with a little help from its friends. These friends are the lawyers who serve as bond counsel who draft them. The Trustee also must enforce their provisions, monitor compliance, and facilitate the process described. The indenture is the heart. The cash flow is the blood circulating through various accounts that keeps the promise to the bondholders alive—to be repaid the money the bondholders basically lend to the issuer by purchasing the bonds.

The Trustee is one party among others to the bond issue. The Trustee does *not* draft the indenture; bond counsel does that on behalf of the issuer. However, it is vital for the Trustee to review the indenture and make substantive comments with the objective of improving the workings of the indenture for the benefit of all. The Trustee must also ensure that proper protections, plus the proper legal rights and authority to act, are present in the indenture. The Trustee must *never* take anything for granted. Therefore, it is vital for the Trustee to properly review any indenture and understand what is expected.

The Structure of the Indenture

To convey the proper understanding of the indenture, I will now discuss the common structure of the indenture with respect to the Trustee. Remember, while no two indentures are ever exactly alike, there are basic similarities and common features.

In issues not qualified under the TIA, such a municipal bonds, some structured finance bonds (ABS, MBS, and CDOS), and other private placements (Rule 144a securities), the same basic information will appear, although there is room for creativity. In general, the indenture structure will contain the following:

Table of Contents: This provides an easy reference point as to what is contained in the indenture.

Recitals: This is the section that names the parties and factors that led to the creation of the indenture. This section contains the purpose of the bond issue and states that all legal requirements and authorizations have been fulfilled or provided for. The recitals will include a paragraph or series of paragraphs often beginning with "Whereas," which will tell the story behind the issuance of the bonds. This is the purpose for which the bond proceeds will be used. Any other pertinent documents to the financing should be incorporated by reference. The issuer will affirm compliance with all regulations pertaining to the bond issuance. The issuer will then authorize the bond issuance. The final recital (especially in a TIA-qualified issue) will denote the indenture as a "valid mortgage and Deed of Trust."

Granting Clauses: In this section, the issuer acknowledges the bondholders' purchase of the bonds and accepts the responsibility for repayment of their loan through principal and interest payments on the bonds. It also lists the properties that are part of the Trust Estate (the security for the bond) and assigns all title to and interest in the Trust Estate to the Trustee for the benefit of the bondholders.

Definitions: A well-drafted indenture should contain a list of definitions and all other documents pertaining to the financing. The definitions give all readers insight into the intent of many of the document provisions and make administration of the bond issue easier.

The Bonds: This section will generally describe the authorized bonds to be issued under the indenture and may allow for more than one series to be issued. There will be a discussion of the bonds' repayment terms, a restatement of the security assignment to the Trustee, and a listing of the details of authenticating, registering, transferring, canceling, and replacing bonds.

Form of the Bond: This will contain a specific format of the actual bonds to be issued, with all provisions listed exactly as they should appear in the actual bonds.

Redemption: All possible types of redemption, whether optional, mandatory, or sinking fund, should be listed here.

Creation of Trust Accounts and Flow of Funds: This section will authorize the Trustee to establish separate accounts in which to deposit the monies received. It should detail the way in which the money is deposited, including: 1) how, when, and on whose instructions funds can be moved; 2) what the disposition should be of income earned in each fund; and 3) the disposition of any monies remaining in the fund when the bond issue reaches its final maturity.

Investments: This indenture section details the permitted investments that the Trustee is authorized to make upon receipt of written direction from the issuer/obligor.

Covenants Between the Issuer and the Trustee: This section will list a variety of duties the issuer agrees to perform, including:

- Maintenance of insurance
- Appointment of a Paying Agent
- Payment to a Paying Agent of principal and interest
- Preparation of statements of transactions
- Payment of Trustee's fees
- Maintenance of existence
- Filing and recording of continuation statements
- Payment of taxes
- Provision of financial reports and information
- Provision of officers' certificates and opinions of counsel
- Default

Events of Default: All things that constitute a default are listed here, along with the remedies the Trustee can take in attempting to cure the default and the actions that require bondholders' consent. Typical Events of Default include:

- Nonpayment of principal and/or interest
- Breach of a covenant by the issuer and any cure period (grace period) before it becomes an Event of Default (i.e., nonreceipt of financial reports)
- Default under corollary documents

Duties of the Trustee: In this section, the Trustee accepts the terms and conditions of the indenture and any specifically related documents. The Trustee is responsible only for the specific actions detailed in the indenture prior to a default. If an Event of Default occurs, the Trustee agrees to adhere to the prudent man/person standard, which states that he/she shall "exercise such rights and powers vested in it by the indenture and use the same degree of care and skill in their exercise as a prudent person would exercise or use under the circumstances in the conduct of his/her own affairs." The Trustee is allowed to rely upon the authenticity of opinions and documents provided in connection with the bond issue and is not liable except for his/her own negligence or gross negligence and willful misconduct. Provisions to be followed in the event of the resignation of the Trustee and appointment of a successor Trustee will be located here. If the bond issue is qualified under the Trust Indenture Act of 1939, the provisions for identifying and correcting conflicts of interest will be listed here. This section will also state that the Trustee has *no implied duties* not specifically stated in the indenture. The Trustee will be required to monitor the issuer's compliance with any covenant only if the indenture specifically states that the Trustee "will" or "shall" receive evidence of compliance.

Miscellaneous Provisions: As the title implies, this section contains items that don't fit elsewhere but are necessary to the legality of the indenture, including:

- Binding effect on successors and assigns
- Severability, meaning if one part of the indenture is voided, then the other parts remain in effect
- Addresses for serving notices
- Governing state law under which the indenture operates

Signatures: This contains attested signatures of the issuer and the Trustee and the seals of each (if required by applicable state law).

Exhibits: This is the actual form of certificates, opinions, and requisitions for payouts or any specific report.

Additional Information on Covenants

Affirmative and Negative Covenants and Covenant Compliance

There are two basic types of covenants by the issuer/obligor: affirmative and negative. Affirmative covenants require the issuer (or parties) to do something while negative covenants prohibit certain actions. Following are some examples.

Affirmative Covenants

- Requires periodic reports be generated, such as financial statements or certificates of default
- Maintains adequate insurance coverage
- Performs servicing responsibilities and provides periodic reports of activity

- Promptly pays principal and interest

Negative Covenants

- Restricts payment of dividends
- Restricts creation of additional debt
- Requires the maintenance of working capital at a specific level
- Restricts the issuer from merging

Examples of Issuer Covenants

Satisfaction and Defeasance: The provisions listed here will specify the steps necessary to satisfy the indenture and release any lien on counselor collateral.

III. The Main Provisions of a Trust Indenture That Concern a Trustee: Key Questions

The main provisions of a Trust indenture that concern the Trustee include:

- The standard of care imposed on the Trustee
- Duties and obligations of the Trustee
- Compensation and indemnity
- Defeasance provisions
- Default provisions
- Bondholder meetings
- Co-Trustee considerations
- Amendment to the indenture

- Creation of accounts

- Investment provisions

- Covenants

- Redemption of bonds

- Operational requirements

- Successor Trustees

- Supplemental indentures

- Officers' certificates and opinions of counsel

Q1. What does standard of care signify?

Standard of care is the level of accountability imposed on the Trustee. On non-TIA issues, Trustees prefer as a standard of care "gross negligence and willful misconduct." A less desirable standard is "ordinary negligence," which means if the Trustee makes a mistake, the Trustee is liable.

Q2. What provisions of the trust indenture concerning Trustee's duties and responsibilities should a Trustee negotiate?

- Duties and obligations of the Trustee should be determined solely by the expressed provisions of the indenture.

- The Trustee should not be required to ascertain or inquire as to performance of covenants or agreements except as specifically provided in the indenture.

- The Trustee need not act until officers' certificates or opinions of counsel are received.

- The Trustee is not liable for anything he/she does in good faith, which he/she believes to be authorized to do.

- The Trustee should not be accountable for the use of proceeds from the sale of bonds disbursed by him/her in accordance with the provisions of the indenture.

- The Trustee is not required to risk his/her own funds or incur personal financial liability.

- The Trustee need not take any action until he/she has been indemnified.

- The Trustee is not required to do anything illegal or anything that would expose him/her to liability.

- The Trustee is not liable for actions taken as directed by a specified number of bondholders.

- Funds held in the Trust by the Trustee should be used for the purpose for which they were received and need not be segregated except to the extent provided by law. The Trustee has no liability for interest on money held by him/her.

- The Trustee can hire agents and is not liable for their negligence if due care was exercised in making the appointment.

- The Trustee is not charged with knowledge of an Event of Default until a Corporate Trust Officer has actual knowledge or until the Trustee receives written notice.

Q3. What are a Trustee's concerns regarding compensation and indemnification?

The Trust indenture should provide for payment of the Trustee's fees and reimbursement for out-of-pocket expenses. The fee agreement itself should be separate from the indenture and provide for renegotiation. The indenture should provide the Trustee's fees, and expenses have a priority claim senior to the bondholders.

Q4. What provisions for defeasance should concern a Trustee? How does the existence of senior debt affect the defeasance of a subordinated issue? Does the Trustee's compensation and indemnity survive the defeasance?

- No bond should be defeased if it will subject to the issuer to arbitrage tax liability or be subject to bankruptcy preference.
- The Trustee should rely on certificates from counsel and independent certified public accountants as to sufficiency of funds deposited to defease an issue.
- Senior debt should always be defeased prior to subordinated debt.

Q5. What are the Trustee's concerns with default provisions?

- Clear definition of "default" and "Event of Default"
- Provision to accelerate due date for payment of the bonds
- Bondholders' rights
- Standard of care imposed on Trustee post-default—prudent man/person
- Provisions to sell pledged property
- Appointment of receiver
- Application of Trust funds
- Notice to bondholders
- Trustee's priority right to compensation and recovery of expenses before payment to bondholders
- Notification of Trustees by the issuer of an Event of Default

Q6. What provisions should be made for amendments to the indenture?
The indenture should provide for certain amendments to be made by the Trustee and the issuer without the consent of bondholders. These include any change that does not

adversely affect the rights of the bondholders. Examples of an amendment that can be made without the consent of bondholders include fixing an ambiguity, defect, or inconsistency. Any addition that increases the security for the bondholders would not require bondholder consent.

However, I would caution that the Trustee be very careful in agreeing to waive indenture provisions without advice of counsel or bondholder consent. An obvious typographical error or needed change in the fiscal year is appropriate for the Trustee to agree to without bondholder consent. Anything else should be considered with caution. When in any doubt, the Trustee should not sign a waiver, as it may lead to consequences in the future.

Q7. What considerations are important to the Trustee in the administration of investments?

The appropriate indenture language should state, "The Trustee should invest only upon written direction in permitted investments." Those permitted investments should be clearly defined with no ambiguity. I particularly dislike language that states, "Investments can be made in any investment type permitted in state statutes for particular issues." This opens the Trustee to risk in possibly making an inappropriate investment, as it is difficult to define under vague or overly broad statute language.

Q8. What Concerns the Trustee about Covenants Contained in the Indenture?

The Trustee must be specifically required to receive evidence of any covenant. The Trustee's responsibility is to match any covenant item received for compliance to the indenture requirements, but the Trustee has no responsibility to investigate or verify any statements provided.

Q9. What is important about the redemption of bonds?

The Trustee must review the provisions to redeem bonds to determine that the proper dates for notices and calls are operationally correct. When bonds are to be redeemed through the operation of a sinking fund, all provisions must be carefully reviewed as to the method of calling the bonds, possible purchase and deposit of securities by the issuer to satisfy the call provisions, and acceptance of tender offers. Call provisions must be clear so that errors can be avoided in redeeming bonds.

Q10. What are operational problems?

Operational problems occur when there are conflicts between sections of the indenture or between the indenture and other legal documents involved with the financing, such as a loan agreement, mortgage, or lease. Other problems occur when there are contradictions within the indenture as to dates for actions to be taken, flow of funds, and bond redemptions.

Q11. What is a Successor Trustee?

A Successor Trustee is a Trustee who serves after the original Trustee is no longer in place. A Successor Trustee is needed if the bondholders, or issuer, remove the original Trustee or the Trustee resigns because he/she has a conflict of interest, becomes insolvent or bankrupt, or becomes incapable of acting as Trustee. The indenture should provide for these contingencies, leading to the need for a Successor Trustee, and also provide for a merger of the Trustee's bank without requiring issuer or bondholder consent.

Q12. When must a Trustee act on a covenant?

The indenture covenants are promises of the issuer to do or not do something. The Trustee must receive evidence of compliance only if specifically required. In other words, the language in the indenture or other trust documents should say the Trustee "shall or will receive a compliance item or perform a certain specific task." If silent, then the Trustee has no responsibility to monitor the issuer and the compliance with a covenant. Making sure the covenants clearly explain the Trustee's responsibilities is also critical to avoiding unwanted duties and liabilities.

Q13. Why does an indenture have a provision for supplemental indentures?

Supplemental indentures are somewhat like amendments. They are divided into two types: 1) those that require bondholder consent and 2) those that require only the consent of the Trustee and the issuer. Supplemental indentures not requiring bondholder approval are: 1) to add to covenants and agreements, 2) to cure ambiguities, 3) to provide for additional bonds, 4) to provide for parity indebtedness, and 5) to provide for exchange of bonds. Any supplemental indenture adversely affecting the bondholder requires unanimous bondholder consent. These are situations such as extending the maturity of the bonds or reducing the interest rate.

Q14. Why are officer's certificates and opinions of counsel important?

Before the Trustee takes action under the indenture, he/she must know that he/she can do so. The Trustee must be able to request an officer's certificate or opinion of counsel at any time in compliance with the indenture. We must also rely on such certificates and opinions to support our actions. As Trustees, it should always be our right under the indenture.

Q15. Why is the miscellaneous provision important?

The miscellaneous provision contains certain important information vital to the Trustee's consideration. The addresses of the parties for official notice requirements are stated. The Trustee must carefully review the addresses to make sure they are complete, especially relating to the Trustee. Individual names should not be used, but enough information should be present to assure delivery.

A Real-life Story

As happened to me once, the notice requirement was sent in care of the general bank address. A subpoena was delivered and never forwarded to Corporate Trust. Yet it *was* delivered to the bank address stated in the indenture. It was simply not specific enough. Needless to say, we did not fare well when we did not respond to the subpoena.

The miscellaneous section also contains the governing law provision. This is important to the Trustee because it will establish which state law or, for international issues, which country law controls the indenture. Therefore, the Trustee must be comfortable with the designated law listed in this section.

A Note About the Exhibits and Why They Are Important

It helps the Trustee immeasurably if copies of required certificates, opinions, reports, and requisitions are included as exhibits. This takes the uncertainty out of determining if what the Trustee either receives or is to provide is the "right" document to meet the indenture requirements. It is crucial for the Trustee to review the exhibits, comment on them, and even provide workable samples.

IV. Tips on How the Trustee Should Review and Comment on the Indenture

The Trustee must live with the indenture for the life of the bonds. Therefore, the Trustee must devote serious attention to properly reviewing the indenture and other relevant documents. The Trustee should read any document that he/she signs and that places a duty or responsibility on the Trustee. The two cardinal principles of document review are:

1. Read the document.
2. Understand what you have read as to the Trustee duties and responsibilities.

It sounds simple, but document review is a task that requires proper focus, dedication, training, and experience. The Trustee must have a sense of urgency when reviewing documents. The reason? We have to live with the documents for a long time. They can be changed but only under certain circumstances, usually requiring bondholder approval and issuer expense.

There is another risk for Trustees. We are usually brought in late in the process, long after the parties involved have negotiated the structure and features of the bond issue. As such, there is often resistance to the Trustee's comments because no one wants to make changes at this point in the financing. The parties also may give the Trustee little time to review the documents. In my experience, this can be as short as twenty-four hours. This makes for a somewhat difficult negotiating position for the Trustee. The Trustee's negotiating position is further complicated by the fact that the Trustee's formal role and authority does not begin until the signing of the indenture. Therefore, proper document review by Trustees requires finesse and courage.

Tips to Review an Indenture in *One* Hour

The following tips are suggested in an effort to help Trustees be more effective in this process. I have employed them and tested them throughout the years of reading literally thousands of indentures and documents as a Trustee. If you follow my tips, you will be able to effectively review an indenture or any Trust document in one hour. Plus you will have your ticklers (reminders) identified. Is this worth it? Absolutely.

1. **Develop your initial mindset:**
   - Review in a quiet place away from the phones, undisturbed.
   - Review at your "best" time of day—when you are at your peak effectiveness.
   - Clear your mind of outside distractions and thoughts. Focus on the document.
   - Visualize the bond structure and how it works.

- Understand the purpose of the financing and what it is designed to accomplish from the issuer's standpoint.
- Understand what the investors gain in terms of security for repayment and the risks they will look to you to monitor. Put yourself in the bondholder's position, and think of what they expect from you for service and protection.
- List the parties to the financing, including:
  a. Issuer/obligor
  b. Company
  c. Trustee or agent
  d. Other parties

2. **Determine your system to record comments:**
- Do not record on a separate sheet of paper to avoid risk of losing it.
- Do not use sticky notes in the pages, as they may fall off or be lost.
- List page numbers and brief notes on the cover of the document.
- List more extensive comments on each page where the language in question appears.
- Compare the language in the Trustee document to your checklist.
- Keep your comments short and meaningful, and avoid observations such as "wow" or "this will never work" or "this is dumb." These will devastate you in litigation, especially if you keep the drafts, which I do not recommend.
- Mark a "?" by phrases or cash flow you do not understand, but be sure to dispose of drafts after comments are made and certainly after closing. Do not keep them. Why? Once again, litigation risks.

- If documents are on email, you can record comments on separate Word documents or by handwritten notes. Then relay them back to counsel.

- If you have counsel representing you (a good idea), then relay comments to counsel and have counsel talk to bond counsel.

- Try to negotiate to remove difficult or unnecessary monitoring responsibilities for you as Trustee.

- Define exactly what you are to receive, when, and from whom.

- Officers' certificates should be direct statements, and the proper parties who sign them should be provided to you in an incumbency certificate.

- Try to negotiate to remove insurance requirements. If insisted upon, try for just an insurance broker opinion with no detail. Here, more detail places more risk and liability on the bank.

- Security interests should be maintained by the issuer, not the bank or Trustee or agent. However, if you as Trustee are required to file Universal Commercial Codes (UCCs), then have that stated directly.

- Identify each tickler as you go through the indenture by marking it with a "T" and including the page number on the indenture cover with your comments.

Comments/Language

Types of comments can be separated into three classes: 1) administrative, 2) operations, and 3) legal. Following are examples of language you should focus on.

Tips Regarding Administrative Comments

- **Cash flow**: Draw a picture to make sure the cash flows without gaps or interruption smoothly to the final conclusion.

- **Investments**: Compare definition of permitted investments to the investment section and identify inconsistencies. Ask for written direction. Get standing instructions. Mention your own money market funds or bank investment products.

- **Covenants**: Review the covenants section, and tickle only those sections stating the Trustee or agent "shall or will" receive. If silent, you have no responsibility to receive.

- **Email language**: State that emails or electronic instructions are allowable under the documents.

Tips Regarding Operations Comments

- Ensure payment dates are clearly defined.
- Make sure record dates are present.
- When funds are to be received by the bank as Paying Agent, ask for payment to be received five days prior to payment date, if being paid by check.
- Lost or stolen security language should be specific.
- Return of funds to the issuer, if required, must be clearly defined.

- Statements for cash and investment activity should be defined as to when and how. Will electronic access be acceptable to the issuer?

- Denominations of bonds should be listed.

- Restricted transfer requirements should be clearly stated if required (e.g., private placements).

- Redemptions, sinking funds, and amortization language should be specific. The selection process for the bonds should be by random by lot selection or fair method as Trustee or agent deems appropriate. A thirty-day notice requirement is standard.

- Interest payment and number of days (actual or bond year) should be calculated. Actual days 365/365 or 30/360 should be specified.

- Wire transfer call backs: State that call back procedures are included in instructions for the issuer or third parties to comply with the banks call back procedures to verify payment instructions.

Tips Regarding Legal Comments

- There should be an indemnity clause for the Trustee or agent to be able to receive indemnity from the issuer or bondholders prior to acting.

- The Trustee should be able to rely on opinions and certificates for which the Trustee is not required to look behind, investigate, or verify.

- The Trustee can rely on direction and can request such direction, which shall not be unreasonably withheld either from issuer or bondholders.

- The Trustee can hire counsel at issuer's expense to render opinions, which the Trustee can rely upon absent knowledge to the contrary.

- The Trustee should look for the governing law: the law you want and understand or can accept.

- Security interests must be maintained as a responsibility of the issuer and assigned to the Trustee. An exception can be UCC filings.

- The Trustee should be protected from environmental law risk by not being required to seize the property if the bank is not adequately protected.

- The Trustee can recover fees and expenses as a priority claim in a bankruptcy distribution.

- The Trustee has a right to reasonable fees and expenses.

- The Trustee should have the ability to resign or seek court appointment of a successor.

- The Trustee requires the issuer or other third parties to the bond issue to provide information as requested by the Trustee in order for the Trustee to comply with Patriot Act requirements.

Negotiation Tips

- Have counsel represent you.
- Have your counsel negotiate directly with bond counsel.
- Work for a lawyer-to-lawyer arrangement, as that is best for a stronger negotiating position.
- List comments in three groups.
  - Throwaways: These are statements that are nice to have but are statements you can live without. Example: gross negligence versus negligence.

- o Substantive comments: Inconsistencies, errors, or ambiguities that need to be cleared up. Example: permitted investments in definitions do not match the indenture language. A second example is inconsistent record dates.
- o Deal breakers: You need these comments to be accepted, or you cannot serve under the Trust documents as written. For example, the document states that you must be backup service, but you cannot perform that role. Therefore, you need the ability to hire an agent to perform the role for you.

- If the underwriters tell you it is too late to make changes due to the fact that the final prospectus or official statement has been prepared, then answer that they can always sticker the disclosure document.

- If the attorneys for the issuer or bond counsel say it is too late to make changes, then have them agree to a "side letter" and have it prepared as part of the closing documents.

- Be strong, direct, confident, and reasonable. Remember, you are all that stands between your bank and the black hole of litigation. Yes, I am being dramatic here, but it is true.

- Protect yourself and your bank by making it your responsibility to review the documents carefully. It could mean your job. It only takes one bad deal to damage the business and your bank.

Other Useful Tips

- Strive for clarity without ambiguity.
- Negotiate for clear, direct language.
- If you do not understand what is stated, ask now. It may be too late at a subsequent date or in litigation.

- Identify ticklers as you go through the documents.

- When in doubt, add a tickler so responsibilities will not be missed.

- Remember, you, your bank, or your successors will have to live with this document for a number of years, so get it right or get it changed.

- Clarify amendment and waiver language so you understand how exactly the documents can be changed.

Indenture Hot Spots of Concern for Trustees

Below are some examples of recent concerns for Trustees in indenture protections and trends.

Expanding Pre-default Duties: Watch for new language being placed in the indenture, expanding the Trustee's role to include new duties. For example, Trustees need to hold themselves more responsible for actions of a third party, such as a servicer in a mortgage-backed bond issue. Try to limit new responsibilities or hire agents to perform additional duties as required.

No Implied Duties: This is one of my favorite protections for Trustees and one that is being eroded. To be safe, include specific language adding to the "no implied duties" by linking the duties you want to avoid. An example is making clear that the Trustee will not review financial statements.

Post-default Prudent Man/Person Versus Fiduciary Standard of Care: The prudent man/person standard involves a higher degree of control and discretion but not to the level of a fiduciary. Be vigilant by eliminating any reference to being a fiduciary. The indenture should clearly state that the standard of care is prudent man/person and not a fiduciary standard.

Reliance on Opinions and Officers' Certificates: The Trustee should be protected in relying on opinions and certificates that meet the requirements of the indenture. Absent bad faith, the Trustee should not have to perform any verification of the validity of any opinions and certificates. Issuers and bondholders are challenging this concept. The Trustee must protect him/herself from language that places any duty to validate or review the facts behind the opinions and certificates.

Actual Knowledge: When does the Trustee know of an event without being specifically informed by written notice from an issuer or third party? The availability of information in the electronic media and press is much more prevalent today; this is eroding the traditional indenture language about what constitutes actual knowledge by the Trustee. A new awareness standard is now being applied by the courts. Trustees must protect themselves from this awareness standard by writing indenture protection language to require written notice of events as actual knowledge.

Covenant Compliance: Exactly when does the Trustee cease to be responsible for monitoring issuer covenant compliance? The Trustee should be very specific about which indenture covenants he/she is responsible for and not assume any "implied duties." The standard should be as follows: unless specifically required to receive a covenant item, the Trustee has no responsibility.

A Word about the Model Indentures

In an effort to simplify the drafting of indentures, the American Bar Association (ABA) and the National Association of Bond Lawyers (NABL) have drafted two model indentures. The ABA model indenture applies to corporate indentures, while the NABL model indenture is designed for municipal indentures. It is important for the Trustee to know of their existence because these models will be used in many bond financings.

The Trustee must proceed to carefully review these indentures and make appropriate comments. The Trustee must also realize that when these models are used, they are done so to expedite the indenture drafting process, which saves on costs to the issuer. Therefore, the Trustee is not expected to have many comments, if any, in these cases. The Trustee must also remember that the legal community drafted the model indentures with their clients—the issuers—in mind, not necessarily Trustees. While Trustee counsel did provide input to the model indenture drafting, these current documents are clearly drafted with the issuer's interests and the investor's viewpoint in mind, not that of the Trustee.

How the Trustee Should React to the Model Indentures Provisions

The Trustee must continue to review the indenture even if it is patterned after the model, as if it is a unique document. Why? Because chances are good that there are differences that impact the Trustee's role. Remember, the model indentures are simply *guidelines*. There is no legal requirement that their provisions be incorporated in any indenture. Bond counsel drafting the indenture may also either modify the model language or selectively use certain sections while ignoring others. Therefore, careful document review still needs to be practiced by Trustees—model or no model.

The Trustee should take note that the overall trend for indenture provisions is to reflect the growing influence and concerns of institutional investors. The Trustee must continue to be vigilant to insure that the following key protections are included:

- Priority claim for Trustee fees and expenses in a workout situation
- Proper indemnity provisions to protect the Trustee prior to taking action
- No implied duties for the Trustee—only those duties specifically stated
- Ability to rely on opinions and certificates the Trustee believes are valid
- The ability to hire lawyers and experts and have this paid for
- No obligation to determine who the beneficial owners of the bonds really are or to assure those beneficial owners receive notification

These are areas that the institutional investors are increasingly becoming more proactive in modifying or eliminating. This presents a difficult negotiation dilemma for Trustees. We want the business, but we also want to receive our traditional protections to help mitigate the legal and business risks of the more litigious and volatile securities markets of today. Powerful institutional investors who push their way to the front of the line increasingly dominate those markets. The Trustee industry cannot afford to let these protections be pushed aside. The model indentures reflect these trends and should be watched by Trustees.

V. Other Trust Documents Impacting Trustees

There may be other Trust documents the Corporate Trust Administrator may encounter. Some examples follow.

Bond Resolution: For municipal issuers, a bond resolution may be the governing document for issuing the bonds. It is a resolution prepared by municipal officials authorizing the bonds.

Collateral or Equipment Trust Agreement: This agreement describes the nature of the collateral and various requirements for depositing, replacing, monitoring, and returning the collateral. Examples of collateral are aircraft or railroad cars.

Custody Agreement: This agreement dictates the responsibilities of the custodian to hold assets on behalf of a third party.

Pooling and Service Agreement: This document details the terms and conditions for servicing assets in a structured finance issue.

Private Placement Memorandum or Bond Purchase Agreement: This is the agreement between the inventors and underwriter in a private placement to buy bonds under certain conditions. These agreements can sometimes contain references to the Trustee's responsibilities.

Escrow Agreement: This is an agreement focused on one specific purpose as established between two or more parties where the bank acts as escrow agent to hold or distribute assets or securities as directed.

Disclosure Agreement: This agreement appoints the Trustee as the disclosure agent for the issuers to disseminate information to the market place per SEC Rule 15c2-12. This may also be referred to as a Dissemination Agreement. One interesting thought is to not allow this agreement to be called a Disclosure Agreement because it is the issuer's responsibility to disclose information under the rule and only name the agreement as a Dissemination Agreement since this is the only role we perform on behalf of the issuer in disseminating information to EMMA.

Loan Agreement: This is a document between the issuer and borrower for purposes of lending bond proceeds to the borrower for a specific purpose. The Trustee is not a signatory to the Agreement, but there often are covenant requirements in the Loan Agreement that the Trustee must monitor. Such requirements include financial reports, insurance requirements, or UCC filings.

Lease Agreement: This is the agreement between the party leasing the plant or equipment and the current owner of the equipment. The Trustee does not sign this document, but once again, there may be certain covenants in the lease agreement, such as insurance evidence or financial reports, that must be reviewed by the Trustee.

Collateral Manager Agreement Found in CDO Issues: This agreement document describes the collateral manager's responsibilities. This can impact the Trustee as a recipient of reports given by the collateral manager who manages the collateral.

Servicer Agreement: Used for structured finance issues, this is an agreement between the issuer and the organization responsible for servicing the assets (e.g., mortgages, receivables, etc.). The Servicer Agreement definitely impacts the Trustee, although he/she does not sign this agreement. It requires servicer reports and financial reports to be provided to the Trustee.

Remarketing Agreement: This is the agreement between the remarketing agent (RA) bond issuer whereby the RA resells the bonds or sets the interest rate on a variable rate demand bond.

Prospectus or Offering Statement: The prospectus, or offering statement, is the disclosure document prepared by the underwriter. This document is to be made available to the investors as per SEC rules (SEC Rule 15) for publicly issued securities. There is controversy in the Trustee community as to whether or not the Trustee should read or comment on this document. Clearly, there is *no legal requirement* for the Trustee to do so. The Trustee is not a party to these documents. The prospectus is for corporate issues. The

Offering Statement (OS), or Offering Circular (OC), is for municipal issues. However, for structured finance issues, it is common industry practice for the Trustee to actively review the prospectus for cash flow information. Otherwise, it is commonly accepted practice in the Corporate Trust industry.

Tri Partite Agreement: This is an agreement among the resigning Trustee, successor Trustee, and the issuer moving the bond issue from the resigning Trustee to the successor Trustee.

There are other agreements that may be part of specific bond issues depending on the nature of the financing, but the ones described above are more common. The Trustee must carefully review *all* relevant documents (the ones we sign or others with references to imposing responsibilities on the Trustee), starting with the indenture. The goal is to understand the duties and responsibilities bestowed upon the Trustee. In addition, the Trustee must assure him/herself that the proper indemnities and protections are in place and stated in the respective documents. The Trustee is not responsible for the content of those disclosure documents, nor does the Trustee draft them.

Conclusion

There is no substitute for a thorough review of the indenture and relevant documents for the Trustee. It is hard work, not made any easier by the usual circumstances of late involvement of the Trustee. The primary culprit is time. The review tips outlined will help the Trustee reviewer to focus his/her efforts and maximize efficiency in the review process.

Chapter Summary

- The indenture is the key document for Trustees to review and understand to define the Trustee's roles and responsibilities for the life of the bond issue.

- The key areas of the indenture for Trustees include the operational and monitoring responsibilities for Trustees of the bond issue (i.e., interest rate, payment frequency, flow of the funds, establishment of accounts, investments, redemptions and sinking funds, other issuer covenants, Trustee duties, and the default section).

- There is a growing list of indenture hot spots, such as "no implied duties," that Trustees must be always vigilant in considering.

- Key document review tips allow an effective, efficient review of an indenture or other Trust document in one hour. Be focused, uninterrupted, and at your best time of day when you review. Yes, it can be done in one hour if you follow my tips.

~ Case Study ~

You are reviewing a supplemental indenture for a utility company that is a major client. You notice that the Trustee's priority claim for recovery of fees and expenses in a bankruptcy is listed last behind the bondholders. This is unacceptable. The Trustee should be first in priority for recovery. You relate this to bond counsel, who tells you that is how it was in the previous issue indenture and that they will not change it.

What would your course of action be?

Answer:

You should refer back to the previous supplemental indenture. There, you find that the Trustee's priority claim was actually in first position. So instead of calling bond counsel a liar, you professionally respond that your position was verified in the previous supplemental indenture. You request the same language be adopted in the new supplement.

This scenario happened to me. Bond counsel apologized by saying that the issuer was a "difficult client" and that they would go back to the issuer and argue our case, which they did successfully. The lesson learned is that you must always carefully review the indenture and have the courage to question language that impacts you as Trustee. Do not be afraid to negotiate and hold firm to important positions. Remember, you will be living with the indenture for a long time.

~ Chapter 3 ~

The Trust Indenture Act

Washington, DC—1995

It is both intimidating and exciting to be in our nation's capital testifying before Congress. The year is 1995, and I am appearing before the House Commerce Committee to present the Trustee's point of view on behalf of the Corporate Trust industry. My testimony is focused on proposed legislation calling for the repeal of the Trust Indenture Act (TIA). In making my presentation to the House Commerce Committee, I do not appear before the Committee directly under the glare of the television lights, but instead I am ushered into a side chamber in the House of Representatives. There, I make my case to three staff members of the Committee, who will report back what they heard to the representatives serving on the Committee.

The staffers are young and bright. I answer their questions about what the role of the Trustee is in a bond issue and discuss why the services provided by a Trustee are necessary and vital to the proper functioning of the securities markets. I try to be factual, yet truthful, honest, and passionate in my advocacy regarding the importance of Trustees and the TIA. I argue, among other things, that the TIA is a necessary act that serves the purposes of issuers and investors well. I give them as many reasons as possible to oppose repeal of the TIA.

As we complete the discussion, which lasts for over two and a half hours, and as I rise to leave after thanking the staff members for their thoughtful consideration, I ask one final question: "I am curious to know who is sponsoring this movement to repeal the Trust Indenture Act." I had previously given some speculation as to who would have objected to the continued existence of the Corporate Trustee as required by the Act. Yet I am shocked by the staffers' responses. They turn to me and smile as they explain, "Oh, didn't you know? It is your customers. Customers, being the 'institutional investors,' the bondholders you are duty bound to protect, who do not think you are either willing to or able to react quickly enough to protect their interests without hiding behind walls of indemnity."

I am stunned. I thank them for their input and leave Capitol Hill with a new outlook. Is it true what the staffers said? I will never forget their words and will continue to take the position that a good Trustee is one who is proactive, takes prompt action, and always considers the position of the people he/she is appointed to protect—the bondholders—both institutional and retail.

In the end, the Trust Indenture Act was not repealed. I would like to believe that my stellar testimony made the difference, but I doubt it. I also believe repeal of the TIA is a threat that someday may return. If we as Trustees forget what our real purpose is—to protect the bondholders—this issue will resurface. I have never forgotten the stunned, sickened feeling I had that day in the outer chamber of the US House of Representatives that at least someone did not think Trustees could do their jobs. It is up to all of us as Trustees to prove them wrong.

Chapter Objective

This chapter will discuss the Trust Indenture Act of 1939 as amended by the Trust Indenture Reform Act of 1990.

To truly understand the function of the Trustee in a bond financing, it is crucial that a basic understanding is gained of the laws that define the role of the Trustee. The most crucial law impacting Trustees is the Trustee Indenture Act of 1939 (TIA) as amended by the Trustee Indenture Reform Act of 1990 (TIRA). In reviewing these acts, I will emphasize how they shape the responsibilities of Trustees and why the capital markets need Trustees.

This chapter will focus on three main points:

I.   The Purpose and History of the TIA as Amended
II. What Trustees Should Know about Their Responsibilities under the TIA
III. The Impact of the TIA and Evolution of the Role of the Trustee in the Securities Markets

I. The Purpose and History of the TIA as Amended

To understand the true purpose of the TIA and why Congress enacted it, we must first understand the intent of the basic securities laws enacted in the early 1930s. The intent of the Securities Act of 1933 was to protect the investing public from fraud. The act was also designed to restore and improve investor confidence in the securities markets by establishing basic standards by which securities are issued, bought, and sold. The overriding intent of the legislators in the early 1930s was to improve the flow of information to the market. By requiring disclosure of timely and accurate information to investors and market makers, the securities laws enhanced the ability of market participants to make informed investment decisions. Therefore, the protection of investors was the main focus of the Securities Act of 1933. Specifically, the Act required:

- Initial disclosure through a prospectus (corporate issues) or official statement (municipal issues) of relevant information about the securities to be issued; and
- Continuing disclosure of material information.

The Securities Act of 1933 was called "the truth in securities act" because of drafter intent to bring truth to the securities markets. The goals of the Securities Act of 1933 were further strengthened by the enactment of the Securities and Exchange Act of 1934, which established the Securities and Exchange Commission (SEC) to enforce the provisions of the Securities Act of 1933.

It is interesting to note that the true purpose of the Securities Exchange Act of 1934 and the intent of the SEC to protect investors has intensified over the eighty-plus years since their creation. This intensity also involves Trustees because of the crucial role played by Trustees to protect the bondholders. The economic crisis of 2008 certainly exposed bondholders to increased risk of default, thereby causing the role of the Trustee to be of greater importance.

Reason for the Trust Indenture Act

Even after passage of the 1933 and 1934 Securities acts, the continued congressional investigations of the securities and banking industries focused on investor protection. A large number of US corporate bonds defaulted during the Great Depression. It seemed obvious that something needed to be done to protect bondholders, who, after all, are creditors of the corporations in whose bonds they had invested. While some corporations appointed banks to act as Trustees for their debt, the practice was not widely used. Even when Trustees were appointed, they had very limited powers and little authority to act. Their responsibilities were strictly limited by broad exculpatory clauses in the indentures, which effectively made Trustees nothing more than bystanders to the proceedings. The exculpatory language severely limited the responsibilities of Trustees and granted no authority for Trustees to take the necessary actions to protect the bondholders' interests in a default.

Bondholders clearly needed protection and assistance in pursuing their rights as creditors. As a result, the congressional committees charged with oversight of the securities laws proposed new legislation that would supplement the investor protections already put in place by the Securities Act of 1933 as enforced by the SEC.

The result was the proposed amendment to the Securities Act of 1933 in the form of the Trust Indenture Act of 1939 (TIA), which was enacted August 3, 1939. The result was a new era of protection for bondholders. This is the basis for the role of the Trustee today.

The Intent of the TIA

The intent of the TIA is to provide a mechanism to protect bondholders' interests. This is achieved by requiring the appointment of an official Trustee. Prior to 1939, a Trustee was not required for any bond issue, although issuers and investors had sought the services and protections offered by a formal Trustee for debt issues. Yet the role was poorly defined and largely ineffective, as was proven by the defaults occurring during the Great Depression. The key objectives of the TIA were to:

- Require an official Trustee be appointed for certain bond issues;
- Establish qualifications that banks and other entities must meet in order to serve as Trustee;
- Define bond issues for which a Trustee is required and exemptions to TIA requirements;
- Formally require registration of a TIA-qualified indenture with the SEC and subject it to SEC disclosure requirements and jurisdiction;
- Define conflicts of interest, which must be avoided by Trustees;
- Establish the duties and responsibilities of Trustees giving them the power and authority to act and carry out mandated responsibilities; and
- Set a formal standard of care to govern Trustee actions—the prudent man/person standard of care.

The overall intent was to require that a Trustee be appointed for bond issues sold to the investing public. Congress had determined that publicly issued corporate bond debt had been subject to the highest incidents of default and that therefore safeguards be put into place.

Congress wanted a formal, professional organization—a bank—to step into the role of the Trustee to protect public investors. Why? Such an organization could:

- Monitor issuer compliance with indenture provisions;
- Provide an intermediary to administer the payments and handle operational requirements of bond issues; and
- Stand in place of the bondholders to represent their interests in pursuing their claim as creditors in a default situation.

Professional Trustees must meet certain requirements in order to serve. Most importantly, Trustees now, under the requirements of the TIA, have the proper authority and responsibility to act to protect bondholders' interests. This was a monumental step in the evolution of the US securities markets. In the course of its seventy-plus-year history, the TIA has worked well to provide standards by which Trustees perform their role in bond financings.

Trust Indenture Reform Act

The Trust Indenture Reform Act of 1990 (TIRA) was enacted on November 15, 1990. The main purpose of TIRA was to modernize the TIA, which had not been updated for over fifty years. The updates brought the TIA into the modern era by permitting banks that act as Trustees to also underwrite, lend, and provide a variety of other banking services to Corporate Trust customers, banks that had formerly been prohibited as conflicts of interest. J. P. Morgan, one of the largest Trustees in the United States, was a driving force behind modernizing the TIA, seeking to be able to provide additional banking services to its corporate clients. With the repeal of the Glass-Steagall Act in 1998, banks were then able to underwrite securities, activities that would have been a conflict of interest before the TIRA amended the TIA.

With the passage of TIRA, the following changes were effected for the TIA:

- Former Section 310(b)'s conflicts of interest were changed to apply only in post-default situations.
- A new conflict provision was added—Section 310(b)(10) for lending. Now, if a Trustee bank loans money to an issuer/obligor and also serves as Trustee, this is an official conflict of interest post-default.

- Foreign Trustees can now act as Trustees in the United States if a reciprocal arrangement exists with that country. This means a bank in Germany can act as Trustee for debt issues in the United States if a US Trustee can serve as Trustee for debt issued in Germany.

- The requirement that a Trustee file an annual Trustee's report formerly required under Section 313 was changed to require a Trustee to file a report only if a "material change" has occurred in the Trustee's position with the issuer/obligor. This largely eliminated the perfunctory annual Trustee reports but did not entirely eliminate the need for Trustees to perform an annual conflict check. The Trustee must still determine if an annual Trustee's report needs to be sent (to bondholders, the SEC, and any exchanges the bonds are listed on) due to significant conflict issues vis-à-vis the Trustee, issuer/obligor, and underwriter.

- The TIA was now included by reference in all TIA-qualified indentures. This cut down on the length of indentures, which no longer had to incorporate the entire TIA. The result was cost savings, yet the parties to the bond issue must realize that every word of the TIA is included in TIA-qualified indentures, even though the TIA isn't physically recorded in the indenture.

- The issuer/obligor is now required to provide an annual officers' certificate of no default to the Trustee stating whether the issuer/obligor has knowledge of a default under the indenture.

- The preferential claims provision of Section 311 was shortened from four months to three months to be consistent with the Bankruptcy Code's preference period.

- Any qualifying entity or financial institution can serve as a Trustee. A Trustee no longer has to be a bank as was the case prior to 1990.

The TIRA amendments to the TIA were designed to more closely align the TIA with current security industry practices and standards. The TIRA also sought to produce cost savings (by, for example, permitting the TIA to be incorporated in indentures by reference) and to make the TIA more efficient by largely eliminating annual Trustee reports. The most significant change wrought by the TIRA, however, was to make certain conflicts of interest, which disqualified Trustees from service as a Trustee, are operative only in post-default situations. This opened the way for banks to provide a broad array of services, including underwriting, to the corporations they were also serving as Trustees. This resulted in more business opportunities for the banks without the fear of a conflict of interest with their role as Trustee.

For the rest of this chapter, I will refer to the TIA with the understanding that it includes all amendments enacted by the passage of TIRA. The Trustee should not confuse the two acts. The TIA is the operative act as amended by TIRA. They are not separate but one.

II. What Trustees Should Know about Their Responsibilities under the TIA

This section will focus on the most significant TIA sections I believe every Trustee should be aware of. A quick reference guide to the TIA, providing a shorthand definition of each section, is provided in Exhibit A. It is vitally important for every Trustee to be familiar with the responsibilities required of Trustees by the TIA. Why? Because many of these responsibilities have become standard in many bond issues not required to be registered under the TIA and have been drafted in the indentures. Let us look more closely at the crucial TIA sections in order to understand their impact on the Trustee.

A Summary of the TIA

As discussed above, the TIA is an amendment to the Securities Act of 1933 and is enforced by the SEC. That is why the TIA begins with Section 301 and ends with Section 328. It is an addition to the Securities Act of 1933.

Exempted Securities (Section 304)

The TIA does not apply to the following securities:

- Government-issued securities, both US and foreign, do not require a Trustee. These include any securities issued by the federal government, state governments, or any city, county, or other political subdivisions of the states. Therefore, US government T-Bills, T-Notes, T-bonds or agency securities, GNMAs, FNMAs, and FHLMBs do not require a Trustee. Also, municipal securities do not require a Trustee. All are exempt from the TIA.
- Certificates of Deposit (CDs), Commercial Paper (CP), or any short-term note of less than eighteen months are exempt from the TIA and do not require a Trustee.
- Private placement issues do not require a Trustee.
- Stock issues do not require a Trustee.
- Securities under $10 million (representing the entire issuance of debt) by an issuer are exempt.

Asset-backed securities, unless they constitute pure debt, are generally considered to be exempt from the TIA. The SEC has issued "No Action" letters indicating that asset-backed securities like issuances of stock do not carry a fixed obligation and therefore are exempt from TIA requirements. To explain it another way, since many asset-backed issues merely entitle holders to whatever amounts are collected on the receivables rather than a specific return or provide holders with a certificate evidencing an undivided interest in a special purpose vehicle (SPV) constituting a trust, these interests may not constitute "debt" for purposes of registration under the TIA. There have been recent court decisions challenging the concept of asset-backed securities to be under the provisions of the TIA even though these issues were specifically designed to not be qualified under the TIA. This is a disturbing development and one I do not agree with. If the bond issue is designed to not be under the TIA, then it should not be pushed into the TIA requirements after the fact, as this may result in unwarranted liability for Trustees who were operating under different provisions of the indentures.

Securities Required to Be Registered under the Securities Act (Section 305)
An issuer must register the indenture pursuant to which debt securities are to be issued with the SEC to "qualify" it under the TIA. The issuer does this by filing a Registration Statement of S-1 with the SEC. This normally occurs thirty to forty-five days prior to issuance of the bonds. This makes the bond issue a "qualified issue," and it is the issuer's responsibility to file the S-1 and qualify the debt securities. An S-3 is filed for shelf registrations and will be discussed in Chapter 8.

Eligibility and Disqualification of Trustee (Section 310)

Section 310 is one of the two most crucial sections of the TIA, the other being Section 315(c), which establishes the prudent man/person standard as the standard of conduct for Trustees. Section 310 covers two areas: 1) qualifications for Trustees and 2) conflicts of interest.

The purpose of this section is to establish formal minimum standards for Trustees and to provide guidelines for assuring that Trustees remain uncompromised and free to use their best judgment in protecting the interests of the bondholders and that they remain free from any conflicts of interest that might impair their judgment. A focused Trustee, empowered to act and not encumbered by any conflicts of interest, is a vital part of the TIA. He/she assures investors of professional protection of their interests.

Qualifications

A Trustee must:

- Be an organization authorized to exercise Corporate Trust powers as granted by one or more states; and
- Maintain a capital and surplus of at least $150,000.

Disqualifying Conflicts of Interest (Section 310[b][1-10])

Section 310(b)(1-10) defines ten specific situations in which a conflict of interest will disqualify a Trustee if at any time the securities are in default. By default, I mean an Event of Default as defined in the indenture. Prior to an Event of Default, these ten conflicts do not disqualify a Trustee from serving. However, once the Trustee becomes aware of the existence of a disqualifying conflict post-default, the Trustee must, within ninety days, either eliminate the conflict or resign as Trustee. Usually, the Trustee will resign because the conflict cannot or will not be cured within the ninety-day period, thereby compelling resignation. Failure to resign or cure the conflict would subject the Trustee to liability and, almost certainly, litigation by the bondholders. In rare cases, the Trustee may obtain a "No Action" letter from the SEC staying his/her obligation to resign. Such stays are granted only if the Event of Default may be cured or waived during a reasonable period and if such stay of resignation is not inconsistent with the interests of the bondholders.

The conflicts described in Section 310(b) of the TIA can be summarized as follows:

- First, a potential conflict situation will arise where the Trustee is a Trustee under another indenture for securities issued by the same issuer/obligor and is at a different level of debt. For example, the bank is Trustee for a secured bond issue and also for a separate unsecured issue with the same issuer/obligor.

- Second, potential conflicts may arise when the Trustee is also an underwriter for the issuer, controls an underwriter for the issuer, or is controlled by an underwriter for the issuer.

- Third, a potential conflict arises in many variations under which there is common control or common ownership between the Trustee and the issuer through common officers, directors, or shareholders and through stock ownership. These potential conflicts arise both in the situation where the indenture Trustee directly or indirectly owns stock in the issuer and where the issuer directly or indirectly owns stock in the Trustee of a certain percentage.

- Finally, a potential conflict exists if the Trustee is also a creditor of the issuer.

Preferential Collection of Claims Against Obligor (Section 311)

The Trustee may have to set aside funds in a special account for any monies the Trustee collects as a creditor during the three-month period prior to a payment default or other Event of Default. This is the preferential claims provision modeled after similar provisions in the US Bankruptcy Code, which is designed to prevent unscrupulous creditors from taking money from the debtor or potential debtor companies to the detriment of other creditors. If the Trustee bank is also a lender to the issuer/obligor, Section 311 must be carefully monitored by both the Trustee side and the lending side of the bank. It may be sufficient reason for the Trustee to resign in advance of a potential default in order to avoid criticism under Section 311.

Bondholder Lists (Section 312)

This is an important section because it was designed to fulfill a crucial bondholder need: to be able to obtain a list of holders to facilitate communication among the holders as a class in a bankruptcy situation. This was a glaring problem in the 1930s whereby bondholders were unable to come together as a class because no entity or individual was charged with maintaining a list of holders. This is now clearly the Trustee's responsibility.

The section provides that any three or more bondholders can petition the Trustee for a bondholder's list, which must be supplied within five business days. In today's world where the securities are held in book entry form at the Depository Trust Company (DTC), the Trustee is only able to provide a "participants listing" from DTC, which does not identify the true beneficial owners. Yet if the Trustee has physical bonds and as such maintains a record of the bondholders' names and addresses, then this section becomes relevant.

Reports by Trustee (Section 313)

This section concerns what was once the Trustee's annual reporting requirement but is now, since passage of TIRA, only required if there is a *material change* concerning the conflicts section. Those items/situations include:

- Any conflicts of interest under Section 310(b)(1-10) that represent any material change to the relationship between Trustee and issuer;
- Any advances, i.e., loans, made by the Trustee if remaining unpaid and totaling more than 1/2 of 1% of the principal amount outstanding;
- Any material loan or credit amount;
- Change in property and funds held by the Trustee for the issuer;
- Any changes in release or substitution of property;
- The appointment of the Trustee as Trustee for additional securities issued by the same issuer/obligor; and
- Any action taken by the Trustee that materially affects the indenture securities.

If the Trustee must prepare an annual Trustee's report, it must be sent to the bondholders, the SEC, the issuer, and any exchange on which the securities are listed.

The significance of this section is that the Trustee must continue to monitor potential conflict of interest requirements under the TIA and may have to provide a Trustee's annual report. The Trustee cannot just ignore this section and assume there is no requirement to produce one.

A Disturbing Story

I was facilitating a training session at a major bank as Trustee in New York, and I was describing the annual Trustee report requirement in the TIA. One of the managers made the statement, "It really doesn't matter if we do a conflict check or send out a Trustee annual report. I do not see the need to do one." I was shocked. As my blood pressure was rising, I replied that it was a requirement of federal law (the TIA) that Trustees still are required to produce an annual Trustee's report as outlined in the Act if certain material events occurred. Failure to do so would be a violation of federal law, not to mention a breach of the indenture.

I would not want to defend a Trustee in court with that position of "who cares?" This demonstrates to me the dangers of misunderstanding what the TIA really requires. I understand the need to cut costs for your business, but you cannot dismiss your stated responsibilities under the law and contract just because it seems unimportant. I can assure you that complying with the TIA is important.

Reports by Obligor: Evidence of Compliance with Indenture Provisions (Section 314)
This section is important for Trustees because it establishes the reports that are to be provided to the Trustee. Part of the Trustee's function is to monitor issuer compliance with the disclosure requirements imposed by the SEC and the Securities acts. As a result, the

Trustee must establish appropriate ticklers to indicate when reports are to be received. Reports that are required to be sent to the Trustee are:

- SEC-required financial reports:
    - 10K—Annual Report
    - 10Q—Quarterly Reports (first three quarters)
    - 8K—Material Event Reports (the 8K is provided only upon the occurrence of a material event, such as a bankruptcy filing, that therefore cannot be anticipated)
    - 10D—Servicer Reporting
- Issuer annual financial report to the marketplace and accountant's certificate regarding the issuer's annual financial statements
- Annual No-Default Certificate
- Any other reports required to be filed with the SEC by the issuer

The Trustee must be sure to monitor receipt of these reports. A further question arises as to what the Trustee should do with the reports once they are received. Should the Trustee read them? This question will be addressed in the risk management chapter (Chapter 7). For now, the reader should assume that the Trustee must, at minimum, receive such reports as required. Current industry practice is for the Trustee to access the SEC EDGAR website, where the reports are filed and printed (front page only) as evidence of obtaining the report.

Duties and Responsibilities for the Trustee (Section 315)

This is the second most important section of the TIA. Why? It establishes the standard of conduct for Trustees. Section 315(a) has two very important protections for Trustees:

1. The Trustee shall not be liable except for the performance of duties specifically set out in the indenture. This is what I call the "no implied duties" provision. It protects the Trustee from being responsible for vague duties that are not directly spelled out in the indenture. In today's modern world where litigation is prevalent, this is an important protection for Trustees.

2. The Trustee can conclusively rely on the truth of statements or opinions he/she receives. This is crucial because it means that Trustees do not have to investigate the statements and opinions they receive but can accept these reports on their face and be protected in doing so. What the Trustee must do is examine the reports/certificates received pursuant to Section 314 to determine whether or not such evidence conforms to the requirements of the indenture provisions. Obviously, this must be done in good faith. Unfortunately, if Trustees have actual knowledge that the information they receive is wrong, the Trustees cannot bury their head in the sand and rely on the face of the certificate. More will be said on this point in the default and risk management chapters (Chapters 5 and 7).

Section 315 is critical because it places a definitive responsibility on the Trustee to provide bondholders with timely notice of default, defined as within ninety days of the occurrence of the event. The Trustee cannot just "sit" on a notice but must communicate it to bondholders within ninety days. This section does allow the Trustee to withhold such notice if he/she deems it is in the best interest of the bondholders. I strongly recommend that Trustees only do so after receiving an opinion of counsel and having consulted senior management and a Trustee committee at the bank.

Section 315(c) defines the standard of care the Trustee must use in cases of default. This is the prudent man/person standard of care. It is operative only after the occurrence of an Event of Default as defined in the indenture. The section reads as follows:

> The indenture Trustee shall exercise in case of default (as such term is defined in such indenture) such of the rights and powers vested in it by such indenture, and to use the same degree of care and skill in their exercise, as a prudent man would exercise or use under the circumstances in the conduct of his own affairs.

While this is the actual language in the TIA, modern-day application of the language is "prudent man/person," and "his/her" is added to the language.

What does this really mean for Trustees? Simply that after an Event of Default, there is an elevation in the Trustee's responsibilities under the indenture. The Trustee assumes a heightened standard of care in pursuing the claims of the bondholders. The Trustee must act prudently—just as if he/she were a person whose own money were at stake—and act accordingly. I know that when my own money is at stake, I am more alert, proactive, and vigilant. The Trustee is in a position of responsibility to act proactively and with discretion to protect the interests of the bondholders.

Section 315(d) states that the Trustee is responsible for his/her own negligent action, failure to act, or own willful misconduct. The Trustee is protected against any errors in judgment made in good faith. The Trustee is also protected in taking action as directed by a majority of bondholders in the principal amount of securities.

Directions and Waivers by Bondholders; Prohibition of Impairment of Holder's Right to Payment (Section 316)

The importance of this section is to allow for bondholder direction to waive provisions of the indenture and to direct Trustee actions. The key is that a majority in the principal amount of securities outstanding must direct the Trustee. The provision is not less than a majority. Some indentures may impose a higher standard of two-thirds or even 100 percent. The Trustee must carefully consult the indenture for the exact requirement and not accept anything less.

This section also states that not less than 75 percent in the principal amount of securities held by bondholders can waive an interest payment, provided, however, that such waivers may not postpone any interest payment for more than three years from the bond issue due date. In my experience, principal waivers generally require 100 percent holder consent.

Special Powers of Trustee: Duties of Paying Agent (Section 317)

This is the last section that will be considered. It provides that the Trustee is authorized to file proofs of claim to establish his/her right as a creditor on behalf of the bondholders in a bankruptcy proceeding.

The rest of TIA covers various miscellaneous topics. All Trustees should read the TIA.

III. The Impact of the TIA and Evolution of the Role of the Trustee in the Securities Markets

The TIA remains the principal framework for defining the role of Trustees. Even though it is mandated to apply only to public, corporate issues, it has become the common framework for other bond issues as well. In fact, today we find many private placements, structured finance, project finance, leveraged leases, and municipal bonds with indentures and other governing documents that contain language almost identical to TIA provisions.

The reason for this is simple: it works—and has done so for over seventy years. Of all the securities laws, the TIA is arguably one of the most successful pieces of legislation. It has served its purpose well: it provides a professional Trustee to serve and protect the investors (i.e., bondholders).

A Threat to the TIA

No discussion of the TIA would be complete without mention of the attempt to repeal the TIA. On July 27, 1995, Representative Jack Fields of Texas introduced the Capital Markets Deregulation and Liberalization Act of 1995. The purpose was to promote deregulation and promote efficiency in the US capital markets. To the surprise of the Corporate Trust industry, the bill contained one sentence providing for repeal of the TIA in its entirety. What was behind this effort? Who wanted to see the cornerstone law of the Corporate Trust industry eliminated? And what would that mean for Trustees?

These are the questions asked by many in the business at the time. As a result of my position as head of the ABA Corporate Trust Committee at the time, I found myself actively involved in lobbying Congress to defend the Trustees' position that the TIA should not be repealed. After two trips to Capitol Hill and discussions with congressional committee members and the SEC staff, I can answer the three questions posed above.

1. The overall effort to eliminate unnecessary regulation was a primary effort of the Republican-controlled Congress under Newt Gingrich. The sweeping deregulation bill was designed as a general catchall for all types of requirements that were perceived to be unnecessary regulation. I found out that the TIA was included, for the most part, because no one really understood its purpose.

2. The institutional investment community was the prime mover behind the perception that Trustees failed to act on what was needed to protect their interests in times of trouble.

3. The repeal of the TIA would not, in my opinion, have been the end of Trustees. The securities markets are now so comfortable with the presence of professional Trustees to handle many pre- and post-default responsibilities that it is inconceivable that issuers and bondholders would want to proceed without them. This is especially true of the structured finance market. However, repeal of the TIA would have raised serious concerns about the overall legitimacy of Trustees and the standards under which they operate.

This story has a happy ending, in a way. The Fields' Bill was changed to HR3005 and became the National Securities Markets Improvement Act of 1996. It was passed and became law in October 11, 1996. It *did not* contain any provision for repealing the TIA nor even for an SEC study of the benefits of, continuing need for, and options for modifying or eliminating the TIA (which an earlier version of the bill had called for). The Trustee industry gave a collective sigh of relief.

Conclusion

The effort to repeal the TIA should serve as a wake-up call for Trustees. Every Trustee must work more diligently to fulfill the responsibilities for which we Trustees are entrusted—both pre-default and post-default. Investors and market participants look to Trustees to do their jobs correctly, as professionals who are protecting the interests of others—the bondholders—who are their real clients. If we do not perform—diligently and proactively—we will be replaced. If the concern about the performance of Trustees could cause an act introduced in Congress to include repeal of the TIA, all Trustees must take notice. The economic crisis of 2008 and the meltdown of the mortgage market and subsequent difficulties with mortgage-backed securities have once again placed Trustees in a difficult position.

Chapter Summary

- The Trust Indenture Act of 1939 (TIA) is the fundamental securities law that establishes the formal role of the Trustee.
- The TIA is part of the Securities Act of 1933, which falls under the jurisdiction of the SEC.
- The TIA was amended in 1990 by the Trust Indenture Reform Act of 1990 (TIRA).
- The most significant changes brought by TIRA were as follows:
  - The conflict of interest situations were made operative post-default from pre-default.
  - The TIA was now incorporated by reference in every TIA-qualified issue—word for word.

- o Trustee annual reports were no longer required to be sent by Trustees unless there was a material/significant change in the Trustee's relationship per the conflict situations in Section 310(b)(1-10).
- o An annual officer's certificate of "no default" was now required.
- TIA exempts different security types of financings (e.g., private placements, municipal bonds, SEC rule 144A, and RegS securities). However, it is common practice for a Trustee to be appointed in these financings because the issuer wants the services of a Trustee and the bondholders desire the protection a Trustee brings.
- Many indentures incorporate TIA language even if they are not TIA-qualified finances because the language works to properly establish the duties and responsibilities of the Trustee.

~ Case Study ~

The TIA defines the conflicts of interest that post-default would require the Trustee to:

1. Cure the conflict or resign the Trusteeship;
2. Give notice of any resignation to issuer and bondholders; and
3. Have a successor Trustee appointed in order to be officially resigned.

The commercial department of the bank approaches you in your Trustee role and relays to you its concerns as to the credit health of the issuer for a TIA bond issue for which you serve as Trustee. The issuer is not in default yet under the bond issue. Answer the following questions:

What actions should you take?

Should you resign as Trustee?

Answer:

As Trustee your first concern is to avoid a conflict of interest as described in the TIA. Lending is certainly a conflict under the Act. However, since no Event of Default has occurred yet, the TIA does not require the Trustee to resign or cure the conflict. The short answer is you are not required under the law (TIA) to take any action at this time.

Yet custom and practice in the industry has also supported the concept of having a Trustee act proactively to resign prior to that Event of Default occurring. The reason is to avoid even the perception that the Trustee's actions were prejudicial by the potential conflict. Therefore, in some cases certain more conservative Trustees will resign or endeavor to cure a potential conflict prior to an actual Event of Default.

As with many instances in Corporate Trust, it all depends upon the circumstances of the situation. My answer would be not to resign too early but get ready to resign by lining up successors in the event that the situation deteriorates quickly. Waiting until the last minute risks the Trustee being criticized for recognizing the conflict too late. The TIA gives the Trustee ninety days to cure the conflict or resign after the Event of Default. It is the wise and, I would add, prudent Trustee who carefully monitors the situation and takes the appropriate actions sooner rather than later.

~ Chapter 4 ~

Pre-default Duties and Compliance Issues

New York, New York—1989

I am sitting in a large conference room on the twenty-third floor of a building, home to a major law firm, in midtown Manhattan, serving as bond counsel. This morning we close a $23 million structured finance issue involving mortgages securitized in a Collateralized Mortgage Obligation (CMO) structure. This complex transaction has taken months to put together, with countless hours invested by bond counsel, underwriters, issuers, and a supporting cast of other attorneys and accountants. We were all up the night before completing a lot of last-minute details and spent some rather tense moments waiting for the rating agency to make its final determination. I went to bed at 4:00 a.m. I am sure others had not slept at all.

As I look at the thirty-five to forty people gathered in the conference room, I identify the representative of a savings and loan as well as the purchaser of the residual bonds. These residual bonds are the last to be paid but will realize handsome returns if the bond issue works as well as we all hope it will. The mood in the room is a mixture of exhaustion, excitement, apprehension, and expectant relief, all encompassed in a slight air of tension as the minutes tick by. Although I play a key role in the transaction as the Trustee, I seem to be a sort of silent partner among all the chatter involving the other constituents.

I get up and walk across the crowded room to a small table replete with the usual token breakfast refreshments—coffee, soft drinks, and stale bagels, a hallmark of these large financial transactions. I pick up a bagel and open my mouth to take a well-deserved bite when I hear the words, ". . . And does the Trustee have the money?"

As I turn to face the room with my bagel in hand and my mouth open, I see forty sets of eyes fixed on me. There is dead silence.

I never do take a bite of that bagel. In order to avoid inflicting panic on all these people, I immediately call our wire transfer room to quietly (and forcefully) ask for confirmation that we do indeed have the funds. Happily, my wire room confirms we have just received the funds. I turn to the people and triumphantly announce the good news. Relaxation and relief flood the room as normal conversation resumes.

I often reflect after closings are done and the celebrations end that the Trustee is the last to be invited to the party but is the one left to clean up after everyone has gone.

It is here that I fully understand my role in the securities process. I am, for one brief shining moment, the real spotlight in the transaction—but not until the very end.

Chapter Objective

This chapter will describe the functions the Trustee performs, from pre-closing of a bond issue to post-closing. These two areas comprise the pre-default duties of the Trustee. Two main topics will be discussed:

I. Pre-closing Trustee Functions

II. Post-closing Administrator Duties

The case study at the end of the chapter will bring to life the pre-closing parties to a bond financing. The objective of the case study is to clarify the roles of the principal parties in bringing a bond issue to closing. It is my favorite exercise in demonstrating the partnership of the Trustee and other key players in the capital market process.

I. Pre-closing Trustee Functions

The closing refers to the day the bonds are issued in the primary market. It's also the official beginning of the Trustee's role under the indenture. The closing is when the Trustee assumes his/her role legally and begins performing all his/her other duties for the bond issue. Prior to the closing, the Trustee has no legal authority to act and technically does *not* exist in the financing. However, prior to the closing, the Trustee plays an unofficial role. During that time, the Trustee takes an active part in working with the parties in the financing to facilitate the issuance of the bonds.

The following are possible tasks a Trustee may undertake in a pre-closing:

- Review the indentures and relevant Trust documents.

- Work with bond counsel, preferably with Trustee counsel, to make comments on the indenture and Trust documents to which the Trustee is a party.

- Authenticate the bonds (either physical bonds or bonds that are issued as one global note).

- Execute documents, usually at the pre-closing or closing. If no in-person closing occurs, then it will take place by mail. Over the years, I have seen a dramatic decrease in face-to-face closings, which were usually conducted in the offices of bond counsel. That is a real shame, in my opinion. In-person closings allowed us, in our role as Trustees, to meet the parties to the financing, the bond counsel, the underwriter, issuer, financial advisors, and others. Relationships were formed that proved invaluable in administering the bond issue post-closing. Over the years, we have certainly lost the personal contacts and in-person interaction. As a result, our partnership with the team that creates a bond issue is not as strong—a real loss for us and the other players in the process.

- File a T-1 with the SEC if the bond issue is qualified under the TIA. This establishes the formal ability of the Trustee to qualify to act as such for the bond issue.

- Provide a Trustee's certificate stating Trustee's officer's signatures as authorized signers and confirming the Trustee's agreement to serve as Trustee for the bond issue and perform the duties required in the indenture.

- Open trust accounts to receive funds at the closing.

- Provide original insurance instructions to operations to establish operational records for the bond issue (e.g., interest and principal dates, record dates, amount to be issued, tax reporting, fee schedules). Also authorizing information to enable the FRAC to take place for any DTC FAST closing issues.

- Perform Know Your Customer (KYC) due diligence and documentation.

- Receive investment direction for execution of investments at the closing.

- Prepare any distribution of funds to the parties for fees or other disbursements, such as for a construction fund, to be made at the closing.
- Prepare to receive any collateral held by the Trustee at closing.

The day before the closing is when the Trustee typically performs the following duties:

- Inspect all financial documents in final form.
- Finalize instructions for funds movement and disbursements.
- Review the closing memorandum (which details the flow of funds), verify the amounts, and wire transfer instructions for both receiving and distributing funds.
- Sign the indenture and other relevant documents in preparation for the closing.
- Deliver the Trustee's certificate.

At the closing, the Trustee performs the following tasks:

- Receive the bond monies from the underwriter.
- Take possession of the closing documents. If all are not available, the Trustee at least takes a signed copy of the indenture and bond counsel's opinion and any other trust documents the Trustee signs.
- Allocate bond proceeds to appropriate trust accounts and disburse funds as required.
- Invest remaining bond proceeds per written direction in permitted investments.
- Take possession and inventory of the global note.
- Issue physical bonds, if required by the financing.

- If the bonds are book entry with DTC, participate in a phone call with DTC and underwriters. In that phone call, the following short conversation occurs:
  - The parties identify themselves.
  - The DTC representative asks if the Trustee has the funds and asks the Trustee to verify his/her DTC account.
  - Once confirmed, the DTC representative states that the bonds will be moved to the underwriter.
  - The call concludes.

The phone call really is a simultaneous transfer of bond proceeds for the bonds. I like to represent it this way:

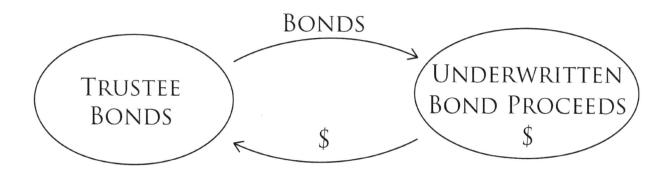

At my first bond closing in New York, I was sitting in one of the largest conference rooms I had ever seen overlooking all of Manhattan, having just completed the DTC call. I had confirmed the deposit of funds in the trust accounts, investment executions, and disbursements of funds. I turned to the other people in the room. Much to my surprise, everyone was leaving. I expected some finale that would punctuate this momentous occasion . . . fireworks, bells ringing, or cameras flashing. Instead, everyone just left. I was very disappointed.

Closing Dinners: A Real-life Story

As in-person closings became a thing of the past, so does the practice of the closing dinner. Hosted by the underwriter, who, incidentally, had the largest fee from the financing, the closing dinner was another unique opportunity for building relationships. Out of the many closing dinners I attended, one stands out above all the others.

The closing was in Mexico City for a first mortgage utility bond issued by a large Mexican company. I arrived late to the opening dinner festivities, as I was busy moving the money. I arrived at the dinner venue in time to witness our branch commercial lender being carried out on a stretcher. It seemed the company had arranged for a mock bullfight with a baby bull for participation by the closing parties. Our commercial officer evidently lacked the required skills and was tossed by the baby bull.

The rest of the evening unfolded in an even more dramatic fashion. After a lengthy dinner, we all embarked to a club with a floor show suitable for Las Vegas. Then we went to several other establishments. We started with thirty-five people represented by company officials, bond counsel, attorneys, underwriters, commercial bankers, and myself as the solo representative of the Trustee. Throughout the evening, various members started literally falling by the wayside. Finally, there were only two people standing: the lead attorney for bond counsel and myself, the Trustee. It was now five o'clock in the morning, and we were sitting in a disco club in downtown Mexico City. I am proud to say that bond counsel was impressed. I had proven that the Trustee had the commitment to perform his duties to the very end.

II. Post-closing Administrator Duties

The Trustee has a variety of post-closing duties to perform as described by the indenture and governing Trust documents. These duties must be *explicitly* stated in the indenture. *There are no implied duties*. Remember, the Trustee is an agent pre-default with limited authority.

A good illustration of the Trustee's role concerns his/her duties in monitoring the covenants in the indenture. The issuer, who promises to do or not to do certain things, makes those covenants in the indenture. The Trustee has no responsibility for receiving evidence of issuer compliance with specific covenants unless the Trustee is specifically directed in the truat documents to receive such evidence. This is supported by both custom and practice and the legal requirements of the indenture (i.e., no implied duties).

One example is the insurance covenant in many indentures where physical property/equipment is collateral for the bonds. There is usually a covenant by the issuer to maintain insurance on the property/equipment. I do not question the fact that this is an important protection for the bondholders in case of a loss of the property. However, if the indenture or other Trust documents do not say the words "the Trustee will or shall receive evidence of the insurance," then it is *not* a Trustee's obligation to receive evidence or try to obtain it. In that case, it is clearly the issuer's responsibility.

Specific Post-closing Duties

I cannot stress enough the importance of performing post-closing duties correctly *every time*. This is not Major League Baseball where you are inducted into the Hall of Fame if you get a hit three out of ten times. In Corporate Trust, we are expected to hit ten out of ten chances.

Below is a list of key post-closing duties. As with everything in Corporate Trust, it is not all-inclusive. Other duties arise, specific to the unique needs of different financings, but the following is a good general list:

- Funds movement
- Covenant monitoring
- Investment of funds
- UCC (Uniform Commercial Code) filings
- Construction fund disbursements
- Valuations and calculations
- Client service
- Redemptions and sinking funds

Funds Movement

The most important Trustee duty post-closing and pre-default is to properly manage the flow of funds for the bond issue. This starts with receiving bond proceeds at the closing and depositing them into the proper Trust accounts, plus making the required disbursements. It continues with the receipt of principal and interest payments from the issuer or collateral and payment of the bondholders. Receiving the right amount of funds when they are due and calculating the proper interest and/or principal amounts to be paid to bondholders are critical steps. The Trustee must make the payments on time as required in the indenture, or serious consequences can occur. Certainly, the word "default" enters the conversation concerning the bond issue. Sources through which the Trustee receives the payments of funds to pay municipal and interest on the bonds include:

- Direct payment by the issuer
- Lease payments
- Letters of credit
- Mortgage payments
- Cash flow from servicers who collect from the assets pledged to the Trust (e.g., credit cards, auto loans, etc.)
- Other third parties, such as guaranteed investment contracts (GICS), SWAP agreements, or escrowed funds

The payment frequency can also vary from semi-annual to quarterly, monthly, or even daily receipts. As with everything in Corporate Trust, the Trustee's duties depend on each specific financing.

In addition to receiving and paying out the funds, which is referred to as "debt service payments," the Trustee is responsible for allocating incoming cash flow to various Trust accounts. This is described in the indenture. It is a critical responsibility of the Trustee to promptly and correctly place the right funds into the right accounts. Therefore, it is also vital for Trustees to clearly understand the indenture requirements for each flow allocation. This is also referred to as "the waterfall."

Another important point to make regarding funds movement is that the Trustee should make sure he/she has "good funds" or "collected funds" before paying out any debt service distributions. Failure to do so could result in potential liability for the bank.

Covenant Monitoring

After funds movement, the second key responsibility post-closing for Trustees is in monitoring issuer covenants. The timely receipt of required compliance items is an important Trustee responsibility. Trustees should diligently tickle all compliance items the indenture specifically requires to be sent to the Trustee. No more and no less. The Trustee must vigorously pursue those items to ensure timely receipt. Such items can include:

- Financial reports
- Budgets
- Officers' certificates (of no default)
- Insurance evidence (policies, certificates, personal property)
- Accountants verifications reports (for refunding bond issues)
- Letters of credit renewals
- Constructions fund/disbursement requests
- Arbitrage rebate requirement
- UCCs

The Trustee is tasked with monitoring certain issuer covenant compliance items because the bondholders want the Trustee to monitor the issuer's compliance with covenant requirements on their behalf.

Failure of the issuer to perform its covenants as evidenced to the Trustee would constitute a "technical default" under the indenture, leading to Trustee action. The Trustee role in this case will be discussed later in the post-default chapter (Chapter 5).

The final requirement for Trustees under covenant compliance duties would be to carefully review the evidence of compliance received. The Trustee must verify that the item meets the requirements of the indenture. Officers' certificates, legal opinions, or other statements must match the indenture language word for word or be sent back for correction.

Investment of Funds

A key fact is that as Trustees, we have *no investment discretion.* The words Trustees live by are that we execute investments only in the case of the following:

- The Trustee receives written direction
- The Trustee can invest in only permitted investments

Permitted investments language appears in both the definitions and the investment section of the indenture. The Trustee must carefully review the permitted investments language in order to allow the investment to be made. Here, the Trustee is the "gatekeeper" for the investments. Let's be clear: the Trustee does not advise or select the investment choices for the issuer. The Trustee, again, has no discretion regarding investment choices. Yet the Trustee is responsible for making sure that only permitted investments are made as described in the indenture.

The overarching principle of investing in the world of Corporate Trust is that bond proceeds and cash flow in a bond issue must not be risked. Only very conservative investments are permitted (no equities) because the monies cannot be lost. They must remain "safe" for the purposes of the financing and for payment to bondholders.

Given the clear responsibility of Trustees to monitor investment decisions of the issuers, the Trustee would be liable for any loss resulting from his/her failure to properly police such actions as required by the indenture. It is also true that issuers have the right to maximize their investment returns, as long as they stay in permitted investments per the indenture. To that end, idle cash should also be invested to the extent possible.

The use of a wider array of permitted investments, including money market funds, presents the Trustee with additional challenges. Add the interesting issue of the use of proprietary money market funds of the Trustee's bank as a permitted investment, and you can see that the Trustee must exercise care in not pushing the issuer into the bank's own funds. Choices should be presented to the issuer at its request (I like at least three choices of funds) to avoid any question of self-dealing. More will be said on this topic in the chapter on risk management (Chapter 7).

Sinking Funds and Redemptions

Many bond issues have sinking fund and redemption provisions. Both are intended to give the issuers flexibility to retire bonds prior to maturity. A sinking fund is a mandatory redemption or "call" of the bonds. It is a scheduled payment of principal representing a partial redemption of the bonds at a set date and usually at par, which is face value of the bonds. "Sinking fund" is the first term I heard when I joined Corporate Trust. My boss said, "Jeff, you need to do a sinking fund redemption." I replied with my usual sense of humor, "But what is sinking? I did not know I was joining the Navy." Needless to say, my boss was not impressed and firmly said, "It means sink the level of debt." His tone implied he thought I was a complete fool.

Redemptions can be either **mandatory** or **optional.**

A **mandatory redemption** can be a sinking fund or a separate redemption either in whole or part of the bond issue. It may be required if certain events occur, such as failure to renew a letter of credit.

An **optional redemption** is at the option of the issuer. It allows the issuer to retire part or all of the bonds at the issuer's discretion. The issuer may choose the option to redeem the bonds in order to:

- Reduce the debt burden of the issuer; and
- Retire higher interest rate bonds if rates are falling.

If the issuer instructs the Trustee to perform an optional redemption, the bonds will be retired at a "premium," meaning the bondholders will receive a bonus amount over the face amount of their bond. For example, a $1,000 bond will be redeemed at a price of 103, which equals $1,030 payment to the bondholder. The premium represents compensation to the bondholders for losing their bond and possibly subjecting themselves to reinvestment risk.

The sinking funds and redemption requirements of the indenture are important parts of the bond issue and are key responsibilities of the Trustee. The basic process to conduct these "calls" is illustrated on the next page.

April 15

- Notice by issuer to Trustee to do an optional redemption

April 30

- Notice to bondholders from the Trustee of the redemption (thirty days prior to call date)

June 1

- Call date and payment to bondholders impacted
- Presentation of bonds, if physical

Between the issuer notification date and the mailing of the redemption notice, the Trustee must do a selection of the bonds to be called if it is a partial redemption. There are two methods of selecting the bonds:

- **Random:** By lot—not all bondholders are selected.
- **Pro rata:** Every bondholder has a percentage selected.

Most indentures provide for the random by-lot selection process or any process deemed fair and reasonable by the Trustee. This selection process is done usually in operations by a computer system, which randomly selects bond numbers and assigns a call amount for that bond. I will explain this process in more detail in the risk management chapter (Chapter 7).

In addition to performing the proper selection process, it is important for the Trustee to properly prepare and mail the redemption notice to the bondholders of the call. The indenture will prescribe the process and any additional information, which usually includes the following:

- CUSIP numbers
- Call amount
- Bond numbers
- Security description
- Price at which the bonds will be paid
- Statements that interest ceases to accrue on payable date
- Presentation of the bonds, if physical, by mail or by hand delivery to the office of the Trustee. If the bonds are not required to be presented, then this is referred to as a "home office payment" with the bondholder noting on their bonds the payment information without presenting the bonds.
- Requirement for bondholders to submit a W-9 to establish their taxpayer IDs on file with the Trustee or be subject to a 28 percent backup withholdings penalty

The Trustee, on behalf of the issuer, usually signs the notice. It is important to note that failure to receive the notice, or any error in the notice, does not invalidate the call for the bondholders. Also, no interest will be paid on called bonds after the redemption date, regardless.

In certain cases, the issuer can purchase the bonds in the open market and present them for sinking fund credit. Other examples of credit against the fund requirement include:

- A conversion of the bond into common stock (i.e., a convertible debenture)
- Property or collateral additions

The above alternatives to cash payments are only permitted if expressly granted in the indenture.

UCC (Uniform Commercial Code) Filings

In many, but not all, cases, the issuer either requests or the indenture requires the Trustee to file the UCC 3 continuation statements, which establish (on record) the first lien on collateral in the form of personal property. Personal property is defined as anything other than the land. Examples would be equipment, such as aircraft or machinery. Revenues are also considered personal property.

If the Trustee is tasked with filing the UCC 3s, then he/she must be careful to do so on time and in the right place. Under revised article 9 of the Uniform Commercial Code (UCC), the lien must be continued every five years. The exception is if the original financing statement designated the issue a public financing, then the period of continuation would be thirty years. The UCC 3s must also be filed in the state of incorporation of the issuer. No filing is required in the local county where the property is located. An exception to that is certain states (e.g., Massachusetts) that may require a county recording under their state real estate law even though UCC Article 9 says this is not necessary. It seems there are exceptions to every rule. It is also best practice for a UCC Termination Statement to be filed at the final payment of the bond issue. It is standard practice for Trustees to tickle the UCC filings even if such filings are the responsibility of the issuer. This will allow the Trustee to determine if the lien has been continued in his/her name.

Construction Fund Disbursement

When monies are set aside from bond proceeds to build a facility, usually in a municipal revenue bond, the Trustee is required to manage the construction fund. The Trustee will invest the funds as directed and disburse them upon receipt of proper requisition documents. This is a major responsibility involving critical decision points for Trustees. I have seen a number of instances where fraud occurs regarding the construction of a project. At the very least, errors can also occur in requisitions and supporting documentation, such as invoices.

The duties of the Trustee for construction fund disbursement include the following:

- Receive the requisition and any required supporting documentation.
- Review the documents for compliance with the indenture provisions, plus the proper authorized signers.
- Add up any attached invoices to make sure they match the total being requested.
- Try to make one payment to the issuer. This relieves the Trustee of the burden of making multiple payments to various contractors/vendors.
- Make the payments promptly after taking the steps above.

Other challenges for the Trustee include the timing of disbursements. A flexible investment vehicle is needed, as construction payouts will vary due to many factors delaying the construction (e.g., weather, supplies, project changes, and unexpected events).

Valuations and Calculations

The Trustee may be required to perform valuations of collateral or reserve funds. This is another of those seemingly minor responsibilities that can have serious consequences if not done properly. The Trustee will be directed in the indenture to value the securities/investments held, for example, in a reserve fund at periodic intervals. If the reserve funds are needed and are not valued properly, resulting in a shortfall that was the responsibility of the Trustee to notice, then the Trustee—not the issuer of the shortfall—may be liable for failure to properly perform the valuation.

The same can apply for any collateral held by the Trustee if the indenture required a valuation or a "mark to market" by the Trustee.

The Trustee must perform the required valuation accurately and in a timely manner. If a shortfall occurs, the Trustee should notify the issuer to restore the fund to the proper amount. If a surplus occurs, then the Trustee typically returns the excess to the issuer. The Trustee must be very careful to fully understand the exact method of valuation or calculation and must do it right.

Client Service

The Trustee does have a responsibility to assist the issuers and bondholders in performing pre-default duties. The Trustee should be accessible and responsive to questions and inquiries. Remember, the role of the Trustee is to act as a facilitator to the bond issue. Of course, legal interpretations should be referred to counsel. The Trustee also avoids making speculations about the issuer or financing. However, prompt attention to issuer questions concerning audit confirmations, investment direction, and fee billing issues should be addressed in a timely manner. It is just good business practice.

There are a number of other pre-default duties Trustees perform, many unique to a particular financing. Here is a short list to consider:

- **Amendments and Supplements:** Changes can be made to the documents requiring issuer direction and possibly holder consent. The Trustee plays a role in these processes of facilitating these changes but is never required to approve them.
- **Waivers:** The Trustee can waive certain minor changes to the indenture but only as strictly prescribed and with caution.
- **Operations Duties:** Many functions fall within the scope of operations, which will be discussed in the chapter on operations (Chapter 11). These duties include the following: debt service payment, keeping bondholder records, tax reporting, processing transfers, fee billing, and escheatment compliance, among others.
- **Tenders and Exchanges:** The Trustee can be a "put" or "tender agent" receiving bonds from the bondholders, who are putting/tendering their bonds to the issuer for payment. There may also be an exchange of one bond for another or for common stock—where the Trustee processes the exchange.
- **Auction Agent:** The Trustee may serve as an "auction agent" and conduct a Dutch Auction on behalf of the issuer to reset the interest rate on the bonds.
- **Custodian or Collateral Agent:** The Trustee may hold assets or collateral in Trust as security for the bond issue. This requires the Trustee to do the following:
  - Receive the collateral.
  - Verify that it meets the requirements of the trust documents.
  - Hold it in safekeeping.
  - Return it as directed.

- **Calculation Agent:** The Trustee performs interest calculations or other required calculations.
- **Disbursing Agent:** The Trustee performs disbursement of funds.

Conclusion

There are a number of post-closing pre-default duties that involve the Trustee. These duties are crucial to the proper functioning of the bond issue and benefit both issuers and bondholders. Trustees are expected to perform those duties correctly and in a timely manner. Trustees are the real link between issuers and bondholders.

Chapter Summary

- The pre-closing role of the Trustee is an unofficial one since the Trustee is not legally appointed until the closing.
- There are a number of pre-closing activities the Trustee is engaged in, which include the following:
    o Review the indenture and other trust documents.
    o Establish operational records and provide original issuance instructions for issuing the bonds at closing.
    o Prepare to receive funds, invest bond proceeds, and make disbursements at closing.
    o Establish the Trustee fees with the issuer.
    o Perform Know Your Customer (KYC) due diligence on the issuer.
- Closing responsibilities include the following:

- Interact with DTC, if it is a book entry issue, to release the bonds to the underwriter. If not a DTC closing, issue definitive bonds to the underwriter.
- Receive bond proceeds.
- Disburse required payments.
- Invest bond proceeds as directed.

- Post-closing pre-default duties are varied depending on the bond financing with the more common being the following:
  - Receive closing documents.
  - Establish ticklers.
  - Facilitate funds movement involving ongoing receipt of monies to pay principal and interest and other cash flow.
  - Monitor covenants to receive and review compliance items the indenture requires the Trustee to receive.
  - Invest funds in permitted investments, upon receiving written instruction.
  - Process sinking funds and redemptions.
  - File UCC (Uniform Commercial Code) forms to establish a first lien position on personal property as collateral.
  - Disburse construction funds upon receipt of proper documentation.
  - Value and calculate performance to value investments, reserve, funds, and collateral or to calculate a rate for payment to bondholders.
  - Provide client services interaction with issuers and bondholders to respond to their needs.
  - Perform operational support duties, such as debt service payments, statement reporting, keeping bondholder records, tax reporting, processing transfers, fee billing, and escheatment compliance.

To properly understand the role of the Trustee, it is important to realize that the Trustee is one of many participants in the process of bringing a bond issue to market. To obtain a true understanding of how the Trustee interacts with the parties to a bond issue, this case study presents a common scenario of how a bond issue comes to market from beginning to end. Starting with the idea for the need to raise capital through a bond issue and ending with the closing when the bonds are sold to investors and the bond issue is in operation, I will discuss the typical timeline for the issuance process and introduce the participants in the general order in which they become involved. It is important for the reader to note *when* in this process the Trustee is brought in. Let's get started.

Putting a Bond Issue Together

Our case study will involve the financing of a new sports stadium. We will start with the origination of the idea that building a new sports stadium will bring forth a number of benefits for the City of Metropolis, its business community, and its citizens. Enter our first participant: **the Mayor of Metropolis.**

The mayor certainly wishes to bring prosperity to the city. What better way than to build a new sports stadium. This new stadium will provide a necessary economic boost to the inner part of the city by creating jobs and attracting businesses such as hotels, restaurants, shopping outlets, and entertainment venues. A new stadium will bring people to the downtown area, create more tax revenue, and provide business revival of the surrounding area (which could use a face-lift). Best of all, it will likely please the citizens, enhancing the prospects of reelection for the mayor. As the vision forms for increased prosperity for the city and a better chance of reelection, the mayor enthusiastically proposes the idea to our next participant: **City Council.**

The city council, comprised of elected members of a city government, also sees the benefits of a new sports stadium and readily endorses the idea. As politicians, the mayor and city council now turn their attention to the challenging logistics of how to make their dream of a new stadium a reality, thereby realizing the economic benefits and reelection prospects. How can they accomplish this daunting task?

The mayor and city council consider their options of finding the best way to finance this large project. Their options are:

- Issue bonds.
- Go to a bank for a loan.
- Sell naming rights to a corporation.
- Raise taxes.

Many politicians would not support a major increase in taxes, because doing so would jeopardize their reelection prospects. Therefore, the last option is quickly dismissed. The bank loan would be expensive and saddle the city with an unwanted debt burden. Selling naming rights is an attractive option but will not finance the entire project. That leaves bonds. Issuing municipal bonds as revenue bonds, supported by the revenues of the stadium (and not as debt for the city), is a viable option and the best one on the list. What happens next?

Enter the **Financial Advisor (FA).** The FA plays an interesting role of facilitating the process and advising the issuer. The FA is a consultant who advises the issuer on a variety of matters—in this case the City of Metropolis. These matters may include the following:

- Structure of the bond issue
- Size of the bond issue
- Identification and coordination of the hiring of an underwriter/investment banker
- Terms of the bonds
- Assistance in dealing with the rating agencies and other third parties, such as credit enhancers
- Hiring of a Trustee

No sports stadium would be complete without a sports team. Enter the **Team Owner.**

The team owner controls the team, hires players, and promotes the team. He/she does not want to pay for a new stadium but does want the benefits a new stadium will bring, including added revenue potential. A new stadium with more skyboxes will create more revenue for the team owner so he/she can pay bigger salaries to star players. If the team wins more games, that will create even more revenue. The elected officials, including the mayor and city council, may get reelected and not have to pay for the stadium either—a win-win for all parties involved. Therefore, the owner enthusiastically supports the idea of building the new structure if financed through alternative means, such as a public bond issue.

In order to create and sell the bond issue, we now introduce another participant in this scenario: **the Underwriter/Investment Banker**.

The underwriter plays a vital role because a private financial organization (e.g., Goldman Sachs, Merrill Lynch, etc.) actually agrees to buy the bonds, with the intent of reselling them. The FA will contact various underwriters to conduct a sort of competition, whereby the potential underwriters will bid on the bond issue. The FA will collect the bids and consult with the issuer and choose a winner. The winning underwriter will become the **Lead Manager** for a syndicate of other underwriters who will sign an underwriter agreement, thereby agreeing to sell the bonds either on a "best effort" or committed sale basis. With this particular bond issue of a larger size ($500 million to $1 billion), the lead manager will spread the risk of underwriting the bonds to other syndicate members. That risk includes changing market conditions or interest rate variation, making the bonds costlier to sell.

The underwriter is responsible for selling the bonds first. The syndicates of underwriters take all the market risks by guaranteeing a price, which is paid to the issuer at closing. The underwriter is also responsible for:

- Creating a prospectus or Offering Statement (OS), the disclosure document to the market and investors, as required by the SEC
- Structuring the bond issue

The underwriter hires separate counsel. The underwriting financial organization can ultimately play three roles: underwriter, investment banker, and broker. The underwriter sells the bonds, the investment banker advises on the structuring of the bonds, and the broker matches buyers and sellers of the bonds in the secondary market.

The next participant to enter the process is **Bond Counsel.** The issuer, for the purpose of drafting the indenture, hires bond counsel to manage the legal process, including preparing legal opinions and assembling all required legal documentation to authorize the issuance of the bonds. Bond counsel manages the closing and is the primary coordinating party throughout the process. Bond counsel is hired by the issuer to coordinate the legal processes and negotiation for issuance of the bonds at the closing.

To enhance the sale of the bonds, another participant enters the process—the **Credit Enhancer**. The credit enhancer is an increasingly necessary party in a bond issue. A credit enhancer can take several forms, including:

- A mono-line insurance company
- A bank providing a letter of credit
- Swap counterparty
- Bank liquidity provider or other third-party guarantor of all or part of the bonds

The credit enhancer will become the bondholder of last resort by paying the bondholders in full and then assuming their position for possible recovery. Credit enhancers really do not want to lose money. Therefore, they are an active participant in the pre-closing process to protect their rights in an Event of Default. They will look to the Trustee to recover on their behalf. Credit enhancers, such as mono-line insurance companies, give the bondholders the assurance that they will be paid. Generally, the bonds are rated AAA as a result of bond insurance. Credit enhancement leads to lower interest expense for the issuer since investors will not demand as high a risk premium (higher interest rate) because they rely on the credit enhancer, not the issuer, for ultimate repayment. Credit enhancers are crucial participants in the bond pre-closing process. Their opinions and document comments are carefully considered. They can literally dictate their terms.

As the above parties enter the financing, the next participant comes in the form of one or more of the **Rating Agencies.** While ratings may not be sought for privately placed bond issues, it is common industry practice to obtain one or more ratings from the rating agencies for all other bond issues in order to increase the marketability of the bonds. Investors want an impartial, professional assessment of the creditworthiness of the bond issue—in other words, the likelihood that the bonds will be repaid. With the view of obtaining the highest possible rating, the underwriter approaches the rating agencies. Why? To lower the interest cost of the bonds and to enhance their attractiveness to investors. The three main rating agencies are: Standard and Poor's (S&P), Moody's, and Fitch. Whichever one is hired, that company will perform an analysis of the bond issue and the structure of the bonds to assign a rating. The rating is a picture in time of the rating agency's assessment of the likelihood of repayment. It is no guarantee, only an assessment. The rating can be changed up or down as future events unfold.

The AAA rating is the highest rating. Everything BBB and above is considered "investment grade." Anything rated below BBB is considered to be high-yield or "junk" bonds. Just because a bond is rated as "junk" doesn't mean it will go into default. Quite the contrary. The historical average of default for junk bonds is, surprisingly, only 10 percent.

The importance of the rating assessed by the rating agencies in the pre-closing process cannot be overemphasized. Everything literally hinges upon receiving the proper rating. The rating impacts the entire process of issuing bonds. The rating not only dramatically influences the ability of the underwriters to effectively sell the bonds, but the rating will also impact the interest rate that determines the amount the issuer will ultimately owe for the life of the bonds.

For structured finance bond issues, one or more **Servicers** are key participants in the pre-closing process. The servicer is the party who actually managers the assets. The servicer keeps the records, maintains security interests in the assets, processes collections, handles foreclosures, generates billings, and may even hold the assets in certain cases. The Trustee may hold the physical collateral and act as collateral agent or custodian, especially for mortgage-backed securities (MBSs) issues with whole loan mortgage files. The mortgage custody function is vitally important to an MBS issue with whole loan mortgages, with extensive interaction with the servicer(s) in verifying the mortgage file, chasing documents for incomplete files (called trailing documents), storing the files, recording the files on a recordkeeping system, and returning files upon default, foreclosure proceedings, refinancing, or final payout.

The servicers will be part of the pre-closing process in contracting through the closing documents (Indenture, Pooling, and Service Agreement or Servicing Agreement) to service the assets, collect payments, forward payments to the Trustee, and provide detailed reports about the cash flow and performance of the collateral.

We are now approaching the end of the pre-closing process. Everyone involved is doing his or her designated job. The issuer is making key decisions about the financing. The underwriters are marketing the bonds and issuing the prospectus/OS. Bond counsel is drafting the governing documents, preparing legal opinions, and managing the closing process. Financial advisors are advising. Credit enhancers are stepping up. Rating agencies are assigning ratings. Servicers are preparing to service. All this activity takes from as little as three months to the more typical time frame of six months to one year or more.

However, we are still missing one more important participant . . . the **Trustee**. Sad but true, the Trustee is often the last party to be brought into the pre-closing process. In some cases, the Trustee will be involved earlier. This is preferable for the Trustee so he/she can be more fully engaged in the whole process of bringing a bond issue to closing. Why is the Trustee brought in later rather than sooner, in most cases? There are a number of reasons why. Some are trivial, and others are more concerning. Reasons include:

- The perception that the Trustee performs a ministerial processing role in the financing and that, as such, he/she is just a passenger in the back of the bus coming along for the ride. While nothing could be further from the truth, the basically passive role of the Trustee pre-default does not result in the respect the Trustee deserves as a vital part of the financing;

- The view that the Trustee role does not officially begin until the closing; thus, it is left to the end to secure the Trustee's service;

- The perception that all Trustees are alike and provide interchangeable services;

- The fact that everyone in the pre-closing process is so focused on creating the bonds for the primary purpose of getting them sold (i.e., issued) that everything else, including the needed services of the Trustee, is left to the last consideration after the work of structuring the bonds is complete; and

- The fact that the parties appoint a Trustee late in the process as an afterthought but also to put pressure on the Trustee not to make substantial comments on the documents.

Of all the above reasons the Trustee is not involved in a bond issue sooner, the most disturbing is the last one. The others can be addressed by Trustees working diligently with all the participants in the marketplace to show their value to the financing as professionals who facilitate a more efficient movement of the bond issue to closing. The real role of the Trustee in a pre-closing is to actively participate in assisting the bond issue—making constructive comments to the documents and properly preparing for the securities issuance and movement of funds at the closing. The goal is to have a more effective bond financing that is more likely to achieve its objective of optimum payout to the bondholders.

The day of the closing, all parties gather in a large conference room to consummate the transaction. Documents are signed, opinions given, and the bonds are distributed to the lead underwriter with bond proceeds paid to the Trustee. The Trustee deposits the funds in the appropriate trust accounts, invests funds as directed, and makes distributions.

Everyone then leaves. Who remains to quietly go about the duties of administering the terms and conditions of the bond issue for the next thirty years? The Trustee. I like to say, "The Trustee is the last one invited to the party and the one left to clean up the mess!" You be the judge.

Timeline: Six to nine months, or even one year or longer, from the gleam in the mayor's eye to the closing of the bond issue. As you can see, the Trustee is usually brought in late in the process.

```
|----------------------------------|----------------------------------|----------------------------|
```

Financing Idea   **Various Parties Involved**   **Trustee Involved**   **Closing**

~ Chapter 5 ~

Post-default Duties and Bankruptcy Responsibilities

Ashwanbenon, Wisconsin—1991

It is a cold, gray November day. My counsel and I have just driven up to Wisconsin from Chicago to visit a large manufacturing building formally owned by Patton Industries, a builder of industrial cranes. Unfortunately, the market for cranes is depressed, resulting in Patton Industries filing for bankruptcy protection under Chapter 11 of the Bankruptcy Code. As Trustee for the facility, I am now the proud owner of the property in this default.

My responsibility as Trustee is to preserve the assets for the bondholders. In order to do so, I have to check off a few items on my "to do" list. A few of these tasks include inspecting the property, meeting with security guards and the power company, and consulting with local realtors.

As my counsel and I walk into the building, we notice a truck outside with workers loading items. The interior is very spacious and nearly bare. We look at each other in amazement when we realize we are witnessing a burglary in progress. The workers are stripping the machinery from the floor in preparation to drive away with the stolen items. Noticing our presence, the workers look us up and down in obvious disapproval of two men in suits who are likely here to officially shut down their place of employment.

In a rather brash tone, my counsel begins to yell at the workers to stop what they are doing. Before this hostile confrontation takes a turn for the worse, I literally drag him out of the building and insist that we promptly go to the police and return with some protection in order to effectively stop the heist without getting our noses broken. We return to the facility with law enforcement and are able to recover a part of the bondholders' assets.

It's all in a day's work when a diligent Trustee enters the Twilight Zone of defaults and is still able to come out on top. There is one thing for sure—there will always be challenging surprises in this industry where every default presents unique challenges. And no two situations are ever the same.

Chapter Objective

When the Trustee enters the realm of post-default, the true role of Trustee changes in that the Trustee assumes entirely different duties and responsibilities. The Trustee is then elevated to a significantly higher standard, the prudent man/person standard, which requires much more vigilance and action on the part of the Trustee.

The analogy is that of Superman. The mild-mannered Trustee in his Clark Kent or her Wonder Woman attire is suddenly called upon to rush into the phone booth and emerge transformed as the Prudent Trustee. Now the Prudent Trustee is armed with new powers and abilities as dictated by the indenture. New powers are accompanied with discretionary responsibilities to take the necessary actions to protect the interests of the bondholders. Naturally, the risks to the Trustee of taking the wrong action or failing to act are heightened. The post-default role of the Trustee requires discretionary powers that require the Trustee to assume a more proactive role. The bondholders expect the protection of the Trustee, who strives to obtain the maximum recovery for bondholders.

The Trustee faces a daunting challenge in the post-default role, made more difficult due to the fact that the Trustee infrequently assumes this role. The transformation to "prudent man/person" is unique in each situation. Truly, no two post-default scenarios are ever the same.

To explore this world of the post-default Trustee, I will focus on three areas:

I. What Constitutes a Default Versus an Event of Default?

II. Post-default Responsibilities of the Trustee and the Prudent Man/Person Standard

III. Best Practices: How the Trustee Complies with Post-default Responsibilities

I. What Constitutes a Default Versus an Event of Default?

To understand what is expected of the Trustee post-default, we must first define what a default is. The word "default" is usually found in the default section of the indenture. The fact that the default section is normally one of the later sections of the indenture does not mean it lacks significance. On the contrary, it is one of the most crucial sections of the indenture and should be treated as such. A default is a situation that arises due to the failure of the issuer to perform as required by the indenture. There are two types of defaults:

- Defaults—which can also be described as technical defaults
- Events of Default

Technical defaults are minor failures of the issuer that may not on their own present a significant risk to the bondholders but that may lead to a significant risk if left unresolved. As such, a technical default has a cure period. A cure period is defined by the indenture as a period of time that passes before the technical default ripens into an Event of Default. In other words, a cure period is the grace period to give time to remedy the noncompliance. Why allow for a cure period? The objective is to cure the technical default without plunging the bond issue into the seriousness of an Event of Default.

As an example, I will use the sports analogy, "no harm, no foul." An example of technical default is nonreceipt of an annual financial report. The dilemma for the Trustee is, first, to recognize that a technical default has occurred and, second, to decide what to do about it. More will be said in the best practices section of this chapter on what course of action should be taken by the Trustee, but for now it is sufficient to say that the Trustee has options.

The important concept for the Trustee to grasp about technical defaults is that the intent is for the Trustee to have options. A technical default does not graduate to an Event of Default without formal *written notice* by the Trustee to the issuer specifically declaring the issue in technical default and officially starting the cure period. I refer to this as "starting the default clock ticking." Some of my students have told me my default clock looks like a pig's butt. However, I can assure you it is an alarm clock and should not be started without careful consideration by the Trustee, plus approval by a review committee (see Chapter 7 on risk management for further explanation of the purpose of a review committee). The only way the default clock is started is by written notification by the Trustee to the issuer that the cure period is starting. Once started, it can only be stopped by compliance in resolving the issue. Once the clock rings at the conclusion of the cure period, the Trustee is now elevated to the prudent man/person standard with all the discretionary responsibility that standard entails. The calling of an Event of Default past the cure period should not be entered into lightly or used to "scare" the issuer. The consequences are too serious. If the issuer remedies the noncompliance during the cure period, all is well again. No notice is required to bondholders. If the cure period expires and the default clock runs out of time, then the Trustee is faced with a more significant decision as to whether or not to declare a formal Event of Default.

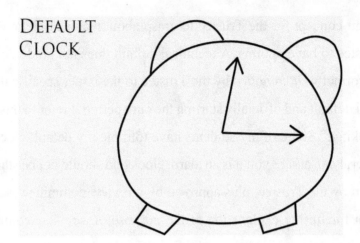

DEFAULT
CLOCK

An example of the technical default process, such as nonreceipt of a financial report, is as follows:

- Determine that a technical default has occurred by nonreceipt of the annual financial report on the date it was due to the Trustee. This would be an item for which the Trustee would have established a tickler.
- Call the issuer to find out why the financial report has not been provided and when it will be forthcoming.
- Decide whether or not to send a formal written notice of technical default to the issuer, starting the cure period.
- If notice is sent, monitor the situation.
- Upon expiration of the cure period, determine whether to declare an Event of Default and what course of action to take.

The key to the resolution of a technical default is for the Trustee to realize that the indenture does allow flexibility for the Trustee and time for the issuer to remedy the noncompliance. The Trustee is not required to immediately send out a formal written notice of technical default. The reason is to allow the issuer an opportunity to remedy the situation. It is common for the Trustee to encounter technical defaults. For example, a nonreceipt of an annual finance report could be caused by a variety of reasons, including unavoidable delays by auditors in gathering all relevant financial information, delays caused by business conditions or merger, or even having a report lost in the mail. The failure to provide an annual financial report may also be due to a more serious issue, such as the issuer not wanting to disclose financial results. Anything is possible, which is why a technical default can present the Trustee with an interesting dilemma as to just how to proceed.

Event of Default

An Event of Default is a serious matter for the Trustee and all concerned. As defined by the indenture, an Event of Default has no cure period. An Event of Default presents a very real threat to the bondholders of potentially not being paid. As such, the occurrence of such a default triggers the immediate transformation of the role of the Trustee from agent to prudent man/person. The following chart should be helpful in differentiating between the technical default and an Event of Default.

Default (Technical Default)

Versus

Event of Default

DEFAULT (TECHNICAL DEFAULT)	EVENT OF DEFAULT
1. Agent standard	1. Prudent man/person standard
2. Cure period or grace period, which varies and requires notice by the Trustee to the issuer	2. No cure period—it is immediate
3. No requirement to notify bondholders	3. Requirement to notify bondholders
4. Nonpayment of interest (however, some indentures list this as an Event of Default)	4. Principal nonpayment, such as a redemption, sinking fund, or maturity principal payment
5. Covenant violation (e.g., financial reports and certificate of no default)	5. Covenant violations that have had the cure period expire after the rendering of formal written notice by the Trustee
6. Failure to provide timely disclosure of information required by the indenture	6. Material misstatements, falsifications, or lies by the issuer
7. Involuntary bankruptcy filing of the issuer under Chapter 7 and 11 of the Bankruptcy Code	7. Voluntary bankruptcy filing of the issuer under Chapter 7, 9, or 11 of the Bankruptcy Code

II. Post-default Responsibilities of the Trustee and the Prudent Man/Person Standard

The major difference between the Trustee's role in a technical default versus an Event of Default is the prudent man/person standard of care. In a typical default, the Trustee is still primarily in an agency standard as governed by the indenture. In an Event of Default, the Trustee steps up to the prudent man/person standard of care. That step up is triggered by the actual occurrence of an Event of Default as defined by the indenture. That definition can change depending on the different indenture requirement as stated.

The Trustee's elevation to the higher standard of care is diagrammed as follows:

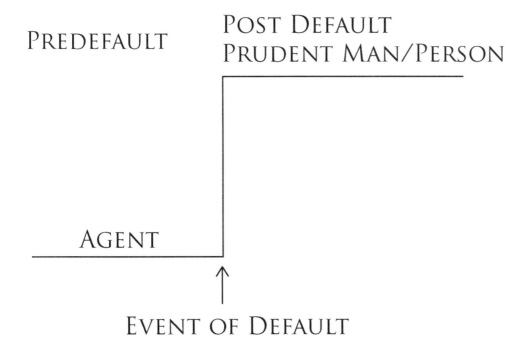

To understand what the prudent man/person standard of care means for the Trustee, it is important to remember what the prudent man/person language says as contained in the indenture.

The Trustee must act as a prudent man/person would act, as defined in the indenture, under the circumstances in the conduct of his/her own affairs. The formal prudent man/person wording is:

> The Trustee shall exercise, during the continuance of a default, as defined in the indenture (and for our purposes means Event of Default), such of the rights and powers vested in it by the indenture, and shall use the same degree of care and skill in their exercise, as a prudent man/person would use under the circumstances in the conduct of his or her own affairs.

This basically means the Trustee must act as if his/her own money were at stake. The Trustee should do the right or prudent thing, as best as he/she can determine at the time and under the circumstances. The prudent man/person standard of care places the Trustee in a more demanding position both legally and practically. Doing the right thing can mean a variety of actions, and even nonactions, all leading to one objective: protecting the interests of the bondholders to maximize their recovery. It is not a guarantee. There is always the possibility that there will be no recovery. I also want to stress that the prudent man/person standard is not a fiduciary standard.

Acting prudently means the Trustee must proactively step up to pursuing recovery for the bondholders. It can be a long process, as I will explore fully in my discussion of bankruptcy. The Trustee must not sit back but must be on constant alert to diligently represent bondholders. This added responsibility for the Trustee of becoming a prudent man/person does not mean the Trustee must be perfect. The Trustee is not being held to an unattainable standard of perfection and, as a result, unlimited liability. The Trustee will be protected under the prudent man/person standard if he/she does two very important things:

1. Hire counsel to represent the Trustee.
2. Act proactively in good faith.

Remedies

The remedies available to the Trustee are:

- **<u>The right to accelerate maturity of securities</u>:** In order to establish an immediate claim on the issuer for full payment of all remaining unpaid principal and accrued interest, the Trustee has the power to declare an acceleration of the debt, thereby notifying the issuer that the Trustee is effectively demanding all debt as now due and payable to the bondholders. With acceleration, the Trustee now formally establishes the claim of the bondholders as creditors to be paid as part of the claim on the assets of the bankrupt issuer.

- **<u>The right to recover judgment</u>:** The Trustee can recover from the issuer based upon any claims under the law as declared by a court in judgment against the issuer. Recovery under judgment would apply to amounts due to the bondholders and for Trustee fees and expenses.

- **<u>The right to sue in equity for a loss under the consent of specific performance</u>:** The Trustee has the important right to bring a lawsuit against the issuer or other responsible third parties as an action "in equity" for recovery. "In equity" means to sue in order to bring about an equitable distribution or payment to justly compensate the injured party (the bondholders). "Specific performance" refers to the right of the Trustee to bring a lawsuit to obtain a targeted or specific result. An example would be to have the court rule that the issuer must maintain insurance or pay taxes on the property serving as security for the bondholders.

- **<u>The right of entry and possession of the mortgage property</u>:** The right of entry and possession gives the Trustee crucial power to take physical possession of the property or other physical assets for the bondholders.

- **<u>The right to sell or dispose of collateral property, with or without entry</u>:** The Trustee has the power to sell the property or collateral even if there is no physical entry by the Trustee to the property. This gives the Trustee the flexibility to liquidate the collateral or property quickly. It is advisable for the Trustee to notify and seek bondholder approval for any sale.

- **<u>The right to exercise ownership with respect to collateral</u>:** The Trustee can now act fully as the owner in order to more fully protect the bondholders' claim and potential recovery from the property.

- **<u>The right to the appointment of a receiver of the mortgaged property</u>:** It is the legal right for the Trustee to appoint a separate third party to manage the property.

- **<u>The right to foreclose by appropriate judicial action</u>:** The Trustee has the important legal right to foreclose and take title of the physical property or collateral. This is a crucial step to preserving and recovering the property for bondholders.

- **The right to participate in bankruptcies and file proofs of claim:** This is the legal authority for the Trustee to file the appropriate claim in the bankruptcy proceeding that establishes the legal bondholder claim as a creditor to the bankruptcy estate of the issuer. Filing a proof of claim is a critical right and duty for Trustees and is coupled with the right to accelerate the debt.

The above remedies are important powers granted to the Trustee to use at his/her discretion.

Discretion

To Trustees in the United States, the word "discretion" is not associated with the Trustee's pre-default role. However, in the post-default world, the Trustee now has the power of discretion under the prudent man/person standard. With that discretionary power comes discretionary responsibility. Trustees have the authority to hire counsel and other experts. They are also given protection in the form of relying upon counsel's advice, seeking bondholders' indemnity, and receiving bondholder direction. As a result, it is now incumbent upon us as Trustees to be proactive advocates for the bondholders—*all* bondholders.

It is interesting to note that in the United Kingdom, Trustees are under the prudent man/person standard at all times—both pre-default and post-default. Having discretion is not in itself something to fear. UK Trustees have been acting with discretion from the closing onward and doing so successfully for many years. Therefore, I do not run screaming in the night from discretion: as long as I understand this heightened role, my responsibilities are clearly defined in the indenture, and I am paid accordingly. Post-default, US Trustees must act with discretion promptly and appropriately.

Notices

An important responsibility for Trustees post-default is giving notices. Information must flow in a timely, accurate fashion to bondholders, especially post-default when the risk of nonpayment is much higher. The Trustee now finds that he/she has the discretion as to what to say and when. The exception is for the initial occurrence of an Event of Default. There, the Trustee is required to render prompt notice to the bondholders, and possibly other third parties, about the occurrence of the event. When to send the notice and what to say should always be decided with proper advice of counsel post-default. The general rule of thumb is, "When in doubt, send it out." The Trustee should send the notice out promptly with as much factual information as possible. There will be more notices to follow. Only in rare instances will the Trustee withhold notice—and only with careful discussions with all parties concerned and with strong support of counsel.

What should be in the notice? The notice should include a succinct description of the nature of the Event of Default, plus actions taken by the Trustee. The notice is the first opportunity for the Trustee to publicly record his/her proactive efforts to protect bondholders. The Trustee should sign the notice. The notice should also contain statements such as:

- The Trustee will provide future notices as events unfold.
- The Trustee will proactively pursue recovery for the bondholders and represent the interests of the bondholders.

128

- The Trustee requests that the bondholders supply their contact information to enable the Trustee to communicate directly with the bondholders.
- The Trustee includes its contact information along with Trustee's counsel contact information.

Additional Post-default Duties

The remaining duties of the post-default Trustee will be dictated by events surrounding the issuer as they relate to ultimate repayment of the bonds. Examples of Trustee conduct include:

- Conducting bondholder meetings
- Joining the creditors' committee
- Protecting collateral
- Maintaining records
- Making distributions

As I have noted before, no two Event of Default situations are the same. Each follows its own path, and so must the Trustee.

III. Best Practices: How the Trustee Complies with Post-default Responsibilities

To successfully negotiate this difficult path the post-default Trustee must follow, there are a number of best practice guideposts to help along the way. No matter what the situation, the Trustee must *take immediate action.* Whether the Trustee receives notification of the Event of Default from the issuer or reads about the bankruptcy filing in the morning *Wall*

Street Journal, the order of the day is that there is no other priority. Actions the post-default Trustee must take include:

- **Get the facts:** Gather all facts possible surrounding the post-default situation by hiring counsel.

- **Hire counsel:** Then contact the issuer or the issuer's counsel to determine the current situation.

- **Be proactive:** Gather all documents for prompt review of the default and remedied sections, and alert bond operations so no inadvertent payments are made.

- **Assess if a conflict of interest now exists:** Determine if you as Trustee have a conflict and must resign.

- **Assess and protect collateral:** Determine where collateral is and whether security interests are properly established (e.g., UCC recordings).

- **Prepare a notice:** Include subsequent notices with advice of counsel.

- **Seek bondholder approval and indemnity:** Hold bondholder meetings.

- **Hire experts:** Bring on board any expert as needed, such as an accountant or other experts.

Get the Facts

The Trustee must immediately gather all the facts concerning the default situation. Much must be done at once, including reviewing indenture provisions and other relevant documents, determining the status of the issuer and collateral, and precisely clarifying the nature of the default and issuer intentions. Counsel can be a valuable partner in this initial fact-finding stage and should play a prominent role in assessing the legal situation as well as business facts of the default. It is important for the Trustee to gather all the facts as completely as possible in order to make appropriate decisions. Also, in order for the Trustee to adequately inform bondholders of the situation, the Trustee needs to have as much information as possible upon which to base his/her actions. In other words, the Trustee should find out what's going on and act accordingly.

Hire Counsel

During the post-default process, it is imperative to hire experienced counsel immediately. Many legal decisions need to be made. It's also important to know whom to call on at this critical time. Counsel should have experience in the bankruptcy process as well as working familiarity with Trustees. Counsel should be someone the Trustee knows and trusts. There is no substitute for experience. A good working relationship between Trustee and counsel is crucial to achieving both maximum recovery for bondholders and to protect the Trustee from failure to take appropriate action. The spotlight is now on the Trustee, and extra care is the order of the day. As an active partner, good counsel is crucial for the Trustee to achieve best results and to avoid the pitfalls of the post-default minefield.

Circumstances may also require the appointment of local counsel (i.e., someone who is familiar with the local laws and, more importantly, the local judicial system). Hiring local counsel can also potentially keep expenses down since local counsel attend local hearings, file motions, foreclose on property, and handle other matters without the Trustee or his/her counsel traveling back and forth. Local counsel can provide valuable on-the-scene contacts and get accurate, up-to-date information to greatly aid the actions of the Trustee to stay on top of the situation as it unfolds. Local counsel can, therefore, provide great assistance to the ultimate success of the Trustee's cause.

Be Proactive

Trustees should take action promptly. Delaying decisions can damage the bondholders' position and ultimate recovery. A record of the Trustee's proactive actions will greatly improve the recovery chances for the bondholders, which, after all, is the primary objective of the Trustee post-default. Demonstrating proactive actions and documenting them will also benefit the Trustee by maximizing chances for full payment of the Trustee's fees and expenses through the creditors' committee recommendations and bankruptcy court approval.

Prepare Notices

The Trustee best practice is to communicate early and often. By often, I mean as many times as relevant information is available. A good best practice can also include periodic update notices, even if not much has occurred, in order to keep bondholders informed of the status of the process. It also shows that the Trustee is being proactive—an obvious plus. Always include a name, phone number, and email address for bondholders to contact. It is preferred to use counsel contact information as the primary focal point for inquiries as it reduces Trustee risk by providing information from legal counsel.

I recommend having legal counsel as the contact to accept bondholder/third-party calls instead of the administrator. This is because the administrator is not trained to answer these inquiries and may disclose nonpublic information.

Hold Bondholder Meetings

The prudent Trustee should always consider holding bondholder meetings for the purpose of both giving information and soliciting direction. An additional benefit for the Trustee is to form a relationship with the bondholders to accurately assess their concerns and thought processes. Counsel should run the meeting, which should be well planned with a carefully prepared agenda. Even if few bondholders actually appear, the bondholders' meeting is valuable for demonstrating the proactiveness of the Trustee.

Join the Creditors' Committee

A best practice for Trustees is to try to join the creditors' committee in a bankruptcy as a voting member. Even if the Trustee participates as a nonvoting member, it is important for the Trustee to be part of the process to more fully represent the interests of the bondholders as creditors.

Protect the Collateral

It can prove difficult for the Trustee in the post-default situation to determine when and how it must protect collateral. Physical possession is always one sure way of protecting collateral but may be impractical. For example, does the Trustee ground all the aircraft and park them in the bank's parking lot in a default by the airline in an equipment Trust issue? This may not be the preferred course of action.

The best practice post-default is for the Trustee to quickly assess the status of the collateral and take whatever action is necessary to preserve it for the bondholders. Hiring third parties is another way for the Trustee to fulfill this responsibility when the Trustee has neither the expertise nor the physical ability to adequately protect the collateral. It is critical for the Trustee to measure the collateral by maintaining insurance coverage and any UCC filings post-default.

Seek Bondholder Approval and Indemnity

It is always a best practice to seek bondholder approval and indemnity whenever possible. The Trustee should always strive to have language inserted in the indenture to provide for both these contingencies. However, due to a variety of factors, there can be times when the Trustee cannot get these protections. The prudent Trustee should be prepared to take proactive action absent direction or indemnity, if necessary. Other factors include the difficulty in identifying and communicating with bondholders and the possible reluctance of one or more bondholders to give direction or indemnity.

Securing these protections can, however, be blocked due to bondholder resistance, delay, or outright refusals to give direction or indemnity for whatever reason. Increasingly, Trustees find themselves in the difficult position of acting without these protections being given. This is when the term "discretion" takes a more heart-stopping meaning for Trustees. Best practice here is to "do what is right," but the prudent Trustee should always receive supporting statements, and opinions, to fortify his/her decision.

Hire Experts

The prudent Trustee should always seek the advice of experts where needed. Examples include: aviation experts for defaulted bond issues backed by aircraft; environmental experts; accountants; real estate experts; and other industry-specific experts. A best practice is to obtain experts' options in writing. Once again, the indenture should allow the Trustee to hire experts at the issue cost or with bondholder indemnity. The prudent Trustee is one who hires the needed experts first and worries about recovery second.

Trustee Default Specialists

The larger Trustees have the resources and activity to justify the creation of default specialists. Whether they are a team or one individual, the default specialist(s) step in to take over the default to conclusion. Some banks transfer the entire relationship to the default team—a concept I refer to as "throwing everything over the wall"—while others bring in the client service administrator.

I have experience with both models and recommend the best practice to be the dual involvement approach. Why? In this approach, you will not lose all the account knowledge, which is the tendency in the "over-the-wall" approach. Also, this approach allows you to spread the workload and keep the mechanical processes with the administrator. This lets the default specialist concentrate on the other default aspects.

A specialty default group provides a better management of the default process by experienced default staff. This experience helps the Trustee to perform prudently.

Some Trustees do not have the resources or expertise to form a default group. The next best option is to hire the best counsel you can to assist your client service administrator (or manager). Counsel has the experience in defaults as well as the time and expertise to devote to properly protecting the bank by directing the appropriate Trustee actions.

Conclusion

The post-default role of a Trustee requires heightened vigilance by the Trustee above his/her former agency role pre-default. Being proactive, heightening communication, and consulting with counsel are the best practices for the Trustee post-default. The Trustee should get help, direction, and good lawyers to assist in successfully performing his/her proper role post-default. More discretion under the prudent man/person standard will elevate the Trustee's authority and responsibilities requiring the Trustee to act accordingly. After all, that is why Trustees exist—to rise to the occasion of protecting the bondholders in the post-default situation when there is heightened risk of the bondholders not receiving the benefit of their bargain. It is a riskier time for Trustees, a time when the Trustees' actions will be placed under a microscope and reviewed critically. Yet it is a role Trustees were meant to play and the one where the Trustee can provide the most value.

Chapter Summary

- The post-default role of the Trustee changes from an agent to prudent man/person upon the occurrence of an Event of Default as defined in the indenture. Four important principles of acting prudently involve the following: 1) be proactive, 2) seek advice of counsel and other experts, 3) communicate early and often with the bondholders, and 4) realize the Trustee is now in a discretionary role.

- The main differences between the technical default and an Event of Default are:
    - Cure period versus no cure period; and
    - Agent standard versus prudent man/person standard.

- Examples of Events of Default are:
    - Bankruptcy filing;
    - Nonpayment of principal; and
    - Lies and misstatements.

- Key best practices for Trustees post-default are to:
    - Take action quickly.

- ○ Hire counsel.
- ○ Be proactive.
- ○ Get the facts.
- ○ Send out frequent notices.
- ○ Seek bondholders' approval and indemnity.
- ○ Hire default specialists to aid your staff.

~ Case Study ~

You are the Trustee for a municipal private activity revenue bond where the tax-exempt bonds were issued to build a warehouse for storing perishable fruit. The warehouse is in Orlando, Florida. Both the warehouse and fruit inventory are the collateral backing the revenue bonds. The private company (obligor) who runs the warehouse has just declared Chapter 11 bankruptcy.

What is the prudent action the Trustee should take and when?

Answer:

The Trustee is now in the prudent man/person standard of care as of the moment of the bankruptcy filing. Since the warehouse and fruit represent the collateral for the bondholders, the Trustee must act immediately to safeguard that collateral. It is July. The temperature in Orlando is over one hundred degrees.

The Trustee cannot wait for bondholders' direction or indemnity. Action must be taken immediately. This involves making sure the electricity bill is paid to keep the air-conditioning and freezer system running. It would certainly be damaging to the bondholders' interests if the Trustee delayed taking action to keep the coolers running. Also, the Trustee must take other immediate steps to have a manager and staff to run the facility, hire security personnel to guard the facility, and continue all insurance coverage on the property. Other tasks would involve both maintaining the facility and finding a buyer.

In short, there's a great deal the Trustee must do to perform as a prudent man/person in an event of a default—and every situation presents its own unique challenges and risks.

~ Chapter 6 ~

The Bankruptcy Process and the Involvement of the Trustee

New York, New York—1996

I am serving as an expert witness for one of the longest lasting and most litigious cases ever involving Trustees to date. The case is called Bluebird[1] and deals with the several successor Trustees to equipment Trust bonds where the Trustees held title to the aircraft and engines for Continental Airlines. Continental filed for Chapter 11 protection in 1991. The litigation began in 1993 and continued for thirteen years.

The viciousness of the litigation is one of the most striking aspects of the case in which several "vulture fund" investors had sued the Trustees for failure to take the appropriate action on behalf of the bondholders, namely to recover their money.

It is a fascinating case with major implications for Trustees. As I read through all the depositions and documentation, I truly feel that the Trustee I am representing had done a great deal to actively protect the interests of the bondholders. The Trustee hired experts, both legal experts and industry consultants, who gave thorough and detailed opinions. The Trustee held periodic meetings with the bondholders to keep them informed. The Trustee also sent notices and asked continually for the opinion of and direction from the bondholders. With all the uncertainties of a bankruptcy, the Trustee never knows exactly what the right course of action should be—every situation is unique. The best the Trustee

---

[1] Bluebird Partners, L.P. v. First Fidelity Bank, N.A. et al., 1 No. 40 (2000).

can do is be proactive, hire experts with whom to consult, and keep the bondholders in the communication loop.

In this case, the Trustee did all that yet was still sued by the vulture fund investors for failure to act prudently. What the case shows me is that the risks in a bankruptcy for a Trustee are subject to twenty-twenty hindsight and will never satisfy a bondholder who is only looking for a deep pocket to sue in order to recover his/her investment. In this case, the vulture fund representative was attending all the Trustee meetings yet secretly meeting with its counsel all along trying to gather facts to sue the Trustee. Every time the Trustee asked for direction from the vulture fund, the vulture fund refused. Yet the vulture fund was always there looking over the Trustee's shoulder waiting to strike. After thirteen years of litigation, this case resulted in a judgment against the Trustee.

Chapter Objective

The above case makes for a very unsettling situation for any Trustee to find him/herself in. It requires expertise, good legal counsel, and a little luck to emerge unscathed. Yet that is precisely why Trustees exist: to serve and protect bondholders to the best of their ability, even if the bondholders do not appreciate the Trustees' efforts or criticize those efforts. Trustees must do the best they can to champion the interests of all the bondholders. It is somewhat analogous to being the parent of a teenage child, a sometimes thankless task but one from which we must not waver. Such is the volatile world of bankruptcy, into which Trustees may find themselves thrown.

The bankruptcy process embodies basic principles of law with its own unique workings. Trustees become involved with the bankruptcy process upon issuer defaults in payment obligations to the bondholders. In fact, the most common Event of Default, where the Trustee steps into the prudent man/person standard, is in a bankruptcy of the issuer. Therefore, it is critical for the Trustee to thoroughly understand the bankruptcy process as it relates to the post-default responsibilities of the Trustee. Fortunately, the Trustee can turn to the real bankruptcy experts—the bankruptcy lawyers—for guidance through the process. Hiring good, experienced bankruptcy lawyers who specialize in bankruptcy practice is the best thing a Trustee can do to successfully fulfill his/her objective of maximizing bondholder recovery in the bankruptcy process.

While a complete analysis of the bankruptcy process is beyond the scope of this book, I intend to educate Trustees as to the following:

    I.   Overview of Bankruptcy Laws and Process as Related to the Trustee

    II. The Trustee's Responsibilities in a Bankruptcy: Best Practices

    III. The Risk to Trustees of Nonperformance of Bankruptcy Responsibilities

When reaching the end of this chapter, the reader will understand how the Trustee is involved in the bankruptcy process.

I. Overview of Bankruptcy Laws and Process as Related to the Trustee

History of Bankruptcy

The evolution of the bankruptcy laws in the United States reflects the constantly changing commercial development of the United States and the blending of economic interests and legal philosophy of the nation. The central definition of bankruptcy, according to the US Supreme Court, is: "nothing less than the subject of the relations between an insolvent or monopolizing or fraudulent debtor, and his creditors, extending to his and their relief." This balancing of creditor and debtor interests attempts to treat creditors fairly while relieving honest debtors from the permanent impediment of existing debts.

In other words, bankruptcy protection is the concept whereby a debtor (the person who owes the money) is protected from the claims of its creditors (the people owed the money). In the United States, a debtor files for protection under a chapter of the bankruptcy laws to create a wall of protection around the debtor. Bankruptcy protection is designated to allow the debtor time to work out its difficulties to continue operating if possible. This is the best chance for the creditors to be repaid. Another option is liquidating the assets, as in a Chapter 7 proceeding.

This concept of giving the debtor a second, and sometimes third or fourth, chance is uniquely American and reflects our ideals as well as our business philosophy. That business philosophy is that anyone should have the opportunity to create a business, to strive to have an entrepreneurial, "let's take a chance" mentality.

Throughout history, the debtor-creditor relationship has consistently penalized the debtor. If a debtor could not pay his debts, the simple solution was to throw him in prison or the dungeon. Debtor's prison was a common sentence for debtors up through the Middle Ages and in England, where the US bankruptcy laws had their roots. Only a few isolated exceptions existed in history, one being the Roman law concept of "Cassio Borrower." The Cassio Borrower was developed in the time of Julius Caesar. It held that if an insolvent debtor voluntarily subjected himself to the proceeding and turned over, honestly and fully, all his property for the benefit of his creditors, he would be freed from threat of execution, imprisonment, or slavery.

DEFAULT PRISON

Jail

This system of execution or jail did not work very well to promote commerce. As a result, with the coming of increasing commerce after the Middle Ages, particularly in England, a new way of looking at the debtor-creditor relationship emerged. Italian merchants called the Lombards were among the first bankers and brokers of Europe. This is where the term "bankrupt" derived from. The breaking or "rupt" of a Trader's table, or "banque," where the insolvent party negotiated his repayment and could not pay his debts became a symbol of financial failure. This signaled a necessary change from the old ways.

The founding fathers of the United States saw things differently. As such, they established a new concept called bankruptcy protection in the United States. In Article I, Section 8 of the US Constitution, Congress was granted the power "to establish uniform laws on the Subject of Bankruptcy throughout the United States." Since the time that the framers of the Constitution in 1787 added this provision, a series of national bankruptcy laws have been enacted. That process continues today.

The bankruptcy laws will continue to evolve in the United States due to the uniqueness of US lawmakers to attempt to strike a balance between the needs of creditors and debtors so that creditors would still extend credit while failing debtors could gain a fresh start. America is the place of business. The bankruptcy laws will continue to evolve to accommodate the changing needs of business. Congress has demonstrated that it will not hesitate to amend the bankruptcy laws if new economic concerns or financing vehicles appear.

Current Status of the Bankruptcy Laws

The bankruptcy laws are also referred to as the bankruptcy code. They represent a series of laws and amendments periodically enacted by Congress. The concept of bankruptcy has evolved for both corporate/municipal debtors and individuals such that it gives the debtor a second chance and fresh start. It is not designed to be a "bad thing" but a process for encouraging recovery for creditors and hope for debtors without punishment or stigma.

The current bankruptcy chapters the Trustee may be involved with regarding a debtor petitioning a bankruptcy court for protection under the bankruptcy laws are as follows:

- Chapter 7: Liquidation
- Chapter 9: Municipal Reorganization
- Chapter 11: Reorganization for Corporate Entities
- Chapter 13: Personal Individual Filing
- Chapter 15: Crossborder Bankruptcy

The Trustee would most likely become involved in either a corporate reorganization filing under Chapter 11 or a municipal filing under Chapter 9. Chapter 11 deals with corporations that file for bankruptcy protection and that seek to buy time to produce a usable plan with their creditors for repayment while continuing to actively continue in business. Examples of companies who have filed for bankruptcy include United Airlines, Enron, Kmart, and USAir, to mention a few. Most of the Chapter 11 filings are voluntary, meaning the debtor seeks bankruptcy protection itself by petitioning the bankruptcy court. While it is much less common, there is also involuntary bankruptcy whereby three or more creditors will petition the court to place the debtor into bankruptcy.

The Chapter 9 protection is exclusively for municipalities because the government recognizes that municipalities are different from corporations. One cannot take over a city, county, or state and simply sell the schools, public buildings, or roads. Liquidation is not an option. Also, the assets themselves cannot be seized. Most municipal financings involve two categories of bonds: 1) general obligations and 2) revenue bonds. Chapter 9 recognizes the unique nature of municipalities and has developed to properly treat municipal financings as such. The most significant municipal Chapter 9 bankruptcy is the city of Detroit. The resolution of that bankruptcy has set the standards for future municipalities.

For corporations, the assets themselves can act as security for the financings and as such can be confiscated, foreclosed, or sold by creditors. For municipal financings backed by revenues from specific assets/projects, the revenue stream is protected for the creditors in a Chapter 9 bankruptcy of the municipality. By protecting the creditors' (i.e., bondholders') claim on the revenues in a municipal bankruptcy, Chapter 9 preserves the unique qualities of municipal financing. An exception is private activity municipal revenue financings in the form of an Industrial Revenue Bond (IDB or IDRB) in which a private corporation leases a plant or facility built for private purposes. In those cases, not only the revenue but the actual property itself can be forfeited in a bankruptcy. This normally occurs in Chapter 11 filings of the borrower.

Chapter 7 is liquidation whereby there is no plan to reorganize the debtor but simply to liquidate the debtor's assets and disburse them among the creditors.

Bankruptcy Courts and Judges

A special bankruptcy court specializing only in bankruptcy enforces the bankruptcy laws. Judges are an extension of the federal district courts. There are eight bankruptcy districts, the primary ones being Delaware, New York, Chicago, and Los Angeles. There is no jury, just a bankruptcy judge who has sole power to grant petitions, overview bankruptcy court proceedings, grant motions, and approve final plans of reorganization. The judge rules on all matters before the court, including fees and expenses paid to all participating parties, which include the Trustee. There is rarely an appeal of the bankruptcy judge's rulings.

The bankruptcy court may appoint a bankruptcy Trustee to act on behalf of the court in overseeing the various aspects of the debtor and creditor or dealings including overseeing the maintenance of the bankruptcy estate. The bankruptcy Trustee is not to be confused with the Corporate Trustee or, as some say, the indenture Trustee.

The Typical Bankruptcy Case

It is useful to give an overview of the steps involved in a typical bankruptcy case. While "typical" is a relative term because every bankruptcy is unique, there is a certain pattern to a bankruptcy case that the Trustee should be familiar with. The bankruptcy process may take anywhere from six months to three years or more depending upon the size and circumstances of the debtor. Prepackaged bankruptcy may take a matter of a few months. The General Motors bankruptcy is an example lasting only sixty days. The trend appears to be shortening the time the debtor is in bankruptcy. The reason: it is expensive to be in bankruptcy. Bankruptcy is also bad for business, as employees, suppliers, and customers may leave. Who would buy a General Motors car while the company was in bankruptcy for fear of uncertain service warranty and parts? Therefore, there is a sense of urgency for all parties. The steps listed below are roughly done in the order described, but the timeline depends upon the unique circumstances surrounding each bankruptcy. An estimate of one-and-a-half to two-and-a-half years is fairly normal from start to finish. From the Trustee's perception, these are the steps in the process:

1. Debtor files a petition with the bankruptcy court.
2. Petition is approved or denied by the bankruptcy court. Usually this ruling occurs within several days of filing or even on the day of filing.
3. Trustee receives formal notice from debtor or becomes aware of the filing through news media or other third parties.
4. Trustee gathers all records and simultaneously hires counsel, who immediately obtains a copy of the bankruptcy filing.

5. Trustee determines if he/she has a conflict of interest that would require him/her to resign in favor of a successor Trustee.

6. Trustee's counsel files a proof of claim with the bankruptcy court and files a notice of acceleration with the issuer.

7. Notice of the bankruptcy filing, which is a formal Event of Default, is prepared by the Trustee's counsel and approved by the Trustee and sent to the bondholders and others as necessary.

8. Trustee secures any collateral, either physically or legally or both as necessary.

9. Trustee seeks appointment to the creditors' committee, if possible.

10. Trustee and counsel monitor the bankruptcy proceedings and report to the bondholders as developments warrant.

11. Trustee may be required to safeguard the collateral and hire experts to manage or maintain it.

12. Trustee may call a bondholders' meeting if events warrant and strives to identify bondholders throughout the process.

13. The debtor to the court presents a plan of reorganization. The creditors can approve the plan or present their own plans to the court. The court will be the arbitrator and work with the parties until a final plan emerges and is ratified by three-fourths of the creditors and half of each creditor class (i.e., secured, unsecured).

14. The plan specifics are implemented by the debtor, which may result in a distribution of cash or securities to the creditors as their various positions warrant.

15. Trustee will make the distribution to its bondholders. There may be several distributions or one final distribution.

16. Trustee recovers fees and expenses as approved by the bankruptcy court prior to distribution to the bondholders if not paid as administrative expenses previously.

Bankruptcy Terms: A Trustee's Primer

There is a unique language specific to bankruptcies. The following terms, among others, are the most important for the Trustee to know.

Proof of Claim: The official filing made to the bankruptcy court formally establishing the creditor's claim in the bankruptcy. The Trustee's counsel files the proof of claim, usually within twenty-four hours, to establish the Trustee's claim as a creditor on behalf of the bondholders for all unpaid principal and interest on the outstanding bonds.

Acceleration: The notice filed by the Trustee to the debtor declaring all principal and interest immediately due and payable. Many believe it is necessary for the Trustee to accelerate the debt to trigger his/her claim as creditor on behalf of the bondholders.

Automatic Stay: The bankruptcy process of stopping creditors from realizing their claims against the debtor. Creditor claims are "stayed" or stopped. This protects the debtor by preserving its assets. It also protects the creditors as a class by preventing any individual creditor from taking assets that might otherwise be available for all creditors. The automatic stay can be lifted in certain circumstances if it is in the best interest of either debtor or creditors at the approval of the bankruptcy court.

Adequate Protection: The concept that the automatic stay can be lifted if a creditor determines that allowing the debtor to continue to hold the assets/collateral would cause irreparable harm to the creditor's ultimate recovery. One example is an airline under bankruptcy protection that fails to adequately maintain the aircraft, which is the collateral for the bond issue. The Trustee leading the way on behalf of the bondholders as creditors can request the automatic stay be lifted and the collateral returned to the bondholders. In other words, take the planes away from the airline. The bankruptcy court will in most cases approve any such motion.

Creditors' Committee: A committee comprised of all creditors of a class of creditors (i.e., secured or unsecured) who come together for the purpose of creating more effective representation of their position with both the debtor and the bankruptcy court. The Trustee often participates as either a voting or nonvoting member. The creditors' committee makes crucial decisions regarding the bankruptcy proceedings and outcome and can also be the focal point for one or more creditor-originated plans for reorganization. Creditors create their own plan of reorganization if they do not believe the debtor plan is sufficient.

Substantial Contribution Section 503(b)(3): The bankruptcy law section directly referencing indenture Trustees and establishing the concept that they are entitled to be reimbursed for their fees and expenses, including counsel fees, if they make a "substantial contribution" to the bankruptcy proceedings. The intent of the wording is to finally establish the right for indenture Trustees to be paid. Yet some bankruptcy courts have misinterpreted this provision by creating an additional barrier for recovery by Trustees, leaving the interpretation of just what actions constitute substantial contribution up to the discretion of the court—an outcome not intended by the drafters of Section 503(b)(3). The Trustee should be mindful of this potential barrier and must thoroughly demonstrate and document his/her proactive, diligent actions in every case to support his/her claims for fee recovery.

Latch On Rights: The priority claims of the Trustee for recovering his/her fees and expenses, plus counsel's fees, prior to any recovery distribution to the bondholders. The Trustee has the right to take his/her money first from any resulting distribution in a bankruptcy before paying the difference to the bondholders. This provision, which should always be part of the indenture, is good business practice because it reduces the risk for Trustees that they will not be paid for their efforts on behalf of the bondholders.

Preference: The bankruptcy concept that provides for the return of certain monies paid by the debtor to creditors ninety days prior to the bankruptcy filing. The purpose is to prevent unscrupulous creditors from stripping the debtor of assets to the detriment of other creditors in the crucial pre-petition period shortly before filing with the bankruptcy court. Any such payments can be determined by the bankruptcy court to be preferential collections (i.e., showing undue preference/advantage to certain creditors over others), which the court can rule should be "disgorged," meaning returned back to the bankruptcy estate for the benefit of all creditors. Some payments to the Trustee, such as fees and expenses or principal and interest payments (not protected by letter of credit claims, which are considered preference-proof), would have to be paid back to the court if they occur within the ninety-day window.

Administrative Expenses: The expenses that the bankruptcy court considers necessary to the continued operation of the debtor under bankruptcy protection. The court pays these expenses during the course of the bankruptcy proceeding. The Trustee tries to have his/her fees considered as administrative expenses so that they will be paid periodically throughout the bankruptcy proceeding and so that the Trustee will not have to wait to final distribution and run the risk of the court reducing the Trustee fees and expenses for whatever reason.

Pre-petition and Post-petition: The time period before the petition for bankruptcy is approved by the bankruptcy court and the time period after the bankruptcy filing has been approved and becomes effective. The Trustee's role is clearly impacted by which side of the bankruptcy approval is operative. The prudent man/person standard post-petition will govern the Trustee.

Substantive Consolidation: The bankruptcy concept whereby assets can be pulled into the bankruptcy estate by the bankruptcy court. It is analogous to a whirlpool pulling all things into its center. The Trustee must protect the assets set aside for the bondholders as security from the desire of the bankruptcy court and other creditors to pull in as many assets as possible to help the debtor operate or maximize recovery for creditors. The real issue for Trustees is for revenue bond issues and structured finance issues. These issues have specifically pledged assets, and the Trustee must fight to preserve the established security lien on these assets for the bondholders and preserve their lien from the clutches of the bankruptcy estate.

Bankruptcy Trustee: The court-appointed Trustee to oversee the bankruptcy process on behalf of the court in working with both debtor and creditors. Bankruptcy Trustee duties could include managing the bankruptcy estate or working with the debtor to manage its affairs. Not all bankruptcies have a bankruptcy Trustee; it just depends on the circumstances and the need for this third-party assistance to the process.

Pre-packaged Bankruptcy: The recent concept whereby the debtor and creditors can avoid the sometimes lengthy and costly bankruptcy process by working together to create a plan of reorganization before the debtor files its petition. Because the debtor and creditors have already agreed to a plan of reorganization pre-petition, the approval of the plan can occur very quickly (within a matter of weeks or a few months, as opposed to years). Obviously, this has major benefits for all parties concerned. The debtor can effectively reorganize and quickly emerge from bankruptcy to continue to do business under the new reorganization plan. This saves time and money and presents less disruption for the business. The creditors benefit by enhancing the prospects of a quicker, smoother transition of the debtor, which the creditors hope will preserve the assets of the debtor and enhance its prospects for success as a going concern. A win-win for all, including the Trustee, who sees a quick resolution to the bankruptcy with its hoped-for benefits for the bondholders. It is a growing trend and a good one.

Plan of Reorganization: The purpose of Chapter 11 of the bankruptcy laws is to give the debtor a chance to reorganize, with creditor approval, while being protected from creditors' assaults on its assets. The bankruptcy law mandates that the debtor must produce a plan of reorganization within 180 days from the date of being granted bankruptcy protection. The court can grant extensions and often does. Also, creditors have the opportunity to submit their own plan of reorganization. The court will then rule on which plan will be used or if there will be a consolidation of the competing plans. The court can also reject any and all plans at its discretion. Any final plan must be approved by three-fourths of the creditors. The resulting one-fourth of nonapprovers will have the delightful experience of having the court "cram down" the plan on them. There is no recourse.

The Trustee's familiarity with the above terms is important to fulfilling his/her responsibilities in a bankruptcy.

II. The Trustee's Responsibilities in a Bankruptcy: Best Practices

In order to comply with the prudent man/person standard of care, the Trustee must be proactive and alert. Keeping in mind that every bankruptcy is unique, there are several best practices, highlighted below, that the Trustee should engage in to successfully perform the role of protector for the bondholders.

Give Notice: The Trustee needs to overcommunicate, rather than undercommunicate, with bondholders and other appropriate third parties, such as credit enhancers. Notice should be sent within twenty-four hours of the Trustee learning of the bankruptcy filing (or as soon as practical). Facts and details need to be clearly communicated without speculation. The Trustee's counsel should draft the notice. The notice should request that the bondholders communicate their contact information directly to the Trustee for building a contact database. The Trustee will need this for future communication in a variety of forms for both passing along updated status reports to the bondholders and requesting possible direction/approval of further actions by the Trustee. As a tip, the notices, which are given by the Trustee, should list contact information—both for the Trustee and the Trustee's counsel. It is preferable to have inquiries funneled through counsel to ensure better legal consistency of response as well as to take advantage of the attorney-client privilege to protect such responses from discovery in possible litigation. The Trustee wants to avoid the "he-said-she-said" difficulties if litigation ensues. The Trustee will also send additional notices at the discretion of the Trustee to keep the bondholders informed of material developments in the bankruptcy.

Hire Counsel: The best practice that is most crucial for the Trustee to employ is the immediate hiring of the best, most experienced bankruptcy counsel available. Time is of the essence, since the notice must be prepared and sent, the bankruptcy petition analyzed, the proof of claim promptly filed, acceleration notice given, and other important duties performed. The partnership formed between the Trustee and his/her counsel is crucial to the Trustee's successful performance of his/her responsibilities in a bankruptcy. The Trustee should look for outside counsel (not inside) with knowledge of the bankruptcy process.

Hire Experts: The Trustee should hire any needed experts or local counsel to render opinions and advice in technical areas. The Trustee should never hesitate to obtain expert help in performing his/her difficult role in a bankruptcy. A common practice is to hire a receiver to oversee the physical property and facilitate a sale.

Get It in Writing: The Trustee should always follow the best practice of obtaining all opinions from counsel, or other experts, in writing. Written direction from the bondholders is also the best practice, although under certain circumstances, it may be more conclusive for the Trustee to employ the "negative consent" in concert with sending written notice to bondholders informing them of actions the Trustee intends to take. The document should also state that, unless directed otherwise, the Trustee intends to proceed along the path described. For example, in a final distribution, the Trustee should proceed with the process as presented by the plan of reorganization. By obtaining opinions in writing, Trustees protect themselves from criticism and demonstrate they are acting prudently.

Form a Review Committee: A good best practice for the Trustee is to create a committee to review and approve actions to be taken as they relate to the bankruptcy and Event of Default situations. Having more people review the events and participate in the decision is better than having less involvement: more involvement ensures that all aspects are considered. No single person should be solely responsible for every decision in this difficult process. The TIA also states that it is important for the Trustee to refer decisions to a "Trust Committee"; this demonstrates prudent conduct by the Trustee.

Secure the Collateral: The Trustee must promptly secure the collateral/security interests in order to preserve the bondholders' rights to the collateral. Legal title should be reviewed and perfected by the Trustee's counsel. Physical possession of collateral, such as mortgage files or securities, may be necessary. Buildings and facilities must be secured by hiring security personnel to ensure UCC filings are checked, thus assuring that proper security interests are maintained. Insurance coverage must be maintained. The security of the collateral is an immediate responsibility for the Trustee and crucial to protecting bondholders' ultimate recovery.

Maintain Insurance: If the bonds are secured by real property in the form of land, buildings, or personal property, the Trustee may be called on to immediately ensure that any insurance coverage is maintained. Often, insurance premiums may not be paid by the debtor, causing cancellation of insurance coverage on the property/equipment securing the bonds. The best practice is for the Trustee to step in immediately to assess what type of insurance is required and then make sure it is continued, even if this means paying the premiums from his/her own funds. This will be added as a reimbursable expense for the Trustee. Do *not* let the insurance lapse, as this may have devastating consequences if a destructive event occurs that damages the property (i.e., hurricane, fire, etc.) or if a liability event develops, such as someone being injured on the property and suing for damages (liability insurance coverage).

Hold Bondholder Meetings: Although it is not required, it is a best practice for the Trustee to hold bondholder meeting(s). The purposes of these meetings are to communicate the status of the bankruptcy proceedings and to seek the thoughts and direction of the bondholders as to Trustee actions or inaction. Bondholder meetings foster better communication and establish a better working relationship with the bondholders the Trustee is striving to protect. Trustee counsel usually runs the meeting jointly with the Trustee. Minutes should be kept and made available.

Participate in the Creditors' Committee: It is a best practice for the Trustee to actively participate in the appropriate creditors' committee. Once again, Trustee's counsel can take the lead on behalf of the Trustee. Active participation as either a voting or nonvoting member will demonstrate active involvement by the Trustee in representing the interests of the bondholders. The creditors' committee is where the action is. Participation by the Trustee is a best practice that keeps the Trustee in the communication and decision-making process throughout the bankruptcy proceedings.

Appear in Court and File Motions: The Trustee through his/her counsel must appear in bankruptcy court to file motions and ultimately to have the court approve his/her fees and expenses. A wise Trustee makes a special effort to be both respectful to the court and to other parties at all times, acting as a positive asset in the bankruptcy process. Presenting a belligerent, obstructionist demeanor will result only in the bankruptcy court potentially denying the Trustee claim for fees and expenses. Being courteous to the judge and respectful of all parties will produce the best results.

Make Distributions Promptly and Accurately: The Trustee will perform any distributions to the bondholders from the bankruptcy proceeds. The best practice is for the Trustee to make any distribution as promptly as possible while being careful to make the proper allocation calculations in the likely event that only a partial recovery is forthcoming for the bondholders. Promptness and accuracy are crucial. The Trustee should verify all calculations with counsel and the court as the court's decision may include a prorated percentage of principal calculations and interest.

Hire a Default Specialist: It is a good practice for any Trustee to have experienced, specialized staff available to perform bankruptcy workouts. Specialized default staff/team can be a real advantage to assist a Trustee in performing well and avoiding risk in bankruptcy.

Manage Debt Service Reserve Accounts: No best practices discussion would be complete without reviewing what a Trustee should do with reserve fund monies in a bankruptcy and Event of Default. The current practice is for Trustees to hold on to the funds and pay the Trustee's fees and expenses. There are variations to this practice depending on the situation. Some banks will pay their legal fees from the funds and withhold paying their Trustee fees until the resolution of the bankruptcy. Others pay their fees as well as counsel fees from the reserve monies in their possession. Others do not use the reserve funds until the conclusion of the bankruptcy or upon court order. In other words, there is no real consistency in approach. The arguments in favor of using reserve fund monies for Trustee expenses are as follows:

- The bondholders want the Trustee to take proactive action on their behalf. Bondholders realize there are Trustee expenses to be incurred that the Trustee will be petitioning for in the bankruptcy. As a result, bondholders may feel that the Trustee should receive just compensation during the process.
- The Trustee has a right to charge a lien on monies prior to distribution to the bondholders.

- The standard indenture language provides that the Trustee does not have to expend his/her own funds without ability for recovery.
- The Trustee is entitled to indemnification before acting and using reserve fund monies that may forestall the need to ask for indemnification.

It does make good business sense for Trustees to be justly compensated for the work they and their counsel do during what can be a long and expensive process. There has been resistance to Trustees taking reserve fund monies from certain bondholders; the rating agencies believe the reserve funds belong to the bondholders first. I would advise Trustees to carefully consider each circumstance, assessing the sensitivity of this issue and acting accordingly. I believe this will continue to be an ongoing point of contention.

Fees and Expenses and How to Recover Them: Best Practices

It is always a possibility that the Trustee will not recover some or all of his/her fees and expenses in a bankruptcy. A number of factors will impact recovery, including the fact that when all is said and done, there just may be no money available to pay the bondholders or the Trustee. How can you maximize recovery? There are several best practices to follow:

1. Have the indenture provide for the Trustee's fees and expenses as administrative expenses in a bankruptcy. If not in the indenture, then have counsel negotiate with the court and the creditors' committee to have the fees and expenses paid as administrative expenses. It is in the best interest, potentially, for the creditors to agree to this since the Trustee's fees and expenses will be paid generally out of the ongoing bankruptcy estate. With this approach, the Trustee's fees and expenses will not remain for the creditors to fight over as just another competing expense when

the plan distribution is made and the available monies are disbursed (i.e., the pieces of the pie are allocated to the hungry creditors).

- The Trustee and his/her counsel should keep very detailed records of all time spent and expenditures made. The best practice here is to create a detailed time log by hour. For example, if a meeting is scheduled, the Trustee not only documents the date and place of the meeting, but he/she lists the parties attending and what was discussed in addition to the time spent. More is more in this case. The more detailed the records substantiating the Trustee's fees, the more likely the court is to approve them.

- Trustees need to make sure the indenture contains "latch on rights," meaning that the Trustee has a first priority claim on any recovery to pay Trustee charges. The Trustee will then be paid first before any remaining monies are distributed to the bondholders. Another designation of this concept is "changing lien" of the Trustee for recovery of his/her fees and expenses.

- Trustee's fees and expenses are submitted under section 503(b)(3), under the substantial contribution wording of the Bankruptcy Code. This avenue is a last resort. This is often referred to as the "substantial contribution" section of the Bankruptcy Code. This is because the courts have taken undue liberties and denied Trustee claims or significantly reduced them, ruling that the Trustee did not make a "substantial contribution" to the bankruptcy process.

III. The Risk to Trustees of Nonperformance of Bankruptcy Responsibilities

A bankruptcy situation clearly places the Trustee in the prudent man/person standard of care, as it is an Event of Default. As such, the Trustee now has heightened duties and responsibilities to act "prudently" and do the right thing for the bondholders. By its very nature, being in the prudent man/person standard of care, which requires discretionary actions by the Trustee, is a riskier environment. That risk can certainly be effectively managed by employing the best practices mentioned previously.

The sins of the past will come home to haunt the Trustee. It is a curious fact that the real risk to Trustees in a bankruptcy situation or any other Event of Default scenario is not often the actual default occurring but what happens prior. After the bankruptcy filing, the Trustee rises to a much higher state of alertness, hires counsel, and is vigilant. The risk that will tend to be most harmful comes from any pre-bankruptcy errors or lapses that occur for a variety of reasons. These lapses and mistakes can and will be used against Trustees in a lawsuit by bondholders or other third parties, who will point to the fact the Trustee did not do his/her job. In other words, Trustees can greatly aid themselves and effectively protect themselves by doing their job correctly before the bankruptcy. Below are representative areas of risk to confront Trustees during the bankruptcy process.

Hearing about the Bankruptcy Filing

While the indenture should state that the issuer is required to give prompt notice to the Trustee of the bankruptcy filing as an Event of Default, this may not occur. The result may be that the Trustee finds him/herself receiving this important information either from someone else or by reading it in the *Wall Street Journal* or seeing it on CNN. The risk is the crucial time lag that may occur: this is time lost for the Trustee to take prompt action, and the Trustee may therefore possibly be criticized. Trustee counsel can assist in aiding the Trustee to receive the crucial information of a bankruptcy filing.

Proactive Shift to Prudent Man/Person Standard of Care

The transformation from an agency role to a prudent man/person role is riskier due to the broad discretionary powers the Trustee now has that he/she did not have before. Everything changes. The Trustee must act proactively instead of sitting back and following directions. A new mindset is now required, and this new mindset does involve risk.

Inexperienced Staff Working on the Situation

It is a difficult task to now assume all the performance obligations and uncertainties of a bankruptcy. Therefore, inexperienced staff can present a risk in that they simply do not know how to manage the risks of a bankruptcy situation from the Trustee's perspective. Help is a must and is available by hiring experienced bankruptcy counsel to advise and represent the Trustee.

Vulture Funds, Private Equity Funds, and Hedge Funds

The Trustee must be alert to the advent of a new class of bondholders who buy distressed debt for the sole purpose of realizing a quick profit. These investors will not hesitate to bring an action against the Trustee as a "deep pocket."

VULTURE FUND

Credit Enhancers

In a bankruptcy, bond insurers or standby letters of credit providers will be called upon to pay the bondholders. These credit enhancers will then look to the Trustee to make sure the Trustee has done his/her job. In effect, the credit enhancer will become the bondholder of last resort and will sue the Trustee for recovery if it feels the Trustee did not perform his/her obligations.

Communications with Bondholders

The Trustee must communicate effectively with the bondholders in a timely and accurate manner. Failure to do so will subject the Trustee to potential litigation. Also, the Trustee must be careful not to give preferential treatment to one bondholder over another. In any communication about a bankruptcy, the Trustee must avoid disclosing nonpublic information that could give someone an unfair advantage. Providing a consistent message and referring inquires to counsel are two preferred options for the Trustee. An initial notice of default should be prepared and sent to bondholders of record as soon as possible after the Trustee is aware of the Event of Default. Subsequent notices from the Trustee should be sent at the discretion of the Trustee to keep the bondholders informed of important developments. I suggest that notices be sent periodically to demonstrate that the Trustee is proactively pursuing bondholders' claims and to avoid large gaps between notices.

Securing of Collateral

The Trustee must adequately secure the collateral for the bondholders in a bankruptcy. Failure to do so either legally or physically will subject the Trustee to a guaranteed lawsuit by the bondholders, who will allege the Trustee failed to adequately protect their security interests as a primary responsibility.

The Risk of Making Enemies with the Bankruptcy Judge and Other Creditors

The Trustee and his/her counsel run a tremendous risk if they act arrogantly, unprofessionally, or with wanton disregard to everyone in the process. Failure to take prompt action, obstructionist behavior, and the running up of unnecessary expenses are several of the ways the Trustee or his/her counsel can bring trouble on themselves. It must be a professional team effort by all parties. I actually saw this occur in one case where counsel representing us as Trustee was obnoxious and combative to the judge. The result was a reduction, also known as a "haircut" to our fee recovery.

Nonpayment of Fees and Expenses

The Trustee always confronts the possibility that his/her fees and expenses will only be partially paid or never paid at all. It is rare for the Trustee to not be paid, but it is more common for the bankruptcy court to give a haircut to the Trustee's fee. There isn't much the Trustee can do to prevent the court from administrating a haircut other than to diligently do his/her job and thoroughly document his/her expenses.

Threat of Lawsuits

The simple fact in a bankruptcy is that some or all of the creditors may not be paid. Unhappy creditors will look for other means of recovery—namely litigation against the Trustee or other deep pockets. It is a risk that cannot be ignored but can be managed. Many lawsuits are brought not to go to trial but to force a settlement. If the Trustee has done everything he/she can to proactively protect the bondholders, there really is little to fear because the Trustee will be able to present a successful defense. The risk arises when the Trustee has failed in some aspect of his/her responsibilities either pre-default or post-default. Once again, the best risk management is for the Trustee to do his/her job right.

Conflicts of Interest

One risk to Trustees in a bankruptcy will arise from the need to promptly determine if there are any conflicts of interest now operative. Since the Trustee is now in the Event of Default category, he/she must determine if there are any conflicts of interest that would prevent him/her from serving as a fair, impartial, and non-prejudiced representative of the bondholders. The conflicts to avoid are listed in Section 310(b)(1-10) of the Trust Indenture Act. The Trustee must resign and a successor Trustee appointed within ninety days of determining the existence of a conflicting interest if the listed conflicts are not resolved. The most common conflict is lending, which would require the Trustee to resign whether a bond is TIA-qualified or not. Failure to promptly determine if a conflict of interest exists and to take prompt resignation action if present would subject the Trustee to the risk of litigation by the bondholders.

Conclusion

The role of the Trustee in a bankruptcy requires heightened awareness and a shift to the prudent man/person standard of care. The Trustee must now act prudently and assume new discretionary powers to use in his/her efforts to maximize bondholder recovery. The key for the Trustee is to hire capable, experienced bankruptcy counsel to mitigate the Trustee's risk in what can be a lengthy process. Yet the duties of the Trustee in a bankruptcy and the responsibility to the bondholders are precisely why the securities markets need Trustees. With the proper diligence and professionalism and with the help of reliable counsel, the Trustee can and does rise to the occasion.

Chapter Summary

- The bankruptcy laws in the United States are based upon giving the debtor a second chance.
- The bankruptcy laws protect the debtor from claims of the creditors by building a wall of protection around the debtor for a period of time while the parties work on a solution.
- The most common bankruptcy chapters involving Trustees are as follows:
  - Chapter 7: Liquidation
  - Chapter 9: Municipal Reorganization (only voluntary)
  - Chapter 11: Corporate Reorganization (both voluntary and involuntary)
  - Chapter 13: Personal Bankruptcy
  - Chapter 15: Crossborder Bankruptcy

- The best ways for Trustees to meet their obligations in a bankruptcy are to:
  - Hire bankruptcy counsel.

- Act prudently.
- Act proactively.
- Provide frequent notices to the bondholders.
- Create a specialized default team or individual with the expertise in this area.

- The risks to the Trustees of not performing their bankruptcy responsibilities include the following:
  - Pre-default Trustee mistakes that will be used against the Trustee in post-default litigation
  - Lack of timely, proactive action
  - Inexperienced staff working on a bankruptcy
  - Aggressive bondholders who may pursue claims against the Trustee to recover their losses

~ Case Study ~

An unusual default has just occurred. Hurricane Andrew has devastated parts of southern Florida. One of the hardest hit areas is a Marine World exhibit featuring a dolphin show. The exhibit is severely damaged. In fact, the tank holding the dolphins is damaged and is leaking. The company immediately files for Chapter 11 bankruptcy protection. You are the Trustee for the bonds, which are secured by both the facility and the dolphins as the critical collateral. Without the dolphins, the facility has much less value.

What do you do?

Answer:

You are now in the prudent man/person standard of care. You hustle down to the facility to make sure it is secured and the dolphins are cared for. Knowing nothing about how to care for dolphins, you immediately must hire caretakers and animal trainers to keep the dolphins alive and happy. It turns out that dolphins need constant interaction, so even if there are no shows, the dolphins exercise as if there were.

You learn a great deal about dolphins before you are through. The ultimate goal is to sell the facility and the dolphins; you do both over the course of time. This case demonstrates the unique situation a Trustee can find him/herself in concerning a bankruptcy Event of Default. No two are alike.

~ Chapter 7 ~

Risk Management for Corporate Trust Pre- and Post-default and Best Practices

Chicago, Illinois—1975

I am a young Corporate Trust Administrator handling a hospital revenue bond issue. There is an active construction fund to pay for the costs of constructing a new wing to the hospital. I am processing one of the requisitions for payout of incurred expenses. Attached to the requisition are invoices to support the requisition amount. As I am paging through the invoice documentation, I come upon an invoice for Mary's Bridal Shop for $5,000. I stop in stunned amazement. What is this invoice doing here? Is it a mistake, or is it somehow part of the construction? Should I pay the requisition? What am I to do?

This situation actually occurred. It has forever influenced my view of risk management and established my strong belief that proper risk management:

- *Starts with the people administering the accounts and their functions;*
- *Is everyone's responsibility, not just that of the manager or compliance officer; and*
- *Takes courage.*

As a young administrator, I had no experience or real guidelines to follow. So I used my own judgment and sense of right and wrong. I thought, "If this money from the hospital construction fund were my money, how would I want it to be spent?" My answer was, *"To build the hospital wing to produce the revenue to pay off the bonds."* Once I answered that question myself, I was committed to taking whatever action I needed to make sure that objective was reached. Anything else would be wrong.

My sense was that something was wrong, and I became determined to resolve the matter—one way or another. I sensed that it was important to do so. It was important for the bank as Trustee, important for the bondholders who bought the bonds, important for the hospital, and meaningful for my career and how I wanted to do business.

This story has an interesting ending. After consulting my manager, calling the hospital, consulting with our commercial officers, and reviewing the indenture and past requisitions, I concluded that the invoice should not be paid. Yes, I did incur the wrath of the hospital treasurer, who had signed the requisition, and the commercial officer, who demanded to know why I was upsetting a good bank client. But I held fast to my conclusions that paying an invoice from Mary's Bridal Shop was inappropriate.

As it turned out, the treasurer was indicted for fraud and embezzlement one month later. I was very happy to have spared our bank's good name and to have avoided any unwanted press attention in connection with the prosecution of the hospital treasurer. This is a good lesson for everyone in Corporate Trust.

Chapter Objective

Risk is an inherent part of any business as it is in Corporate Trust. This chapter will explore the unique aspects of the various risks impacting Trustees pre- and post-closing. This chapter will also discuss post-default risk and best practices for risk control. The purpose is to better understand how the Trustee should act in a variety of risk scenarios. Understanding what the risks are and how to successfully manage them is a crucial part of everyday life for the Trustee.

To understand the risks facing the Trustees of today, I will focus on these key areas:

I.   Defining the Key Areas of Risk and the Overall Risk Climate

II. Administrative Performance for Pre-closing, Post-closing, and Post-default

III. Post-default Risk Management

IV. How to Successfully Manage Risk in Corporate Trust: Top Ten Best Practices

I. Defining the Key Areas of Risk and the Overall Risk Climate

The overall risk climate facing Trustees today is fraught with hazards. It is characterized by four overall factors. The first is today's unforgiving business climate. I call this the "Economic Crash of 2008 Factor." It is much more than a regulatory and marketplace backlash against deceit, greed, and blatant disregard for the law. It is an ongoing business climate that increases pressures from all sides—pressure to not make a mistake. It is a singularly unforgiving business environment, where second chances are rare and the penalties for failure are swift. The business will simply leave for a competitor. Old loyalties are a thing of the past in this "what have you done for me lately?" environment.

Second, there is more litigation. The unforgiving marketplace has produced a new class of investors who will not hesitate to sue the Trustee, and anyone else, for recovery.

Third, the increased speed of the marketplace has created enormous risk for the Trustees. Technology has played a major part in speeding up all aspects of the securities markets and business practice in general. The Trustee has less time to review documents, which are revised and sent with the touch of a keystroke. The lack of time to think, analyze, and seek advice has introduced more risk for Trustees who must carefully consider many factors in both the creation and life cycle of a bond issue. In short, speed can kill.

Fourth, increasing pressures on resources for both people and systems have had a major impact on the Corporate Trust business. Trustees are faced with having to do more with less and in a shorter time. This spells risk. Everyone is stretched to the maximum. In such a business environment, it is easy to see how mistakes can be made. Add the increasing complexity of the securities markets and the structures the Trustee must deal with and you have a difficult challenge for Trustees to effectively manage the financial, legal, and reputational risks they face.

Given this overall business environment, which does not appear likely to change in the near future, what is the Trustee to do? This chapter will supply some answers.

The key areas of risk I will explore will be divided into the following five categories:

- Regulatory requirements
- Administrative performance for pre-closing, post-closing, and post-default
- Operational functions
- Legal litigation

- Business risks

The risks will be defined in each of these categories for Trustees, with the recommendations to successfully manage those risks following in the second section.

Regulatory Requirements

The various regulators that impact Trustees require compliance in certain areas. The Securities and Exchange Commission (SEC) is the main securities market regulator and focuses on disclosure, current compliance with the new laws under Dodd-Frank, and all operational requirements for processing securities and payments as Transfer Agent per the Securities Amendments Act of 1975. These operational functions will be covered in the operations chapter (Chapter 11). The SEC also focuses on all TIA requirements. The Office of Comptroller of the Currency (OCC) is the regulator for all national banks and focuses under Reg. 9 on all compliance procedures, administrative and operational procedures/policies, investments, and overall risk management, including Know Your Customer (KYC) procedures. The Federal Reserve and state regulators focus on Trustees' conformance with federal and state laws. The Internal Revenue Service (IRS) is concerned with compliance with arbitrage laws, municipal tax-exempt requirements, and tax reporting requirements. Finally, the Trustee bank's own internal auditors try to cover all the above regulatory concerns in addition to conformance with the internal bank rules, such as KYC compliance, administrative and operational procedures, and proper documentation.

Overall, the Trustee must demonstrate to all regulators proper risk control awareness, which includes:

- Knowledge of and compliance with the relevant rules and regulations

- Proper documentation proving compliance, such as written policies and procedures and proper files of governing documents and compliance items
- Complete files
- Balanced and reconciled cash and securities positions

II. Administrative Performance for Pre-closing, Post-closing, and Post-default

The key to proper risk management for administrative performance is based on proper activities in the three phases of administration. It is my opinion that, surprisingly, the greatest risks occur for Trustees in the order of pre-closing, post-closing, and post-default. At first glance, it would appear to be just the opposite, with the most risk occurring post-default rather than during active administration. Finally, it would seem there would be reduced risk for pre-closings when the Trustee has not assumed his/her formal responsibilities. I would submit that the Trustee of today must recognize the true risks in importance of the order I suggest—pre-closing, post-closing, and finally post-default.

Why? Because real risk management for Trustees begins at the account acceptance, KYC, and pre-closing stage of fully understanding and negotiating the proper responsibilities that the Trustee must now live with over the life of the bond issue. It all starts with managing the pre-closing risks and forms the basis for all that follows. I like to say good deals usually stay good whereas bad deals always stay bad. So be careful what you accept.

Pre-closing Risk Management

The basic and crucial risk management practices for Trustees involve a rigorous process as follows:

Know Your Client (KYC): It is vital for Trustees to perform due diligence on the identity of all clients to comply with both bank procedures and regulatory requirements. Proper documentation is a must. Information to be verified includes the name and address of the client. A search should be conducted on an identification database such as LexisNexis® to determine if any improper events surround the client. Forms must be completed for the type of business conducted by the client. Other necessary documents include W-9s, financials, and articles of incorporation. This rigorous process is also applied to individuals for escrow relationships. All clients are checked against the Office of Foreign Assets Control (OFAC) list. This new client adoption process is required under the Patriot Act passed in October 2001. For Trustees, there is simply no excuse or second chance for failure to comply with KYC requirements. Doing business with a prohibited organization or individual will result in fines, jail terms, and massive reputational damage. This is the most important risk management item for Trustees today, and it all must take place immediately at the point of first contact with the client. It is also an ongoing responsibility.

Account Acceptance: This second crucial step for Trustees involves analyzing both the nature of the bond issue or transaction and the responsibilities and services to be performed by the Trustee. Proper risk management practice requires the Trustee to promptly analyze what he/she is signing up to do and whom he/she is doing it for, then matching all this to defined account acceptance criteria. A good checklist that defines the new business acceptance parameters that are in agreement with the bank's business practices is recommended. In addition, it is important for the Trustee to have a formal approval process whereby an acceptance committee both reviews and gives final approval for accepting the business. Every piece of new business must go through this formal acceptance process. To comply with regulatory requirements, the board of directors must ultimately approve all new Trust business.

Document Review: The third pre-closing risk management area is performing proper document review of all relevant Trust documents impacting the Trustee. A thorough review of the indenture is necessary and should be completed as early in the drafting stage as possible to give Trustees the best chance of successfully negotiating any changes. Using legal professionals, either outside counsel or internal counsel, is a recommended best practice for Trustees. Since Trustees will be living by the indenture and other governing Trust documents for the life of the bonds, it is imperative for the Trustee to review the documents completely and effectively. In some cases, experienced administrative staff can effectively review the documents without assistance from counsel, but having counsel review documents only strengthens the Trustee's comfort level. The key question for the Trustee to ask him/herself is, "Can I perform all the responsibilities from a legal, processing, and systems capability?" If the answer is "no," the Trustee must be able to hire a third party, eliminate the responsibilities (from the documents), or simply not accept the business. The other question is: should the Trustee hire counsel to review the Trust documents? The answer depends on the experience and capabilities of the Trustee and the type of transaction.

Closing Responsibilities: The Trustee must identify all funds movement specifics, securities issuance instructions, investment instructions, and any distributions to be made at closing. Proper risk management controls for the Trustee require prompt, early identification of all these aspects, such as proper pre-work to include accounts to be established, instructions given to DTC and the broker, plus preparation of checks or wires for any distributions. The Trustee must be precise in these areas; this may require constant attention and diligence in extracting this information from bond counsel and brokers early enough to avoid errors. Much embarrassment, and potential claims, can be avoided by the Trustee's relentless persistence to gather pre-closing information as soon as possible in order to smoothly execute his/her crucial duties at the closing.

Closing Risk Management Concerns: Escrows and Paying Agent deals do not generally need counsel review. However, as a best practice, employing outside counsel to review Trust documents is recommended. The closing requires the Trustee to not only execute on the items outlined previously but also to assure him/herself that the documents are properly signed, appropriate legal opinions given, and the legal title to collateral properly established to the Trustee. Best practice is to receive signed copies of all original documents the Trustee executes. It is important to reiterate that the Trustee is not obligated to look behind the legal opinions given or to be responsible for their legal conclusions. Neither is the Trustee responsible for the safety, soundness, or structure of the securities transaction as to its economic viability. Those are the sole responsibilities of the issuer, bond counsel, and underwriters, respectively.

Post-closing Risk Management

When the bond issue has closed, the active role of the Trustee begins. That role will be made all the easier if the pre-closing risk management practices are done properly. Given that, I will review some of the post-closing risk areas for the Trustee. These areas are representative but not all inclusive, as each securities issue will have possibly unique responsibilities facing the Trustee. This in itself is another area of risk.

Ticklers: Establishing ticklers is the most important post-closing task for Trustees. All administrative activities should have ticklers that identify all Trustee responsibilities, such as covenant compliance, payments, sinking fund/redemption duties, and others. Ticklers should be set up promptly after closing within thirty to sixty days to assure proper administration of the bond issue. Ticklers should be complete, reference the indenture section from which they originate, and describe the task to be performed. The rule is: when in doubt, establish a tickler. Proper Trustee risk management starts with establishing the right ticklers and then performing accordingly. Major risk occurs when ticklers are not properly established or followed. That is why a proper second review of the initial set-up of the established ticklers is a good best practice. I call this a "secondary review." I also recommend that the review be done by a separate party and not by a peer administrator. I have found peer reviews are not effective due to time pressures as well as peer pressure. Some Trustees follow this with an annual account review, which I recommend only for the first year or for watch list accounts.

Covenant Compliance: The Trustee must meet his/her responsibilities by monitoring covenants that the indenture specifically requires the Trustee to follow. Another concern is that there may be other covenant or monitoring duties in other documents that the Trustee must find and tickle. An example is insurance monitoring, which may be specified in a loan agreement, where it references that the Trustee must receive evidence. This is an example of a document the Trustee does not even sign, yet a Trustee is responsible for certain duties in the document. One way to catch these hidden responsibilities is to ask bond counsel if they exist. The risk for ticklers is that the Trustee fails to follow-up and to review what is required. This will certainly damage the Trustee in a post-default role by demonstrating a failure to perform given defined responsibilities. Another risk is the failure of the Trustee to properly review items received such as opinions, no-default certificates, and reports. The

Trustee is required by all documents to review any item received to determine if it meets the requirements of the governing document. This means the Trustee must do enough review to make that determination. This takes time and the need to make the proper comparison, which could mean going back to the document language to make sure the item received complies with that language.

If the Trustee does not take the time or care to properly review the items, this may result in liability for the Trustee. An example I witnessed was the failure of my administrative coworker to properly review an officer's certificate of no default. My coworker received the certificate, glanced at it, and put it in the files. The certificate appeared at first glance to have the same words, to be the same length, and to be properly signed as previous certificates had been. In reality, the middle of the certificate read "and a default has occurred," where it should have read "and there is no default which has occurred." My coworker missed those words. The issue did go into default. The bondholders brought suit, and we lost because we had written notice of the default and did nothing. Needless to say, this was a bad result for the bank and for my friend's career.

A second example is a legal case called the SemiTech case.[2] In this case, the court ruled that the Trustee failed to receive the proper officer's certificate because he/she was missing several key sentences.

I cannot strongly emphasize enough the following recommendation: review *every word* of the required certificates, opinions, and requisitions—and match the exact wording to the indenture. Any discrepancy should cause the Trustee to reject the document and request a correction. Anything less presents real risk for the Trustee.

---

[2] SemiTech Litigation LLC v. Banker's Trust Company 234F. Supp. 2nd 297 (2002).

Sinking Funds and Redemptions: This key responsibility for Trustees contains significant risk if not performed properly. The Trustee must tickle and execute. Failure to do so will result in money claims against the Trustee and damage to the entire bond issue if bonds are not redeemed promptly and accurately.

Cash Flows and Debt Service Payments: The proper management function for the Trustee in processing flow of funds and making payment to the bondholders is a critical responsibility. It is the first duty on every Trustee's list and simply cannot be delayed or handled in error. Money claims, overdrafts, and damage to the bond issue are key risks for the Trustees. Proper attention to payment deadlines and understanding of cash flows are required. Structured finance bond issues are especially vulnerable to significant risk for Trustees if the "waterfall" (i.e., cash flow) is not properly administered.

Investments: It is the Trustee's responsibility to execute investments as directed in keeping with the investment provisions of the documents. While the Trustee does not bear the risk of selecting which investment is to be made, as this is the responsibility of the issuer, the Trustee must be very diligent in receiving proper and timely direction and must always check to see that the investment is permitted under the documents. Failure to do so will result in potential liability for the Trustee if an improper investment is made. The Investment Company Act of 1940 requirements may also be breached by the Trustee for failure to facilitate required disclosure of fees charged and to provide prospectus copies to the issuer. A further risk is the Trustee "pushing" issuers into his/her own proprietary money market funds. The Trustee can educate, but not "advise," on investment choices by the issuer. The Trustee should also communicate with issuer to assure timely investment of funds to avoid having uninvested funds, resulting in lost investment income for the issuer. It is wise for the Trustee to avoid this risk by actively communicating with the issuer

180

or, at the very least, maintaining standing instructions so that funds will not be left uninvested.

Insurance: Often, due to a covenant requirement, Trustees may be required to receive evidence of insurance. The first real risk for Trustees is that they do not receive what is required. Second, they do not realize the insurance coverage mandated is not accurately reflected in the evidence of insurance. If insurance coverage seems inadequate, the risk is that there will be a loss that is not properly covered. The Trustee can be severely criticized or possibly held negligent for not receiving proper evidence of insurance matching the governing document language. By not "catching the discrepancy," the Trustee may be charged by unhappy bondholders for failing his/her responsibilities. The Trustee is not required to obtain the proper insurance. The issuer is responsible. The Trustee is not an insurance expert. However, the Trustee must realize there is risk in not properly maintaining insurance covenant requirements as related to the Trustee receiving proper evidence of insurance. Remember, the Trust documents must specifically state that the Trustee shall or will receive evidence of insurance. If silent, then the Trustee has no responsibility for receiving any evidence of insurance.

A Real-life Example

This brings me to a real-life example I often use to bring home the importance of receiving proper evidence of insurance. And it's also a reminder that the Trustee must remember to match that evidence to what the indenture requires so there is no difference for which the Trustee may be held liable.

I sat next to an administrator who had the bond issue for the McCormick Place Convention Center in Chicago. He was watching TV on a Sunday night when a news flash showed a huge fire at the McCormick Place facility. He immediately turned pale. Did he have the evidence of insurance in his files as required by the indenture? He spent a sleepless night, and first thing in the morning when the bank opened, he burst through the front door, climbed eleven flights of stairs not waiting for the elevators, and frantically searched his desk files.

To his great relief, the proper evidence of insurance was there. He was saved. The moral of this story is: don't let this happen to you. Make sure that you have the proper evidence of insurance—no more and no less—if required by the Trust documents.

Insurance is one of my greatest risk concerns because we Trustees are certainly *not* insurance experts. It is the responsibility of the issuer, not the Trustee, to properly insure the property. My strong advice is to not receive evidence of insurance at all as this is a potential land mine for Trustees who are not educated in the types of insurance, especially against vague, unclear indenture language.

My motto is, "When in doubt, negotiate it out of your documents." Let the issuer take the responsibility—not the Trustee.

Uniform Commercial Code (UCC)

The filing of UCC continuation statements may or may not be a duty of the Trustee. The governing documents will decide. In either event, there is real risk for the Trustee if the UCC continuation statements are not properly filed. The resulting risk is that the first lien on the property/collateral in favor of the Trustee will lapse. Someone else may intercede in front of the Trustee as senior lien holder; this would have severe consequences in a default if the Trustee must seize the collateral on behalf of the bondholders. The new UCC filing requirements enacted in July 2001 make proper UCC filing even more of a challenge to match the state of incorporation.

The other risk for Trustees is if the issuer fails to file. It is then appropriate for the Trustee to step in and make the filing on behalf of the issuer. This is proper risk management by the Trustee since the alternative is a serious risk for bondholders in losing their first lien on the collateral.

Some basic explanation of UCC Article 9 requirements is needed here. Revised Article 9 (RA9) to the Uniform Commercial Code was adopted in 2001. Fundamental changes were made regarding how UCCs were processed for what, where, and for how long.

- **UCC/Financing Statement:** Usually filed by bond counsel, the financing statement establishes the initial lien on the property in favor of the Trustee as secured party.
- **UCC 3 Continuation Statement:** Under RA9, all state filings are to be made every five years.
- **Place of Filing:** RA9 dramatically changed this to the "state of legal incorporation of the issuer," not the state where the property is located. I call this the "Delaware Full Employment Act," since most issuers are incorporated in Delaware. The second big change was to eliminate the requirement to file UCC 3s in the county (counties) where the property is located. One exception is if certain states classify the property filings as "real estate" under their state law. Then the UCC 3 may have to be filed in the county recorder's office as well. Massachusetts is an example.
- **Public Financings:** Under RA9, if an issue is a "public financing," it could have a thirty-year filing period. My concern here is that bond counsel should give strong

assurance that the issue qualifies as a thirty-year filing under the Code. The risk is that it doesn't and the lien lapses after five years, leaving the Trustee vulnerable.

- **Property Description:** The description of the property is incorporated by reference.
- **Uniform Form:** Instead of fifty different forms, there is now only one form. It is also filed electronically.

UCC Termination and Changes

Do not forget to file an amended UCC if there is a change in the Trustee's or issuer's name; this will ensure that the lien is recorded to the proper owner—the Trustee. Also file a UCC Termination Statement when the bonds are paid in full. The Trustee does not find him/herself in a favorable position if the property is being sold and the Trustee is still listed as senior lien holder. This happened to me once, and it proved both embarrassing and potentially harmful in holding up the property sale. I also do not want to be the titleholder of record on property if there is a problem, such as an environmental risk that arises.

Letters of Credit Draws

In bond issues where letters of credit (LCs) exist, the Trustee finds him/herself confronted with several significant risks. To be clear, there are two types of LCs:

- **Direct Pay:** This is a type of LC where periodic draws are made to primarily pay principal and interest when due. These LC banks are then subsequently reimbursed for the draw amount. This type of LC is used to assure timely payment of principal and interest due to cash flow difficulties in receiving the necessary funds in time to pay principal and interest. A good example is a housing bond issue where collections from the mortgage holders or renters can be delayed.

- **Standby:** This LC is not drawn on periodically but is there to pay for the bonds if there is a default. In other words, the LC simply "stands by" until needed in a default. The reality is that it may never be used.

There are several additional points to be made regarding LCs:

- Any draw on an LC is *preference-proof* under the bankruptcy laws. This means the payments cannot be seized in a bankruptcy proceeding. Therefore, any LC payment is protected from being potentially returned to the bankrupt estate. This is good protection for payments to bondholders.
- LCs are subject to *downgrades* if the LC bank has its rating dropped. This could trigger the need to replace the LC with one whose sponsoring bank has the appropriate rating.
- LCs *expire*. It is common for LCs to expire prior to the maturity of the bonds. They must therefore be renewed periodically. The exception is an "evergreen LC." These LCs automatically renew; this is similar to an evergreen tree, which is always green. The exception would be a Charlie Brown Christmas tree, but that is beyond the scope of my experience.

For standby LCs requiring periodic drawdowns by the Trustee to pay debt service, the Trustee faces the risk of making an improper draw request. Failure by the Trustee to *precisely* execute the draw request in accordance with the LC documentation can result in the failure of the LC bank to honor the draw. Such a failure would mean no funds to pay bondholders. Need I say more? Trustees do not realize how precise and accurate they must be in executing these draw requests. This is due to the strictness of the International Letter of Credit Rules governing the banks. The Trustee should understand completely what is required to make the draw and also realize this must be done within the stated time frames. Failure to do so, again, can result in denial of the request by the LC bank.

This would be a very bad day for a Trustee. I refer to it as "Former Administrator Time." In other words, it could cost you your job. This happened to one of my administrators. He was one hour late in delivering the LC draw request to the LC bank, which denied the draw. We had to make the debt service payment from our bank funds. We did recover the funds several weeks later when the LC bank agreed to honor our draw request, but it was a frightening position to be in. Don't let it happen to you!

Another risk for Trustees is that the LC can expire. While it is clearly not the Trustee's responsibility to renew an LC, the Trustee should tickle the expiration and diligently communicate with the issuer to assure that it is renewed in time. Failure to renew the LC or replace it with the properly rated LC bank will result in a serious risk to the bondholders. Their credit enhancement is now diminished. This may also trigger a mandatory redemption of all the bonds, so the Trustee must be diligent in seeing that the issuer takes appropriate action to renew or replace the LC.

I strongly recommend that the administrator conduct a practice run of making the LC draw just to be sure he/she has the proper draw method, address, and timing. You do not want to be guessing the draw process on the due date and find you haven't dotted all "i's" and crossed all "t's." The result could be denial of the draw.

Secondary Market Disclosure

The SEC adopted Rule 15c2-12 to the Securities Exchange Act effective in July 1995. This rule established new disclosure requirements for municipal issuers. The purpose of the rule was to address the need for more information on municipal security issues to the market place. The SEC had no direct jurisdiction over municipal issuers. In order to achieve the objective to require more disclosure from municipal issuers, the rule prohibited broker dealers from selling municipal issues for which certain disclosures were not forthcoming from the issuer. The result was to effectively require municipal issuers to disclose in two key areas:

- Provide *annual financial reports* (not required to comply with GAAP).
- Provide information on *material events* and *other events* as listed in the rule but not limited to that listing.

The impact on the Trustee of SEC Rule 15c2-12 is to potentially have the Trustee appointed as Dissemination Agent under a separate Dissemination Agreement. The duty of the Trustee as Dissemination Agent is to facilitate easier compliance for the issuer with the disclosure requirements under 15c2-12. This is done by acting as an agent for the issuer to receive annual financial reports and material event information and to pass those documents along to the marketplace by reporting them to the Municipal Securities Rulemaking Board (MSRB) and electronically filing them into the Electronic Municipal Market Access system (EMMA®).

The risk for the Trustee is any failure to promptly pass along the disclosure information from the issuer. There could be liability for the Trustee for unwarranted delay or failure to properly communicate the disclosure information from the issuer to EMMA®. Therefore, any information received should be passed along promptly.

The Trustee faces one additional risk as Dissemination Agent. Failure of the issuer to provide the required annual financial disclosure information is an unpleasant event that the Trustee would be required to communicate to the marketplace. The Dissemination Agent is required to file with EMMA® a "failure to file" notice if the annual financial report is not provided. Therefore, the Trustee must be aware of the importance of his/her role as Dissemination Agent and have proper procedures in place to fulfill this new role. Failure to do so could subject the Trustee to liability claims by the bondholders or enforcement action by the SEC. I will emphasize that the Trustee should include specific language in the Dissemination Agreement stating that the Trustee has no duty to review or approve any disclosure information provided.

Disclosure under the rule is the responsibility of the issuer—not the Trustee. I make this point because I was personally involved in the drafting of Rule 15c2-12. I advocated for several key concepts in the rule, including the following:

- The Trustee is not responsible for the content of the disclosure information or the timeliness of the issuer filing it.

- The Dissemination Agreement is not part of the indenture but is a separate agreement that stands alone. The role of Dissemination Agent is not a Trustee role, but an agent role, which limits the Trustee's liability.

- Any failure of the issuer to disclose under the rule is not an Event of Default because it is outside the indenture.

- Finally, the issuer is responsible for disclosure under the rule and the content of any disclosure—not the Trustee.

I worked very hard to have these principles employed in the implementation of the rule. I even drafted the original ten material events, which are now expanded to fifteen, with some of the disclosure events no longer required to meet a standard of materiality—just that they have occurred.

Cash Flow Movement

The Trustee has significant responsibilities for properly receiving funds, allocating them to the right accounts, investing the funds as directed, and ultimately disbursing the funds. Timeliness and accuracy are required. Improper allocation of funds to the proper accounts can cause significant harm. An example is allocation of principal and interest monies. Receipts of segregated principal and interest funds on housing bonds or structured finance issues and misallocation of those funds would, dramatically, alter the cash flow waterfall and ultimate debt service payment to the bondholders. In short, don't mix them up, or you will be short on principal payments and in excess of interest payments or vice versa.

Understanding the flow of funds or waterfall cash flow, as it is often referred to, is crucial to proper risk management of this important Trustee function. The importance of timely adherence to when the funds are to be received, and making timely disbursements accordingly, is vital to proper administration of a bond issue. Overdrafts cost the bank money, give an impression of poor service to issuers and third parties alike, and must therefore be avoided.

I recommend that all cash flows for each issue be diagrammed to assure complete understanding. If there is any lack of clarity, the administrator should question bond counsel to resolve any open questions.

A Real-life Example

I was once asked by an administrator to review the cash flow for a proposed sports stadium bond issue. I worked all night diagramming the movement of funds, but in the morning I had to admit defeat. The cash movement just did not work and had many gaps. I told the administrator to push back to seek clarity. She replied that she had tried and was told to just live with it. As is always the case, this was an important bond issue for the department, so there were political pressures to take the deal.

Luckily, the bond issue never came to fruition. The risks to the Trustee not being able to process the cash flows are:

- Timeliness of the funds movement;
- Accuracy of the amounts allocated to various Trust accounts; and
- Overdrafts, resulting in improperly funding the wrong accounts and either investing or disbursing monies that are not there.

My strong recommendation is to seek clarity around funds movement and cash flows. Double-check your work. Diagram your cash flows. Pay close attention to the whole process, as it is one of the most critical functions performed by Trustees.

Collateral Management and Substitution

One dangerous area for Trustees, and one of great concern for me in my experience, is involving collateral management (or custody). When the Trustee is required to hold collateral, either physically or in book entry form in a certain amount, it is vital to do it right. The Trustee simply cannot lose the collateral or improperly record and account for it, as this is the security for the bondholders. Proper custodial facilities, vault facilities, and systems are needed, in addition to having the proper staff to manage and keep the collateral safe. Mortgage files are a particularly difficult example requiring the following multistep process:

- Review the collateral.
- Verify the completeness of the collateral, which may entail rejecting it if it is incomplete or identifying the missing documents to be supplied and following up to receive them.
- Record the collateral properly on a system.
- File the collateral in the properly secured storage facility or vault.
- Be able to retrieve the collateral when required.

Multiply these responsibilities by volume that may reach millions of files, and it becomes obvious that this is an area of risk for the Trustee for what appears to be on its face a simple task of just holding collateral. It is anything but simple.

The other grave risk Trustees face in this area is substitution of collateral. Many bond issues backed by collateral provide for the substitution or replacement of the collateral under certain circumstances. This is all well and good if the collateral substitution requirements are properly defined and followed. The risk is that they are not. Numerous cases exist where collateral has been substituted to the ultimate detriment of the bondholders because of failure of the substituting party to properly follow the document guidelines. The result is replacing good collateral with lesser quality collateral, thus weakening the security for the bondholders.

The Trustee finds him/herself in the middle of this controversy as the gatekeeper for the collateral. It is the Trustee's job to ensure that all required documentation is received and that the issuer meets all requirements before releasing or substituting collateral. Anything less is simply unacceptable.

Therefore, it is a major risk for Trustees to inadequately monitor any collateral substitutions and make sure they are fully documented and meet all requirements. An unfortunate example that I have experienced is the Continental Airlines bankruptcy situation in 1991 where aircraft were initially the collateral of collateral Trust and equipment Trust bond issues. Unfortunately, Continental substituted the original aircraft, newer DC-9s, for older aircraft, 727s, which later proved to be of lesser value. The Collateral Trustee did not stop the substitution due to vague document language and unawareness, which was compounded by incomplete substitution documentation. Obviously, this became a point of contention later in subsequent litigation brought by the bondholders after the bankruptcy filing by Continental.

In short, the responsible Trustee must pay very close attention to any collateral substitutions. The Trustee must follow the trust document requirements to the letter. The standard is that the new collateral must be of *equal or greater value* than the collateral it is replacing; otherwise, the substitution should not be made. Once the collateral is gone, it is *gone*.

Valuations

In certain circumstances, Trustees are required to value securities or collateral as required by the Trust documents. The risk to Trustees occurs when the Trustee either fails to perform the valuation or does it incorrectly.

To avoid this risk, Trustees should carefully review any valuation requirements in the Trust documents prior to closing to make sure the method of valuation is *precisely* spelled out. There can be no ambiguity. It must be crystal clear so that the Trustee knows exactly what, when, and how the valuation will be performed. It is wise for the Trustee to insist on specific information such as which index or valuation source to go to in order to obtain the exact valuation of the security or collateral to be valued. Specific direction as to when the valuation is to be performed is also a must.

Failure by the Trustee to properly perform valuations will present liability exposure to the bondholders. The most common area of valuation occurs for Trustees in cases where a reserve fund is present. Valuing the reserve fund and properly notifying the issuer to either add more collateral or return excess is a crucial role for Trustees. Failure to properly do so will potentially diminish security for the bondholders if the reserve fund is insufficient to make a required payment and will result in liability for the Trustee.

Construction Fund Withdrawals

Trustees often find themselves in the position of managing disbursements for a construction fund. Whether for a construction fund or any other disbursement, the process involves real risk for the Trustee. The central concept is that monies are set aside for constructing a facility or purchasing equipment. If the funds are not used to do that, then the bondholders are at risk since the bond issue will not have achieved its purpose of creating the required security (building or equipment) for the bondholders. In other words, if the funds are not used to build the facility as envisioned, there will be no method of repayment for the bondholders.

The Trustee is then put in an important position of bearing the responsibility of monitoring construction fund disbursements. The Trustee is required to receive requisitions and other supporting documentation, such as an architect opinion or invoices, as part of the requisition request for disbursement of funds. First, there is a timing issue. The Trustee is pressured to disburse the funds promptly, usually within a day or two, as vendors and contractors need to be paid. Second, invested construction fund monies must be made available either through sale of securities that the funds are invested in or through a more liquid investment such as a money market fund. Construction fund withdrawals are often delayed due to scheduling delays in building the facility, thereby causing uncertainty as to when the funds will be needed. Third, multiple disbursements may be required of the Trustee if the indenture allows for the Trustee to pay vendors and contractors directly. This is time-consuming and prone to error as the Trustee may make ten to fifty separate disbursements to a wide variety of parties. Fourth, and most important, the Trustee must receive all required documentation, properly signed by the authorized representative, in order to make the disbursements. Failure by the Trustee to obtain the required documentation will subject the Trustee to liability if improper payouts are made.

The real issue is the potential for fraud. The construction industry has had an unfortunate history of inflated invoices, fraudulent or bogus charges, and just the opportunity for dishonest individuals to try to take advantage of the situation. Remember, the Trustee acts as the gatekeeper for construction fund payments. It is clear that the Trustee is *not* required to do due diligence behind the requisition documentation or to determine if the charges are reasonable or proper. The Trustee must rely on the requisition documentation and should not be further liable if improprieties occur. However, the Trustee *must* make sure the proper documentation is received and properly executed by the authorized parties before release of funds. If fraud occurs and improper use of funds uncovered, the Trustee should be protected if the Trustee has precisely followed the document requirements for all requisition documentation. Unfortunately, it all will depend on what a judge or jury decides. They will look to see if the Trustee had documentation or knowledge of impropriety. One very disturbing issue for the Trustee is to what extent the Trustee must review the supporting documentation. Obviously, the requisition must say what it is supposed to and must be signed by the right party. The real issue is when invoices are required to be attached. What is the Trustee to do? To what extent should the Trustee review the invoices? What liability could occur as a result of the Trustee's actions in reviewing the invoices?

There is no comfortable answer for Trustees in this situation. Reliance on the representations is the first line of defense, and certainly the Trustee does not have the expertise, time, or ability to analyze every invoice. However, there is the risk that an invoice could be so blatantly wrong that its inclusion into the requisition could raise questions. As mentioned in the story at the beginning of the chapter, the Mary's Bridal Shop invoice present in the requisition could raise questions and highlights the potential risks for Trustees in construction fund disbursements.

To this day, I am grateful I took that action as it saved the bank not only the embarrassment of the situation but potential liability for making this payment. But the whole issue raises some interesting questions for Trustees. Can you really just rely on the representations of the parties when you have other documentation or information that casts doubt on the propriety of what is being requested? Not an easy issue to resolve.

Environmental Risk

It is a Trustee's worst nightmare to become embroiled in the cost of cleaning up an environmentally contaminated property. The potential risk arises if the Trustee becomes an "owner operator" of contaminated property under the environmental laws. The key environmental law is the Comprehensive Environmental Response, Compensation, and Liability Act (CERCLA), commonly known as Superfund, enacted in December 1980. As the name implies, the act established prohibitions under federal law for polluting the environment. The act also provided for liability of persons responsible for the pollution. A Trust fund was established to fund cleanup operations. The Superfund Amendment and Reauthorization Act (SARA) amended this act in 1986. The Environmental Protection Agency (EPA) enforces the environmental laws.

Simply stated, the danger for Trustees is that a default occurs in a bond issue that is secured by property. If the Trustee forecloses on the property as is required by the indenture, then the Trustee becomes the "owner operator" of the property and a potential target for any environmental problem.

The real risk for Trustees occurs not from the law but from the courts that enforce the law. This risk arises because there is no source of funds generally to clean up an environmental mess. The Superfund Trust Fund is underfunded as a source of cleanup monies. The party that caused the problem is also usually long gone, in bankruptcy, or lacking the resources to fund the cleanup. That leaves the Trustee as a deep pocket and the only source of funds.

Recommendations for Trustees to avoid environmental risks are as follows:

- Identify the accounts that have secured interest in property, and increase your vigilance to environmental risk if a default occurs
- Establish protective language in the indenture, such as:
  - The Trustee shall receive periodic reports as to the status of the property concerning any environmental problems.
  - The Trustee is not required to foreclose on property if there is an environmental problem without bondholder indemnity.
  - Prior to accepting the bond issue, the Trustee is to be provided various environmental reports concerning the current status of the property.
  - Phase I Report: A report by an environmental expert disclosing details of the environmental condition of the property.
  - Phase II Report: A detailed report with core soil drilling analysis.
  - Phase III Report: This is the cleanup plan for a contaminated site.

The good news for Trustees is that in 1996 Congress passed the Asset Conservation, Lender Liability, and Deposit Insurance Protection Act, which provided considerable comfort for Trustees in two important areas:

- The Trustee would not be liable for environmental problems if it became "owner operator" of property in its normal course of business (e.g., foreclosing on property for bondholders in a default).
- Any liability is limited to the assets of the Trust.

While helpful, several court decisions have eroded these protections for parties pursuing the deep pocket in the case, as I have stated before. Therefore, my standard joke regarding environmental risk for Trustees is, "If it glows, don't foreclose." This is probably good advice.

UCC 4A

The Uniform Commercial Code states in Article 4A that organizations must develop procedures around sending and receiving wire transfers or they will be subject to potential loss. Simply put, Trustees send and receive wire transfer payments as a normal course of business. To avoid the risk of being responsible for a claim because a wire transfer payment was improperly sent to the wrong party by the Trustee or, worse yet, fraudulently wired, Trustees must be aware of the need to have written procedures in place to properly identify instructions around wire transfers. For many Trustees, the wire room has such procedures. What the Trustees need to realize is that those procedures depend upon the Trustees properly verifying both sending and receiving information. Failure to do so will subject the bank to liability. Trustees today are increasingly becoming targets for hackers who provide false wire transfer documentation due to the large amounts wire transferred by Trustees. To guard against this increasing risk, Trustees are instigating detailed transfer fund agreements to protect against this new threat.

Trustees today are increasingly becoming targets for hackers who provide false wire transfer documentation attracted by the large dollar amount of funds moved by Trustees. To guard against this increasing risk, Trustees are establishing specific language in Trust documents providing for callbacks and other verification information from authorized parties prior to transferring funds. Some banks are even developing separate wire transfer agreements to accomplish this enhanced due diligence in order to counteract the threat of wire transfer fraud.

Hackers are targeting Trustees because of the large amounts of monies being transferred from Trustees in the course of business for bond issues. Examples are construction fund disbursements or escrow disbursements. Trustees

III. Post-default Risk Management

Heightened awareness is required for Trustees in a post-default environment. I will discuss the main areas of risk facing Trustees in such situations.

Events of Default

When an Event of Default occurs, the Trustee is thrust into the prudent man/person standard of care. As such, the Trustee must now exercise considerable discretion on behalf of the bondholders to protect their interests. With expanded authority to act and broaden responsibility, the Trustee is now in a riskier position. The Trustee's actions or lack thereof will be highly scrutinized in light of developing circumstances surrounding the Event of Default. In these situations, the Trustee must exercise good judgment backed by advice of counsel plus good business sense in working through to a successful conclusion for the bondholders. Focused attention, assistance from knowledgeable experts, and experience will greatly aid the Trustee in performing prudently given the circumstances in a bankruptcy proceeding—the most common Event of Default.

Resignation and Conflict of Interest

In the post-default world, the Trustee may have no choice but to resign due to a conflict of interest. The risk to Trustees is not in the actual resignation process, which is fairly straightforward, nor is it in finding a qualified successor, as there are a number of candidates to step in. The real risk is determining quickly and decisively that a conflict exists and promptly executing the resignation. Remaining in a conflict situation may lead to liability for the Trustee, who will become a target for disgruntled bondholders for not doing enough on their behalf due to the existence of the conflict.

The best course of action for Trustees is to quickly focus attention to determine if any conflicts exist by researching all the conflicts under Section 310(b) (1-10) of the Trust Indenture Act. Special focus should be on determining whether or not the Trustee bank has any lending relationship with the defaulting issuer. Remember, the Trust Indenture Act and the indenture states that the official conflict of interest prohibition is not triggered until an Event of Default (e.g., bankruptcy, nonpayment of principal) occurs. Then the Trustee has ninety days to resign or cure the conflict. The motto of "when in doubt, get out" applies here unless there are very strong business reasons backed by a solid opinion of counsel saying there is no material conflicting interest.

Backup Servicing

A standard requirement for Trustees in structured finance bond issues (asset-backed or mortgage-backed bonds) is to be responsible for performing the role of backup servicer or servicer of last resort. Inability of the current servicer to perform will lead to responsibility of the Trustee to replace that servicer, either by assuming servicer duties him/herself or finding another third party to perform servicer responsibilities. Backup servicing is the most crucial risk area for Trustees in structured finance issues and must be managed well.

The risks come from several areas. First, the timing of the transfer of servicing responsibilities is critical. Prompt and immediate action on the part of the Trustee is required. The servicing transfer must occur to provide continuity in collections of funds and other servicing duties. Any delay can result in lost collections, interrupted cash flow, and potential loss to the bondholders. One only has to envision thousands of individual receivable assets, such as credit cards or home equity loans, to realize the daily work of monitoring, billing, and collecting. This is what servicers do, and this work cannot be interrupted for long. Even a few days can make a difference. So the Trustee must be prepared to step in immediately, with no delay, to perform or engage a third party to pick up where the nonperforming servicer left off.

Second, the risk to the Trustees is how they find out that the servicer is nonperforming and must be replaced. Servicer nonperformance could evolve over time or occur through one main event such as a bankruptcy filing. Therefore, sometimes it is difficult, and potentially risky, for Trustees in determining just when to step in.

Third, the Trustee may not have the proper authority to act in removing a nonperforming servicer. The documents and deal structure may not give the Trustee the power to remove servicers; this could further complicate the Trustee's role of when and how to assume the responsibilities as backup servicer.

Fourth, Trustees find they do not have the staffing, systems, or expertise to perform servicing. Therefore, the Trustee is faced with the risk of both not being able to do the job of servicing and being faced with the need to find third-party servicing organizations to step in on behalf of the Trustee. This obviously involves research, planning, and negotiation by the Trustee in what could be a very pressurized, time-sensitive situation.

I recommend the Trustee have a list of third-party backup servicers he/she can call on to step in at a moment's notice. If possible, the Trustee should try to negotiate protections in the Trust documents to have any backup servicer fees paid for from the cash flow of the transaction at current fee rates. Even better would be to have a backup servicer appointed and ready.

I cannot emphasize enough that it is critical for the Trustee to have in place a viable third-party servicer to immediately step into the servicer role to avoid liability for the Trustee in not acting promptly enough to replace the defunct servicer.

Policies and Procedures

It is a given that Trustees must have written policies and procedures to govern their conduct of business. Such policies and procedures should be clear, concise, and well written. A policy should be a short, targeted statement of action to be taken. One example is, "No principal or interest payment will be made without the receipt of good funds in the bank." A procedure should be a step-by-step process to accomplish a certain function. An example would be to outline how monies are received, cleared, and paid out for principal and interest payments.

The policies should usually be backed up by a procedure. I like procedures clearly defined and written in numerical steps to avoid any confusion. Exhibits, screen prints, and checklists are very helpful.

The policies and procedures should be reviewed annually and constantly updated to remain current. The risks for Trustees in the area of policies and procedures are:

- Lack of procedures for key functions
- Poorly written statements that cause confusion and inconsistent application
- Lack of staff awareness of the policies and procedures, resulting in inconsistent application
- Failure of staff to follow the policies and procedures
- A writer who does not understand the business

My recommendation is to appoint someone to manage, review, and update your policies and procedures. Create your core policies and procedures, but do not produce more than are needed. This leads to overkill and liability for Trustees in documenting processes they do not follow. More is less in this case. Use procedures in training as well to promote awareness. Have them accessible online for easy access.

And finally, I always enjoyed writing policies and procedures. No, I am not crazy. You can become an expert in a function. Being an expert is a good place to be these days. Also, it develops your writing skills and critical thinking. Plus, you control the process and not someone else. These are all benefits.

Well-written policies and procedures are a must for controlling risk in Corporate Trust. I do not know how a Trustee would pass an audit, either internal or external, without them. But be aware that they can be used against you in litigation if you are not following them. That is why some Trustees call them "guidelines" instead of procedures. This is a play on words to avoid strict liability.

Every Trustee should have well-written, current policies and procedures in place.

Operational Risks

There are a number of operations risks that fall into several general categories, including:

Conversions: Any system conversions involving operational systems can be a risky time for Trustees. Lost records, poor data, inadequate staffing resources, and costs are just a few areas of risk facing Trustees in any system conversion.

Processing Risks: Operational workflows for payments, transfers, recordkeeping, reconciling, balancing, and all general processing functions contain the potential for risk.

Clear processing structure, trained staff, effective procedures, and proactive management are needed.

Custodial and Safekeeping Risks: Operations bears the risk of safekeeping securities, records, and collateral. Proper vault facilities, maintenance of proper security access, and well-established recordkeeping systems are needed to avoid losing or improperly accounting for all safekeeping items. The result would be liability for the Trustee.

Tax Requirements: Operations is usually charged with all tax reporting compliance responsibilities. As such, operations must meet all IRS requirements for providing tax information to the IRS and to bondholders within IRS guidelines. Failure to do so will result in IRS penalties, which could be fifty dollars per item. Customer service problems of bondholders can also arise from either not receiving their tax forms (e.g., 1099s) in order to do their taxes properly or errors in those reporting forms. Both the monetary and publicity risks are severe for Trustees who fail in these areas. Also, keeping current with changing IRS tax code revisions is difficult. The Trustee is faced with costly recordkeeping duties, such as receiving certified TINs (Taxpayer Identification Numbers) and Social Security numbers and keeping them on file. If the Trustee does not have the TIN information, it may be required to perform backup withholding of any payment to the offending bondholders. Another area of concern is cost basis accounting requirements. This IRS ruling requires the Trustee to report the cost basis to bondholders on a 1099-B form. A Separate area of concern is under the Foreign Account Tax Compliance Act (FATCA). This IRS provision targets tax noncompliance by US taxpayers with foreign accounts. Once again, the Trustee may be in a position to report payments made to US taxpayers who have foreign accounts. More will be said on these areas in the operations chapter (Chapter 11).

Therefore, preparing, reporting, and filing all the required tax information and forms can be a risky and daunting task.

SEC Transfer Agent Requirements: Operations serves to process transfers of bonds for buyers and sellers. As such, the Securities and Exchange Commission (SEC) has a series of rules governing the recordkeeping and processing of transfers that operations must comply with as registered Transfer Agents. The risk is that operations is not in compliance; this can result in the SEC fining or prohibiting the Trustee from being a Transfer Agent.

Second-class Citizens: One final risk for operations is the unfortunate fact that operations is a cost center, not a profit center. As such, operations is often viewed as a necessary evil that is under constant pressure to reduce costs. Operations may then become starved for resources and find themselves ill prepared to meet the growing demands of the Trustee business with new products, new regulations, and heightened liabilities. Systems can be part of the solution to meet these operational challenges, but *people* are still needed—the right people. Experienced people. Operations is in itself a risky area for careers in that it is an area that usually suffers most in a merger or sale of the business. Operational people have wonderful backgrounds to go into administration, already knowing much of what goes on in the "back office" supporting the business, but the transition can be difficult and opportunities limited. Operations is such a vital part of any Trustee's business. Trustee organizations simply cannot afford to *not* devote the resources for both systems and people needed to have a well-functioning operations support group. The success of the Trustee's business depends squarely on good operations support. Without operations, the entire service level that clients demand for basic payment, recordkeeping, and processing will be jeopardized.

Legal Risks

Trustees face a variety of legal risks that stem from several sources. Regulatory requirements must be abided by and require Trustees to be continually vigilant to new changes in laws and objectives of the regulators. For example, the ongoing efforts of the regulators to require more timely, accurate information and better disclosure will impact Trustees for years to come. An example is the Dissemination Agent role under SEC Rule 15c2-12. Legal risks also arise from the Trust documents Trustees live by. The more litigious society we live in also contributes to Trustee's legal risks and the chance to be sued. There are several other legal risks facing Trustees as summarized below.

Proper Lien Risks: Trustees may be required to maintain properly recorded UCCs in order to assure the correct legal lien is maintained on collateral as the security for bondholders. The Trustee must keep pace with current recording requirements under the Uniform Commercial Code. The Trustee must also make sure the issuer is in compliance with proper UCC filings if the issuer is the primary responsible party under the documents. Any attempt by a third party to establish a lien senior to the Trustee's lien on collateral or impairment of that lien by the issuer would require prompt and decisive Trustee action. The risk for Trustees is in finding out about such action and then moving aggressively to resolve the issue.

Doing What You Are Supposed to Do under the Documents: This is a simple concept but accurate in describing the legal risks facing Trustees. This involves both understanding what is required of Trustees and then performing those duties. I strongly support the position that Trustees are required to perform the duties that are strictly recommended in the indenture. If the indenture is silent, then the Trustee has no duty. Receiving required financial reports and other documents, as described specifically in the indenture, is the first responsibility. The second is to review said documentation to see that it meets the stated requirements of the indenture. An example is an officer's certificate of no default. The Trustee must compare the certificate language to that required by the indenture. Any discrepancies should result in the Trustee rejecting the certificate and requesting a new one that contains the proper language. Failure to do so will subject the Trustee to litigation, damages, and loss in the form of costly legal settlements or, worse, a court decision against the Trustee.

Target for Lawsuits: Trustees do represent a deep pocket to bondholders and other parties involved with these bond issues. The smart Trustee knows he/she can be a target for litigation, which may be brought for several reasons, including: 1) the wronged parties feel the Trustee failed to perform and 2) the wronged parties (who usually are not receiving their money under the deal) are casting about hoping to uncover wrongdoing by the Trustee. Everyone knows Trustee banks are averse to bad publicity and want to keep their names out of the press and out of court. So there is the prospect that lawsuits are begun with the goal of forcing a settlement by the Trustee organization. There is always risk of being sued. Wise Trustees guard against this risk by doing their job right, protecting themselves by relying on counsel and other experts, and recognizing that they can be a target when things go wrong through no fault of their own.

Legal Precedents and Litigation Risks: While it is true that most lawsuits never go to trial or reach a verdict, there is always the risk that a lawsuit will be adjudicated with an unfavorable result for the Trustee. Legal precedents are thereby set that can impact all other

Trustees for years to come. The Dabney v. Chase[3] decision in 1952, which is still law today, is an example. The Dabney v. Chase case established in common law the concept of the Trustee having a conflict of interest in an Event of Default situation where the Trustee bank was also a lender to the defaulting issuer. This precedent has firmly established this lending conflict post-default and requires any Trustee in such a situation to resign or have the lending relationship extinguished. As such, legal precedents will always be a potential risk for Trustees. It is important for all Trustees to know this and conduct themselves accordingly in an effort to *avoid* setting these dangerous precedents whenever Trustees contemplate their options in litigation. In my experience serving as an expert witness defending Trustees, I can assure you that the legal environment is becoming increasingly unfavorable for Trustees. I have seen several reasons for this. They include the following:

- Banks are unsympathetic defendants due to the economic crisis of 2008, which banks were partially blamed for.
- Banks want to avoid the reputational risk of a trial.
- The time commitment and cost of defending themselves in litigation is substantial for the banks.
- The banks represent a deep pocket for recovery of a deal gone bad.
- There is a lack of understanding of the true nature of the role of the Trustee and the limitations inherent in that role.

For these reasons, Trustees find themselves in a difficult position. It's imperative they do their jobs correctly; this is the best protection of all during litigation.

---

[3] Dabney v. Chase National Bank of City of New York 196 F. 2nd 668 (1952).

Due Diligence: One disturbing legal risk currently developing for Trustees is the concept of due diligence by the Trustee. The issue is whether the Trustee has the responsibility to look behind the economics of a deal or the basis upon which legal opinions are given. The Tremble v. Holmes[4] case involved a municipal bond issue, which was to fund an office complex near Seattle. Unfortunately, the developer stole the bond proceeds, and the complex was never built. The bondholders sued everyone involved, including the Trustee, alleging that the Trustee should have known the legal opinion stating the bond issue was properly issued under state law was wrong and that it is common industry practice for Trustees to do due diligence on the legal requirements for bond issuance. The case was settled but introduced a very dangerous premise that the Trustee pre-closing had extensive duties to review the legal underpinnings of the financing. This is simply not true. This case clearly highlights this concern. The market participants seem to be sending Trustees to this dangerous area of liability. Trustees clearly do not have the expertise or resources to do these things and certainly are not paid enough to undertake such liability. Yet the potential risk remains and must be carefully watched by the Trustee community.

Priority of Fees and Indemnity Risks: Trustees need to establish their position as being first in line in the Trust documents for fees and expenses in an Event of Default (e.g., bankruptcy). Failure to be first will put the Trustee at substantial risk of not being paid for all his/her work in a bankruptcy. It is what I call a "deal breaker" in being appointed Trustee. By deal breaker, I mean that, in my opinion, the Trustee should refuse to accept the appointment unless he/she has a priority first position on receiving his/her fees and

---

[4] Tremble v. Holmes Harbor Sewer District, et al., Island County Case No. 01-2-00751-8 (2003).

expenses first before any payout to the bondholders or other third party. Indemnity language should also be present to avoid substantial risk for Trustees. There is pushback to giving Trustees the right to such indemnification from issuers and bondholders in an Event of Default or other circumstances; this may put the Trustee at risk. The smart Trustee will recognize this risk and insist on proper indemnity language in the Trust documents to protect him/herself before taking action. It should be the Trustee's right to ask for indemnity before he/she acts.

Business Risks

The Trustee is subject to a variety of business risks, described below.

Pricing: The pressure on Trustee fees from a number of sources has resulted in reduced pricing, lower revenue, and heightened risk for Trustees despite our efforts to continue to provide the optimum services required. The Trustee organization will not support the business if it cannot produce the desired returns, and the organization will allocate capital and resources elsewhere. Trustees can fight this trend by working to be more efficient, developing new sources of revenue, and simply refusing to underprice the business for the sake of market share. Getting paid well for what we do is a must. Educating issuers, providing good service, and establishing strong client relationships will counter the negative trend in pricing.

Being Under-resourced: This applies to both staffing and systems. The right people and the right systems are crucial to properly managing risks in the Trustee business. The solution is linked to maintaining profitability, seeking more varied revenue opportunities, and convincing senior management of the viability of the Trustee business. More will be said on this in the chapters on management and future of the business (Chapters 13 and 14).

Training: Poorly trained staff are an obvious risk to the business. Changing laws, more complex transactions, and new systems require well-trained people at all levels. Attention to training and developing expertise are key focal points for any Trustee to more effectively manage risk. You simply have to do it through a combination of inside and outside sources.

The Business Not Being Understood by Senior Management: How do you educate senior management about the Trustee business? Also, there is a crucial need to educate the rest of the bank, our clients, and third-party influencers. Everyone in the Trustee business must educate others on a continuous basis. It is a daily task, not just at conferences, meetings, closings, or client events. Constant repeating of the services we provide and the value added is the answer, backed up by actual performance. Senior management is always looking for successful businesses. Proving the Corporate Trustee business can produce attractive annuity revenue, excellent profit margins, long-term returns, and good client relationships that can be a platform for selling other bank services and support for other bank products will get their attention.

New Products Risk: Developing a new product and devoting the time and resources to establish a new product is always difficult. The risk is in first being able to identify a business need and properly assessing your capabilities to meet that need through existing staff or through the addition of new expertise or systems. The risk is that this is new for you and that you do not know for certain if it will produce the revenue desired or involve unanticipated risks. Trustees must develop a mechanism for assessing new service needs and manage that process more effectively through proper risk analysis, establishment of proper procedures, and training. I believe a dedicated project manager is the best way to develop new products, but this is certainly is a luxury many Corporate Trust business do not have.

Reputational Risk: Of all the risks, reputational risk is the most devastating of them all. It arises from unfavorable publicity, which damages the bank's name in the marketplace. Litigation or regulatory fines or failed regulatory exams can produce such risk for the business and the bank. In short, we in Corporate Trust do not want to be the cause of the bank appearing in the front page of the *Wall Street Journal* as occurred with Chase in the mid-1990s. The article had a cartoon of a teacher at a blackboard with a dunce cap on (meaning you were not too smart) adding 1+1=3. The article was about a system conversion in Corporate Trust where the bank confused "issued" versus "outstanding" amounts of bonds and was out of balance. This is the most damaging case of reputational risk I have seen, although there have been others. To avoid this risk, we must do our jobs appropriately and, if a problem occurs, promptly address it and communicate it to senior management and impacted clients.

IV. How to Successfully Manage Risk in Corporate Trust: Top Ten Best Practices

There are a number of best practices I can recommend for Trustees to follow to successfully manage risk in the business. I have listed my top ten suggestions to follow. The remaining suggestions are listed in Exhibit C, for your consideration.

1. Know your **documents**, and negotiate good documents with the proper protective language that is clear and understandable from the Trustee's perspective.

2. Know your **clients**, their business, and what they hope to accomplish by their financing.

3. Know the **deal**, why the bonds were issued, and what the financing is designed to accomplish.

4. Get the **best people** you can find from a variety of backgrounds. Expose them to multiple parts of the business. Train them and support them on an ongoing basis. Keep them as long as you can by creating the best working environment possible that presents them with the opportunity to continuously learn, grow, and be successful.

5. Create the proper **risk control environment** by having dedicated risk/compliance staff. Have updated written policies and procedures that are practical and thorough. Establish a **review committee** and **watch list** to review defaulted accounts and risk situations as they arise. Have written **account acceptance** criteria and a new business acceptance committee to review and approve all new business with the objective of accepting the right business for the organization (not the risky business that you will not be able to service or for which you will find yourself in litigation).

6. Have enough **resources** to properly do the business—both people and systems. Do not "starve" the business or overburden existing staff with excessive workloads, as this inevitably leads to turnover and errors that cost time, clients, and money.

7. Develop an ongoing **training plan**, which includes orientation, business training, system training, and specialty instruction on key aspects of the business. Utilize both internal and external resources. Vary the training between on-the-job, classroom, e-learning, and written materials.

8. When in doubt, utilize **counsel** to assist in reviewing documents and supporting actions taken by the Trustee. Always hire experienced **bankruptcy counsel** to represent the Trustee in a bankruptcy situation.

9. Always require **good funds** to be received before releasing any debt service or other payment. Always have written direction in accordance with the documents for any disbursement of funds because once it is gone, it is gone.

10. Always **ask questions** and gather all the facts you can about any situation. Do not hesitate to **escalate** the situation to your management immediately and/or seek counsel's advice to determine the course of action to follow. If you are not clear or do not understand what is being asked of you or what is proper under the documents, do not act without doing the above.

Conclusion

Trustees are faced with a multitude of risks in performance of services during the life of a bond issue. Trustees can successfully manage these risks but only if they hire, train, and support the right people. Systems will greatly help, but at the end of the day, there is no system that can review an indenture or negotiate with counsel or serve the clients. Only people can do that. Corporate Trust professionals who know their documents, know their deals, and know their clients are your best protection from risk. They have a sense of responsibility and urgency in providing all the services the marketplace requires of Trustees. The ultimate service is representing the bondholders' interests to maximize their recovery in a default. With the proper attention to risk management, Trustees can both provide the services needed in the securities markets and produce sustainable revenues as a profitable business for their organization.

Chapter Summary

- An unforgiving business climate with more litigation has required Trustees to be even more diligent in performing their responsibilities both pre- and post-default.

- Regulatory requirements have been heightened with the OCC, SEC, and state examiners all increasing their scrutiny of Trustees.

- The two main pre-closing areas the Trustee must oversee to manage risk is in the KYC process and in proper document review.

- The post-closing areas requiring Trustee attention to managing risk are varied but center on proper ticklers, covenant monitoring, flow of funds, and establishment of proper policies and procedures.

- Key best practices are outlined, with the most important being hiring and training the best people and having enough people to do the job.

- Operations risks center on having the proper systems and well-documented processes with the proper controls for recordkeeping, funds movement, tax filings, and reconciliation.

- Utilizing legal counsel for reviewing documents where necessary and advising in a default situation can manage legal risks. Performing all responsibilities under the Trust documents is a must to avoid litigation risk.

- Business risks for Trustees include reputational risk, primarily through litigation, money loss, and nonperformance of duties prescribed by the Trust documents.

- The Trustee who hires experienced default counsel and avoids conflicts of interest mitigates post-default risks.

~ Case Study ~

A Corporate Trust Administrator approaches you with a situation developing with an issuer. It seems that the issuer is instructing the administrator to not draw on a direct pay letter of credit on a bond issue for the upcoming debt service payment. The issuer has said it will wire funds to cover the payment. Answer the following questions:

What would be your concerns regarding this request?

What if you advised the administrator to follow the issuer's direction and not draw on the LC?

What are the risks in following such advice?

Answer:

The direct pay LC was put in place for two specific reasons:

1. To smooth out the cash flow in order to assure timely debt service payment.
2. To maintain the draw in an LC, which is preference-proof under the bankruptcy laws. As such, a bankruptcy court cannot reclaim it.

These reasons are important safeguards for the bondholders to get paid and keep those payments even if a bankruptcy occurs. If the Trustee were to ignore the ongoing draws on the LC in favor of the issuer paying directly, he/she would circumvent the protections provided by the LC and cause potential harm to the bondholders.

If the manager's advice to the administrator were to follow the issuer's directions, I would advise that the administrator question the advice and escalate the issue to upper management and counsel. The risks are simply too great for the bank, the bondholders, and the administrator.

Following the issuer's direction would directly violate the LC purpose as established by the parties to the bond issue. If the issuer then defaults and files for bankruptcy and if the filing is within ninety days of the payment, then a bankruptcy court can seize the money.

The risk is too great. Also, when an issuer directs the administrator to do something contrary to an established practice in the bond financing, I would encourage the administrator to think very carefully about following that direction and to ask for counsel's opinion. This case shows the administrator must always be considering the facts of any situation. In this case, it is highly likely the issuer is in financial difficulty (the financials may show this) and intends filing for bankruptcy within the ninety-day preference period to get back the debt service funds. You do not want to take this chance.

~ Chapter 8 ~

Products for Corporate Trust

New York, New York—October 2008

I am working with my account administrators in conjunction with our Deutsche Bank Operations and Auction Rate Team in New York to try to resolve the crisis of the meltdown of our variable rate demand bond issues. Due to the market crisis, investors have lost faith in their continuing holding of variable rate demand bonds. The result is a flood of puts by the bondholders who no longer wanted their bonds, just cash. This is a scenario that never could have been anticipated.

Since no one now wants to hold these variable rate bonds, no one participates in the Dutch Auction, which is normally held to reset the bond rates. Auctions fail, and a liquidity bank is now forced to pay for (and own) the bonds, thus coining the term "bank bonds." Issuers now are required to substantially increase the interest payments on these bank bonds per the requirements of the Trust documents, another unanticipated occurrence.

The end result is the overnight demise of several bond products—which we are including in our revenue stream. In the space of three months, from October to December 2008, the market for variable rate demand bonds evaporates. The need for our services as agent for all the Dutch Auctions associated with this formerly popular bond product also dramatically reduces. Therefore, in a very short period of time, two profitable products for

Corporate Trust, the variable rate bond Trusteeships and the Dutch Auction agent services, virtually disappear. What were once good sources of revenue are suddenly gone. The challenge remains of how to replace that lost revenue.

The reality is that bond products might come and go with startling suddenness, thereby forcing Trustees to seek other sources of revenue.

Chapter Objective

My objective for this chapter on Corporate Trust products is to give a brief overview of the most common products found in Corporate Trust. I will also describe the general Trustee duties for serving these products. There are, of course, other specific services that various Trustees may perform, and these services evolve into new products as created by the securities markets and client demands. This will always be an ongoing evolutionary process for Trustees. It is why I have remained fascinated by the business—because it is always changing.

The basic products I will describe as typically part of the Corporate Trust business are:

      I.   Municipal Bonds

      II. Corporate Bonds

      III. Escrows

      IV. Custody

      V. Additional Corporate Trust Products

Structured finance products (e.g., ABSs, MBSs, CDOs, CMBSs, and CMOs) will be covered in a separate chapter (Chapter 9).

General Corporate Trust Services

Before describing the products, a good general list of services provided in most cases across the products is as follows:

- Receipt and disbursement of funds from one party to another

- Recordkeeping of payment information, bond certificates, bondholder records, cash movement in trust accounts, and investments
- Tax reporting to investors and the IRS
- Compliance monitoring of various Trust document requirements

Other more specialized functions, depending on the product, could include:

- Filing of UCC forms to maintain the lien on property and collateral
- Investing funds as directed
- Receiving financial reports, certificates, and opinions
- Disclosing information to investors and the marketplace (e.g., Electronic Municipal Market Access systems [EMMA®] for municipal bonds)
- Holding collateral

The final service that may occur in any of the products is the action of the Trustee in a default or actions required of his/her role as an agent (e.g., escrow or custodian if the provisions of the agreement are not fulfilled). Let's briefly review the products.

I. Municipal Bonds

Cities, counties, states, or other governmental entities such as conduit issuers (e.g., state housing authorities) issue municipal bonds. They come in two versions:

- **Tax-exempt:** Not subject to federal taxation and possibly state taxation
- **Taxable:** Subject to federal and state taxation

Most municipal bonds fall in the tax-exempt category. They can be exempt from federal taxes or in some cases state or local taxes as well, referred to as double-tax-exempt bonds. Other municipal bonds can be taxable for federal tax purposes.

There are several main categories of municipal bonds. They include:

Revenue Bonds: Bonds where payment to bondholders is derived solely from the revenues of a project or assets. These are nonrecourse to the issuer of the bonds but paid only from specific revenues of what is financed. These are considered secured bonds and have a Trustee.

GO Bonds: Known as general obligation bonds and backed only by the general financial resources (e.g., tax collections and other income sources) of the municipality. These are unsecured and do not have a Trustee. They only have a Paying Agent to receive and pay funds. As Paying Agent, the bank plays a limited role confined to receiving and paying funds with no other responsibilities (e.g., default duties).

Industrial Development Revenue Bonds (IDRBs): Revenue bonds issued for a private activity—usually by a for-profit corporation that leases the facility built by bond proceeds and is obligated to pay for the bonds, versus the municipality that issues the bonds.

501(c)(3) Bonds: Bonds issued by charitable/not-for-profit entities (e.g., churches, schools, hospitals, colleges, and universities) under IRS code section 501(c)(3). These bonds receive favorable tax-exempt treatment due to their very nature.

Refunding/Defeasance Bonds: Bonds issued to pay off an existing bond issue over a period of time or in some cases at a designated time. The intent is for the issuer to reduce its cost of financing by providing for payment of an older, higher-rate bond issue with a new bond issue with a lower interest rate. I liken this process to an individual refinancing his/her mortgage with a new mortgage at a lower interest rate. However, in a bond refunding, the old bonds may not be paid off immediately. The Trustee has a limited role for the refunded/defeased bond; this role is largely confined to investing funds, then paying off the bonds as required. The specific investment is usually made in State and Local Government Securities (SLGSs); their interest is exempt from IRS arbitrage rebate requirements.

Housing Bonds: Municipal bonds backed by revenues from residences. There are two types:

- **Single-family**: One-family residences
- **Multi-family**: Apartments, condominiums, and duplexes

A state or local housing conduit authority usually issues bonds as they are a government entity with bonding authority to issue bonds for the purpose of funding housing. There is no recourse to the conduit authority, only to the properties and their cash flow. The Trustee assumes a wide variety of duties with respect to housing bonds, including monthly cash flow receipt and processing of funds; possible holding of mortgage collateral or securities; investments; disbursements; redemptions and sinking funds; covenant monitoring; and possibly servicer replacement. In a default, the Trustee may be involved in foreclosing on the properties, maintaining them, and selling them.

Additional Municipal Bonds

Below is a list of additional municipal bonds the Trustee may encounter. A listing of additional municipal bond products can be found in Exhibit D.

Variable Rate Demand Bonds (VRDBs): Bonds with a variable rate with a put option for bondholders. These bonds may include a Dutch Auction process to reset the interest rate. They will include a liquidity provider to pay for put bonds if they cannot be remarketed (i.e., resold once put back to the issuer). Failure to remarket results in the bonds being purchased by the liquidity provider; thus, they become "bank bonds."

BAB Bonds: Known as Build America Bonds, taxable municipal bonds that were briefly issued in 2010 under the American Recovery Reinvestment Act (ARRA) stimulus legislation with a government subsidy for interest payments. There were various categories of government subsidy bonds for schools, environment projects, and economic development. BAB bonds may be similar to revenue bond duties with the added prospect of submitting a tax form, which is to be signed by the issuer for payment of funds from the government as the interest subsidy. Original subsidy varied but generally was 35 percent, which was reduced by the government sequester for the years the sequester was in place. This is in keeping with my experience that in some cases "the government giveth and the government taketh away." It has happened before.

II. Corporate Bonds

In general, corporate bonds do not require the variety of duties from the Trustee as municipal bonds. Most corporate bonds are unsecured and do not have a construction fund, frequent cash flows, UCC filings, insurance requirements, EMMA® disclosure duties, variable rates, puts, credit enhancement draws, or investments. In other words, they are more straightforward and simpler to administer.

However, corporate bonds have a higher possibility of a bankruptcy (i.e., default). Corporate bonds are also subject to the Trust Indenture Act requirements if they are publicly issued whereas municipal bonds are exempt from the TIA. Corporate issuers are also subject to SEC oversight whereas municipal issuers are not. The standard duties for Trustees with a corporate bond are paying debt service, usually twice a year; monitoring covenants for reviewing financial reports, receiving an annual officer's certificate of no default, and administering sinking funds and redemptions. If qualified under the TIA, the Trustee must also perform reviews for potential conflicts of interest that are material and are required to be reported to bondholders and the SEC annually.

Types of Corporate Bonds

The following are types of corporate bonds:

Debentures or Notes: A form of unsecured bonds that are backed by the general financial strength of the company. They are unsecured and have no specific assets or collateral backing them. They are generally issued to the public.

Convertible Subordinated Debentures: A debenture that can be converted into common stock of the issuing company at a certain price.

Commercial Paper (CP): An unsecured corporate note less than 270 days in maturity. CP issues are usually issued in programs with a continuous issuance process.

Medium-term Notes: An unsecured corporate bond issued for a medium term anywhere from one to ten years.

First Mortgage Bonds: A secured corporate bond issued by a utility (e.g., power company or telephone company). The bonds are secured by a first mortgage on the property, plants, and equipment of the company. The bonds are usually issued by a number of supplemental indentures over the years to finance the acquisition and replacement of the physical assets of the company.

Equipment Trusts: A bond issue secured by specific equipment, which is leased by the company using the equipment. Examples are aircraft, rail cars, ships, or any other equipment.

Leverage Lease Bonds: A bond issue secured by equipment but with added parties who purchase an equity interest in the equipment being financed by the bonds. These bonds usually represent 80 percent of the purchase price of the equipment (e.g., aircraft is financed by bonds and 20 percent is financed by one or more equity participants). There is an indenture Trustee for the bonds and an Owner Trustee to hold legal title to the equipment.

144A and Reg S Bonds: SEC rules governing private placement bond issues. The 144A bonds are issued in the United States while the Reg S bonds are issued offshore. Under these SEC rules, the bonds must qualify to be issued as such, meaning they can only be sold to institutional investors called QIBs (Qualified Institutional Buyers). The bonds are restricted in that they can only be sold (i.e., transferred) to other QIBs and have restrictive legends on them stating this. Issuers can avoid SEC registration if they can qualify to issue bonds under these rules so they can get to market much more quickly and avoid the SEC disclosure requirements. Another common feature of these types of bonds is that they tend

226

to have an exchange after the initial issuance to a public issue, which now must qualify under the TIA.

Project Finance: A hybrid finance structure, which can be regarded as a very large bond issue accompanied by a group of lenders to finance a project with both bonds and loans. The project can be overseas or in the United States. Typically, these transactions finance infrastructure projects such as power plants, gas pipelines, waste disposal facilities, telecommunication systems, mining, roads, or dams. These financings can be over $1 billion and have a variety of roles for the Corporate Trust business area to play. They include duties such as:

- Construction agent to disburse construction monies
- Depository
- Account bank
- Trustee

Expertise is required to administer these financings as they are complex and involve different third parties (i.e., lender banks, project sponsors), all with the added twist of overseas processing challenges. These challenges include time zone issues, language issues, cultural impact, foreign law issues, and funds movement.

III. Escrows

There are many types of escrow transactions commonly administered in Corporate Trust. Here the Trustee acts as an "escrow agent" for a short-term transaction between two or more parties. The following is my somewhat humorous definition, but it has a ring of truth: An escrow is an agreement between two or more parties who do not trust each other.

As escrow agent, the Trustee acts upon direction and has no discretionary authority. The Trustee is simply an agent doing what he/she is directed to do according to the escrow agreement and the parties involved. The Trustee usually provides a specific service either to hold cash, securities, or assets and distribute or release them upon instruction or occurrence of an event.

The escrow agreement is usually very short—six to eight pages. The escrow agent is usually paid a minimal fee. Here are some of the more common escrows:

- **Merger and Acquisition Escrow:** Cash or securities deposited pending the completion of a merger. Company "A" holders deposit stock or cash to be given to company "B" stockholders when the merger occurs. If the merger doesn't occur, then the shares or cash are returned to the original holders.

- **Litigation Escrow:** Funds deposited by a defendant or other litigants pending the outcome of a litigation proceeding to be disbursed as required by the court.

- **Subscription Escrow:** A group of investors subscribed to an offering to purchase shares in a company or project such as an oil and gas property. They will receive the shares or ownership rights upon reaching a certain fixed amount, which is referred to as "breaking escrow." If the fixed amount is not reached, then the transaction does not occur and investors' funds are returned.

- **1031 Like Kind Exchange:** Funds are deposited in an escrow account upon the closing (sale) of property A, which is going to be exchanged for property B in 180 days as a like kind property. The name "1031 Like Kind Exchange" refers to the IRS code section allowing this transaction, which would avoid capital gains tax. Funds are deposited with the escrow agent, who can also serve as a Qualified Intermediary (QI) to properly hold the funds as required.

- **Reinsurance Trusts:** A Trust in which insurance company A deposits funds in an escrow to compensate insurance company B, which in turn assumes the insurance risk of insurance company A. This is called insurance for insurers. Funds are paid out to insurance company B if, for example, a hurricane occurs. Periodic deposit or disbursement of funds can occur as part of the escrow agent's duties.

- **Funeral Trusts:** An escrow established to hold funds pending a funeral and paid out to cover such costs.

- **Construction Retention Escrow:** Funds retained or withheld from a construction fund as a holdback pending completion of a project (e.g., 10 percent holdback). These may be periodic holdbacks when disbursements are made until the project is finished. Then remaining monies are disbursed as directed.

- **Qualified Settlement Funds Escrow:** A fund authorized by the US Treasury created by court direction to hold monies in a lawsuit to be used to resolve claims and possible settlement of a litigation proceeding.

- **EB-5 Escrow:** A government-sponsored program for foreign nationals to obtain a visa if they qualify with a deposit of $500,000 and promise to create a certain number of jobs in the United States. The escrow agent would hold the funds.

- **Mini-lease Escrow:** An escrow established to hold a deposit of funds from a municipality that leases equipment or property for a public purpose. For example, the lease can finance buses or snow plow equipment.

- **ESCO Escrow:** A government-sponsored program referring to Energy Service Companies. Under this program, if a company can qualify as an ESCO, the government sponsors the company to receive a bank loan to pay for a project, which will be required to save 35 percent as energy costs. The 35 percent savings pays off the bank loan. The escrow agent holds the funds.

- **Environmental Escrow:** An escrow established to hold funds pending disbursement to pay for an environmental cleanup.

Escrow Agent Duties and Risks

Escrows are a key business for Corporate Trust, and they entail a variety of duties and risks. Even though an escrow is only an eight-page document with limited duties for the escrow agent, it can still cause problems. I have seen this occur in a number of situations where a Trustee is acting as a simple escrow agent but fails to understand that, even with this limited role, there is much that can go wrong to cause liability for the Trustee if he/she does not perform. Add to this the fact that the parties to the transaction may not be in agreement with the intended outcome, and then you have a potentially dangerous situation with potential liability to one or more of the parties, including liability to their escrow agent. Following is a brief summary of both the duties and risks of serving as escrow agent.

Duties

- Receive funds, securities, or assets either in one deposit or periodically.
- Hold and invest funds as directed.
- Verify documentation received in accordance with the escrow agreement.
- Distribute funds or assets as directed in one disbursement or upon occurrence of an event either all at once or periodically.

Risks

- Valuation of securities or assets held in escrow.

- Extension of a subscription period without proper authorization from *all* the parties or in the escrow agreement.

- Improper disbursements that cause harm to one or more parties to the escrow agreement.

- Failure to properly tickle responsibilities in the escrow agreement.

- Failure to perform proper due diligence for KYC on all parties to the escrow.

- Escrow occurrence with little or no warning, which places the escrow agent in a time crunch to properly review the transaction.

- Failure to carefully read the escrow agreement, resulting in lack of proper language protections (i.e., who directs the escrow agent and indemnities).

- Failure to understand the duties required, resulting in nonperformance.

One other risk is to guard against what are referred to as "funny money escrows." These are fraud schemes perpetrated by scam artists who are trying to defraud third parties by representing themselves as having established a legitimate bank account with you as escrow agent. They usually represent themselves as having a very large deposit to make (e.g., they have $1 billion and want you to open an escrow account). They will then use that account to defraud others. Don't do it. Remember, if it sounds too good to be true, it is fraud.

A Real-life Example

Once, I received a call from an individual who represented himself as having had $2 trillion of expatriated funds from Russia. He wanted me to open an escrow account. He said he knew Mr. Putin and was having dinner with George W. Bush. I did not open the account.

I later discovered by initiating a Suspicious Activity Report (SAR) that this individual had attempted to defraud this bank several other times. So beware.

IV. Custody

Custody is a product in Corporate Trust whereby the Trustee holds assets or securities in custody for a period of time. The Trustee acts as a custodian under a custody agreement or collateral agreement. Once again, the Trustee acts as an agent and has no discretionary authority. The Trustee follows the direction of the custody agreement language.

Simply put, as custodian, the Trustee does the following:

- Receives securities, assets, or files.
- Verifies that what he/she receives is complete according to the custody agreement.
- Holds the assets, securities, or files in safekeeping.
- Returns the assets, securities, or files as directed.

Sounds simple, doesn't it? In reality, it is anything but simple. To be a custodian requires good people, proper systems, and good controls over the whole process of receiving, verifying, tracking, holding, and disbursing the items described.

The major custody product is mortgage custody. In this case, the custodian must perform a variety of functions, including:

- Receiving mortgage files.
- Verifying that all proper mortgage documents are present and complete.
- Chase missing mortgage documents.
- Log files into a system, usually by bar-coding each file.

232

- Placing the file in storage.

- Removing and returning files when requested as mortgages are refinanced, foreclosed upon, or sold.

All of the above functions must be performed in compliance with the custody agreement. Usually, temporary staff are employed as volumes fluctuate, adding an additional training and managerial challenge.

The standing joke I employ in explaining the duties of a mortgage custodian is that a mortgage custodian never loses a file. The file is only "locationally challenged."

V. Additional Corporate Trust Products

Below are some additional products that may be found in Corporate Trust.

Structured Finance: Issues backed by specific assets that produce a cash flow. Examples are:

- Mortgage-backed Securities (MBSs), also referred to as Residential Mortgage-backed Securities (RMBSs)

- Asset-backed Securities (ABS)

- Collateralized Debt Obligations (CDOs)

- Commercial Mortgage-backed Securities (CMBSs)

- Collateralized Mortgage Obligations (CMOs)

Global Products: Bond issues and other overseas products, such as offshore Trusts and directorships.

Successor Trustee/Default Administration: A separate service provided by a Corporate Trust business in which a bond issue is resigned from one Trustee to a successor Trustee. Most successorships are a result of the existing Trustee resigning due to a conflict of interest, a situation which arises in an Event of Default (i.e., bankruptcy). To avoid a conflict of interest, the original Trustee resigns to a successor and a Tripartite Agreement is executed to move the Trusteeship. In order to take on this business, especially when a bankruptcy occurs or is imminent, the successor Trustee must have properly trained, experienced staff to correctly administer a defaulted issue and must work closely with counsel throughout the entire bankruptcy process. More risk can occur in a default for a Trustee, especially if there is a financial loss to the bondholders. Higher incidence of litigation by unpaid bondholders or other third parties is always a possibility that must be recognized. However, the service of successor Trustee is needed and can generate attractive fees for the Corporate Trust business unit.

Directorships for Various Trusts: Another interesting service that can be categorized as a separate product. It is a specific Trust when, for example, a special purpose vehicle is established in a tax-free or advantaged location either in the United States or offshore. These Trusts require the services of a director to establish and manage the Trusts. The director holds board meetings, keeps minutes, legally holds assets or cash, and performs a number of duties as directed by the Trust. Interesting legal responsibilities for someone serving as an official director are required; these responsibilities include a fiduciary role.

Auction Rate Agent: The product by which the auction agent processes the Dutch Auctions involved in certain securities structures.

Conclusion

There are a wide variety of products that can be found in Corporate Trust. Some products can come and go due to economic conditions or changes in tax law. The one certainty in Corporate Trust is that there will always be new products evolving as the securities markets create new instruments, thus presenting new opportunities for the business.

Chapter Summary

There are a wide variety of products that a Corporate Trust business will service that expand beyond the traditional products that form the core of the business.

The traditional products involve the services of a Trustee, Registrar, Transfer Agent, and Paying Agent for bond issues, including:

- Municipal bonds, both revenue and general obligation bonds.
- Corporate bonds, both secured and unsecured.
- Escrows in which the bank acts as an escrow agent for a short-term transaction as directed by the parties to the escrow agreement.
- Custody, that is holding cash, securities, or other assets for the benefit of other parties.
- Structured finance products of collateralized bond issues with assets that produce cash flow.
- Global products.

Other products will evolve as new security structures are created and services required for recordkeeping, funds processing, and valuation services.

There is no limit to what the Corporate Trust business can and will become involved with. Overall, that is a good outcome for the business and assures growth for the future.

~ Case Study ~

You receive a phone call from someone who asks you to open an escrow account for $1 billion. The person further says he is representing "the sheik," who wishes the account to be opened immediately for purposes of holding the money with instructions to follow. The person wants the account opened today and requests documentation from the bank confirming the account opening. When you ask the person for documentation as to what the escrow will entail or who the parties are, he replies that will not be necessary.

What do you do?

Answer:

This is an obvious fraud or "funny money" deal. You cannot obtain any documentation to establish the legitimacy of the transaction or where the money is coming from. You do not know who "the sheik" is. The dollar amount is staggeringly high and probably fictitious. What this person wants is for you to open an account so that he can represent himself to other third parties as having a legitimate account established at your bank. He will then use this to defraud other parties and disappear.

You must decline this opportunity and be very careful not to send anything that could be interpreted as acceptance or opening of an account by the bank. You must also initiate the filing of a SAR report. I have actually received this exact phone call. One billion dollars is certainly tempting when your business needs revenue, but you cannot take this on.

~ Chapter 9 ~

Structured Finance

Charlotte, North Carolina—August 2000

I am waiting for a phone call that all asset-backed Trustees hope they never receive. The call is taking place to inform us that the Trustee is going to step in as backup servicer and physically take over the servicing of the assets behind our Trusteeship. In this case, it is furniture receivables for Heilig-Meyers Furniture, which had suddenly filed for bankruptcy Chapter 11 protection two weeks earlier. Since the furniture receivables are being collected in over seven hundred Heilig-Meyers stores spread over numerous states, someone has to step in to do the collections (i.e., servicing in the local stores since there is no centralized billing system). Payments are usually made in cash at each store, which further complicates matters. The furniture is generally of lower quality, and there is a corresponding high volume of receivables accounts. The stores are located in rural areas and college towns.

Since Heilig-Meyers is unable to continue servicing, the Trustee is required by the trust documents to step in to do the servicing or have an agent do it on our behalf. But all the legal language does not begin to make one realize just how massive an undertaking it is to actually do servicing until one is faced with the very real prospect of doing so. The Trustee is now responsible for seven hundred stores and $1 billion of furniture receivables. Our management alerts us to be ready to actually travel to designated stores to man the *cash registers and keep the lights on. I am curious as to which state and stores I am to be assigned. This is not how I had planned to spend my next month.*

Fortunately, that call never comes. Due to the terrific efforts of a few people, the crisis is avoided. The company continues to provide personnel to keep the stores functioning, and qualified backup servicers are engaged by us to continue the servicing. But what the situation teaches me is the harsh reality of actually becoming a backup servicer. I also learn how critical the type of assets can be to a backup servicing role. I certainly never contemplated that, as a Trustee, I might be involved in repossessing furniture.

Chapter Objective

Bonds backed by collateral are certainly not a new concept. However, the structures of these bonds and the impact they have had on the world of financing have been extraordinary. Due to the unique requirements for the Trustee in structured finance, this topic deserves its own chapter.

Certain structured finance bonds were a contributing factor to the economic crisis of 2008. As such, Trustees found themselves in the uncomfortable position of defending their role regarding the resulting meltdown of these financings as the real estate markets declined, bringing a wave of foreclosures. The collateral for many mortgage-backed bonds was therefore impaired. The fallout from the defaults of mortgage collateral will be a long and difficult process and a challenging one for Trustees.

This chapter will explore the following topics regarding structured finance:

I. Securitization and Basic Structured Financings
    - MBS (Mortgage-backed Securities)
    - ABS (Asset-backed Securities)
    - CDOS (Collateralized Debt Obligations)
II. How Structured Finance Bonds Work
III. The Role of the Trustee in Structured Financings
IV. Challenges Facing Trustees with Structured Financings and Managing Risk
V. The Misunderstood Role of the Trustee

I. Securitization and Basic Structured Financings

Structured financings are a classification of bond issues collateralized by assets that produce cash flow. They are, therefore, secured bonds with specific assets pledged as collateral. The bondholders are paid from the cash flow generated by those pledged assets. As such, there is no recourse to any other entity for payment. In other words, the originator of those assets acting as servicer collects the cash flow and is not obligated to pay the bondholders. An exception would be if a third-party credit enhancement were involved and ultimately responsible to pay the bonds in an Event of Default.

The key concept of a structured finance bond issue is that the bondholders only look to the assets themselves for repayment. The process by which bonds are issued to investors backed by pledged assets is called *securitization*.

Securitization

There are several key aspects and definitions of securitization that Trustees need to consider.

True Sale: The assets are irrevocably sold (conveyed) to the Trust.

Bankruptcy Remote: The assets are legally separated from the assets of the originating entity. Therefore, if the originating entity enters bankruptcy, the pledged assets to the bonds are not subject to being pulled back into the bankruptcy estate of the originator.

Off Balance Sheet: The assets are moved off the balance sheet of the originator and are no longer owned by the originator.

Special Purpose Vehicle (SPV): This is the legal entity created to hold legal title to the assets pledged to the bondholders. This legal entity can be created onshore or offshore. The pledged assets can also be assigned to the trust in the name of the Trustee or physically held in custody by the Trustee, such as is common with Mortgage-backed Securities (MBSs). The SPV may be a corporation, partnership, limited liability company, or Trust, depending on the transaction. Several types of SPVs include grantor trusts, pass-through trusts, pay-through trusts, and owner trusts.

Cash Flow: The cash flow from the assets is collected by a servicer or servicers and relayed to the Trustee.

Waterfall: The term is used to designate the order and amounts of the collections (i.e., cash flow generated by the pledged assets and administered by the Trustee once received from the servicer[s]).

Issuer: This is the entity, usually the SPV, that issues the bonds.

Originator: The originator is the entity that generates the pledged assets, which are securitized.

PSA: The Pooling and Service Agreement may accompany an indenture describing the structure of the bonds and duties of the servicer(s) and Trustee.

Servicer(s): These are the entities responsible for collecting payments on the pledged assets, notifying delinquent parties, foreclosing on collateral, preparing periodic servicer reports to investors and the Trustee, and taking all other actions to service the pledged assets. In many cases, the servicer is also the originator of the assets.

Pool: This is the grouping of the collateral, which is referred to as pooling the assets in the trust.

Tranche: The French word for "slice" refers to each series of bonds in a structured finance bond issue. An example is with a CMO, which is divided into a number of tranches or bond series, each with their own interest rate and maturity:

- A Class—6 percent due 2015
- B Class—7 percent due 2017
- C Class—8 percent due 2020
- Z Class—0 percent due 2030 (zero-coupon bond)
- R Class—12 percent due 2035 (residual class; is paid last)

Pass-through: This is the designation of the structured finance bond issue in which all payments and prepayments of principal pass directly through to all classes of investors.

Pay-through: This is the designation of the structured finance bond issue in which payments and prepayments of principal are prioritized in terms of which tranches are paid first.

Trigger Event: A document provision requiring the Trustee to take certain action in the event that a certain delinquency percentage of the collateral is reached. For example, if 10 percent of the collateral becomes delinquent/nonpaying, then this triggers Trustee action either to redeem bonds or require the deposit of more collateral.

Definitions of Structured Finance Bond Issues

There are three main structured finance bond issues: Mortgage-backed Securities (MBS), also referred to as Residential Mortgage-backed Securities (RMBS), Asset-backed Securities (ABS), and Collateralized Debt Obligations (CDOS).

Mortgage-backed Securities (MBS): Bonds backed by mortgages. As such, these bonds have a wide variety of collateral and subcategories, including:

- Residential Mortgage-backed Securities (RMBS): Bonds backed by private homes/residences.
- Commercial Mortgage-backed Securities (CMBS): Bonds backed by commercial properties (e.g., strip malls or office buildings).
- Collateral Mortgage-backed Securities (CMOS): Bonds backed by mortgages.
- Real Estate Mortgage Investment Conduits (REMIC): A designation for a CMO meaning special tax treatment as established by the Tax Reform Act of 1986. This designation for a CMO was designed to assure that the tax liability for the pledged assets passed to the investors of the bonds and not to the originator of the assets.

Asset-backed Securities (ABS): Bonds backed by assets that produce cash flow. Anything producing a cash flow other than mortgages can be categorized as an ABS securitization. The most common examples are:

- Credit card receivables
- Auto loans
- Healthcare receivables
- Equipment leases

Collateralized Debt Obligations (CDOS): Bonds securitizing specific collateral in a more unique structure. Subcategories include:

- Collateralized Loan Obligations (CLO): Bonds backed by bank loans, both revolving and term loans.
- Collateralized Bond Obligations (CBO): Bonds backed by other bonds, either domestic or foreign.

II. How Structured Finance Bonds Work

It is vital for the Trustee to understand first why these bonds are issued and how they work.

Why Are Structured Finance Bonds Issued?

Structured finance bonds are issued in order to raise capital. Banks, financial companies, and mortgage originators find this type of financing particularly attractive for a number of reasons.

Lower Cost of Financing: Because these are secured bonds, the interest rate is lower due to perceived less risk for investors, who have a secured interest in specific collateral for repayment.

Off Balance Sheet Financing: Since the assets are moved off the originator's balance sheet, this saves on taxes and allows the banks to not be required to reserve capital against these assets.

Bankruptcy Remote: Investors are more confident they will be repaid even if the originators go bankrupt because the assets are not consolidated as part of the bankrupt estate of an originator.

Higher Bond Ratings: The rating agencies have rated the bonds in the highest categories due to their structure, collateral, and third-party credit enhancement; this also reduces the cost of financing for the originator, resulting in lower interest rates.

Liquification of an Illiquid Asset: These assets are illiquid as they are sitting on the balance sheet. To securitize them results in making them a source of capital funding for the originator.

The concept of securitization has been well accepted by the securities markets, resulting in over $1 trillion of securities issued and invested in largely by institutional investors.

How Do These Bonds Work?

The way structured finance bonds work is fairly straightforward. The complexity comes in with the wide variety of collateral employed, including the servicer performance, system requirements, and legal structures.

From a processing standpoint, the workings of a structured financing flow in this order:

1. Assets/collateral are held in a Trust (e.g., SPV) and generate a cash flow—usually monthly in accordance with the asset type, such as mortgages or credit cards.

2. Servicers bill for and collect the cash flow and pass it along to the Trustee along with servicer reports detailing the nature of the cash flow payments.

3. The Trustee receives the cash flow and reports and deposits the funds into the various Trust accounts, invests funds as directed, and makes required disbursements.

4. The Trustee may also be required to physically hold assets in custody, such as mortgage files for an MBS issue.

5. Servicers are responsible for any delinquencies or foreclosure action required.

6. Once the bonds are paid off, the collateral is released back to the originators.

7. The Trustee has no independent duty to investigate or review/approve the collateral or servicer performance.

Most structured finance bonds never reach maturity because they always have more collateral than is needed. This concept is called overcollateralization. The riskier the collateral, the more excess collateral is pledged. The purpose is to provide excess collateral to cover for possible delinquencies and losses in the collateral pool.

A second structural feature of structured finance bonds is they can be multi-tranched, as I referred to earlier. In other words, there may be a number of differing series or tranches of bonds within an overall bond issue. This is common with MBS securities. I have seen an MBS issue with over fifty different tranches (series) of bonds. Obviously, this adds to the complexity of the issue from a Trustee perspective. The reason for the multi-tranche structure is that it increases the diversity of the bond financing to appeal to different investors to meet their specific investment needs. Some investors may want the safety of AAA-rated bonds and are not attracted to a higher interest rate. Others want a higher interest rate but are willing to take more risk of repayment and therefore purchase the lower tranches.

A third structural feature of structured finance bonds is the senior/subordinated structure. Here in a multi-tranche issue, the higher tranches of bonds have a senior claim to the asset cash flow than the lower classes, which are subordinated. Obviously, the bond ratings of the lower tranches are lower than the highest tranches, which are usually AAA.

A fourth structural characteristic for a structured financing is the priority of cash flow to the different tranches. Especially in MBS issues, which have multi-tranches, the cash flow from the mortgage collateral for principal repayments is prioritized. Any repayments on the mortgages (e.g., refinancings or foreclosures) are paid first to the top tranches only. The lower tranches are not paid by any collateral prepayments, thus protecting them from redemption. This is especially valuable for investors in an MBS security who do not want their bonds prepaid due to falling interest rates when mortgage holders will refinance their mortgages, thus paying them off. The investors would then have their bonds paid and be subject to reinvestment risk of finding similar investments at a lower interest rate. This was one of the main reasons the multi-tranche sequential pay structure was created for MBS securities.

CDO Structure

The CDO structure is unique in structured finance. The complexity of this structure is one reason CDOs were blamed in part for the economic crisis in 2008. Briefly stated, the CDO structure differs from the other structured finance bond issues in three ways:

- **Ramp-up Period:** Unlike other structured financings, CDOs have what is called a ramp-up period. This is a sixty- to eighty-day window of time after the closing whereby collateral is added to the collateral pool supporting the bonds. As much as

60 percent of the collateral needed to support the bonds is purchased by a portfolio manager and added to the pool within this period.

- **Trading Period:** This is a one- to three-year period after the ramp-up period, during which time collateral is traded. The portfolio manager actively purchases collateral to constantly upgrade the collateral pool or substitute underperforming collateral (bonds or loans). Tests of the substituted collateral are required to be made by the Trustee to verify if the new collateral meets the criteria established in the Trust documents. Therefore, the Trustee as collateral administrator acts as the "gatekeeper" for the collateral pool. As such, the Trustee verifies the acceptability of the collateral, performs the appropriate tests, and settles the trades with the portfolio manager. If the new collateral fails the tests, then the Trustee will not approve the trade.

- **Stabilization Period:** This is the remaining life of the CDO after the trading period when collateral is not traded and remains stable as in the other structured finance bond issues.

III. The Role of the Trustee in Structured Financings

There are a variety of roles performed by the Trustee in a structured finance bond issue. The frequency of the cash flow processing (usually monthly) and frequent monitoring responsibilities and servicer interaction require constant attention by the Trustee. Following are the more common responsibilities for Trustees.

Cash Flow Receipt: The Trustee receives funds from the servicers on a timely basis, usually monthly.

Waterfall Management: The Trustee allocates funds received to the proper trust accounts.

Debt Service Payments: The Trustee makes principal and interest payments to the bondholders.

Trigger Event: This is the occurrence of a percentage of the collateral becoming delinquent, thereby triggering action by the Trustee to redeem bonds or require the deposit of more collateral.

Investing Funds: The Trustee Invests monies in permitted investments per written direction.

Monitoring Servicer Reports: The Trustee is to receive servicer reports on the cash flow and performance of the collateral.

Modeling and Analytics: The Trustee is usually called upon to produce reports on the cash flow as compared to the original projections made at the beginning of the bond issue. Other special reports on the valuation and performance of the collateral may also be required. These reports may be made available on a specific website for access by investors.

Backup Servicer: This is the crucial role that the Trustee may be obligated to assume if the servicer either goes out of business or needs to be replaced. The three standard levels of backup servicing are as follows:

- Hot: Running parallel to the servicer's systems-monitoring collections, delinquencies, and cash flow
- Warm: Having the data but not running parallel
- Cold: Not performing any activity but just standing by

Document Custody: The Trustee may hold physical mortgage files in custody. This requires the Trustee to have dedicated resources to receive, verify, hold, and return the files when requested. People, systems, and facilities are needed.

Advancing: Certain issues may require the original servicers, as well as any successor servicers, to advance funds to make scheduled payments or repurchase nonconforming assets. If the Trustee becomes a backup servicer or a servicer of last resort or is designated as the party to advance funds if the cash flow is inadequate, the issue becomes whether or not the Trustee wants to assume this responsibility and in essence become a temporary lender. So it is up to the Trustee as to whether or not he/she wants to agree to advance funds.

Tax Reporting: In this role, the Trustee represents the SPV for the trust in all tax matters and is responsible for preparing, signing, and filing federal and state tax returns and schedules. The four basic tax concerns for structured finance are:

- Determination of ownership
- Assurance of only one level of taxation on income when an entity holds multiple classes of pass-through certificates
- Calculation and reporting of income to the trust
- Reporting Original Issue Discount (OID) taxes

IV. Challenges Facing Trustees with Structured Financings and Managing Risk

Needless to say, there are a number of challenges facing the Trustee with regard to a structured financing. To help combat these challenges, the first order of business is to understand all required duties. Second, the Trustee must carefully review the trust documents to include the needed protective language commonly found in all Trustee documents and to go even further to define what he/she is responsible for. The complexity of these financings has made this an increasingly difficult challenge for Trustees.

To more effectively manage the growing risks to Trustees for administering structured finance issues, I would make the following recommendations in the following key areas.

<u>Backup Servicer</u>: Of all the risks associated with structured finance for Trustees, this is the most critical. It is standard industry practice that the Trustee assumes this role in a structured financing. The reason? There simply is no one else. To assume this role, the Trustee must understand what servicing requires: an army of people, specific systems, billing capabilities, collateral, monitoring tracking systems, foreclosure expertise, and collections capabilities. Clearly, most Trustees do not have these specific resources. What to do? The solution is for the Trustee to hire an agent to perform as backup servicer. The documents should provide for this as well as provide payment to a backup servicer at the current market rates. The Trustee must not be put in the position of paying for a backup servicer. The Trustee must have in place the contact for someone to assume the backup servicer role immediately. There can be no gap between the original servicer leaving and the backup assuming the servicing duties. Disruption of cash flow and delinquencies will occur if servicing isn't provided on a continuous unbroken process. Clear notice requirements should be put in the trust documents, or specific triggers should be clearly stated as to when and how the Trustee must assume the backup servicer role. My experience has shown that the backup servicing responsibility is the most critical risk for Trustees in a structured financing. Agent backups must be established for immediate action. This is the only way to avoid significant liability for Trustees.

Servicer Conduct: The Trustee must not be held to analyzing or verifying servicer conduct; the document language should clearly state this. The Trustee has neither the resources nor expertise to verify servicer operations, underwriting, or processing functions. Servicers must stand on their own and perform separately from the Trustee. The Trustee cannot and should not be put in a position of directing servicer actions. The Trust documents must clearly exempt Trustees from such a duty.

Document Custody: There are many risks with performing the custody function of receiving, holding. and returning millions of mortgage files, which are what the few large document custody businesses do. Proper systems, people, and expertise are required; this is why there are so few document custody providers.

Modeling and Analytics: The unique aspects of various structured finance bond issues require specialized reporting capabilities. In my experience, reporting requirements have always stayed ahead of system capabilities. Excel spreadsheets tend to fill the gaps. This is an obvious control risk. The calculations—that is, the reporting analysis of cash flows as projected against the original assumptions in the prospectus—require precise and accurate reporting by Trustees. Timing is also an issue for producing these reports, which are carefully analyzed by investors. Errors are a serious matter.

CDO Special Requirements: CDOS are such complex instruments that they are very labor-intensive for Trustees. Because the collateral undergoes a constant turnover in the trading period, the Trustee must approve the trades within a very short time frame—usually within twenty-four hours or less. This requires the Trustee to run reports immediately to test whether the substituted collateral passes certain tests as required by the Trust documents (e.g., not more than 5 percent of the portfolio of a CDO ontains Greek bonds). This places enormous pressure on the Trustee in administering these issues requiring intense administrative activity.

V. The Misunderstood Role of the Trustee

In structured finance, enormous pressure has been placed on Trustees, primarily focused on MBS transactions. A result of the real estate meltdown in 2007-2008, a number of pools of MBS securitizations became nonperforming. While centered on MBS issues backed by subprime mortgages, the overall real estate decline, along with the dramatic increase in foreclosures, led to defaults in a number of MBS issues.

Sometimes in the case of a default where they are not paid, investors may look to litigation as a means of recovering their losses. The MBS securitizations with pools of subprime or nonperforming mortgages have become a target for such litigation. Unfortunately, the Trustees have become a target after the originators of these mortgage pools.

I would like to reemphasize the true role of the Trustee in a structured financing, especially an MBS, to clarify what Trustees can and cannot do.

Servicer Performance: The servicers have the staff, systems, and expertise to serve as mortgage collector. It is the job for which they are equipped and for which the Trustee is not. Pushing Trustees into assuming a greater oversight role on services is simply not workable. Trustees do not have the resources or expertise to monitor and control all that the servicers do. The Trust documents do not place such a role or even authorize the Trustee to assume such responsibilities. If investors other than the rating agencies or other third parties wish Trustees to assume greater servicer oversight, then Trustees must be compensated significantly more. Since no one wants to pay Trustees what such an effort would cost, it is a nonstarter. No Trustee bank would stay in the business of being a Trustee for MBSs or other structured financings as the cost and liability of doing business would be prohibitive if more extensive servicer monitoring and due diligence are required.

Fiduciary Responsibility: The Trustee is not a fiduciary in a structured finance transaction. Pre-default, the Trustee is an agent performing those duties specifically described in the indenture and PSA. No implied duties beyond those expressed in the Trust documents exist. There is fundamentally little discretionary authority for Trustees pre-default. Post-default the prudent man/person standard applies. This is the legal standard under which the Trustee operates as supported by federal law (the Trust Indenture Act of 1939), by court precedents, and by custom and practice in the industry. Pushing Trustees into a fiduciary standard for which we would assume much greater liability without the authority or resources to perform such work would be unacceptable. The Trustee is not compensated for such work.

Discretionary Duties Outside the Indenture or PSA: To require Trustees to assume discretionary responsibilities outside the provisions of the Trust documents is also unacceptable. The Trustee is not responsible for the underwriting standards or for the quality of the collateral placed in trust. The Trustee has no control or input into the collateral pool or its assumptions. To state that the Trustee has such responsibilities is simply wrong.

Conclusion

The Trustee must have very specialized resources, systems, and capabilities to successfully perform the required duties for structured financings. The cost, the risk, and the need for specialized processing capabilities is the reason just a few larger Trustees engage in structured finance business.

The role of the Trustee in structure financings is complex and demanding. The Trustee cannot be blamed for the problems that have arisen in the MBS issues due to nonperformance of collateral or servicer difficulties. The Trustee fulfills a vital role in structured financings to facilitate the processing of the cash flow and security interests in the collateral. The Trustee does not have the authority, resources, or expertise to do more than his/her defined role no matter how tempting it is for outside parties to demand more from Trustees. Compensation and legal authority would be required for an increased role for Trustees. Only time will tell the eventual outcome.

Chapter Summary

- Bonds backed by assets with a cash flow are said to be securitizations and comprise the overall bond financing called structured finance.

- The types of structured finance bond issues Trustees encounter are:
    - MBS (RMBS and CMBS)
    - ABS
    - CMOs (REMICs)
    - CMBS
    - CDOS (CLOs and CBOs)

256

- The basic structure is that assets are sold to an SPV trust, which legally holds title to the assets in the name of the Trustee.
- The greatest risk for Trustees in a structured finance bond issue is becoming backup servicer when a servicer defaults.
- Trustees are being challenged to assume greater responsibilities for servicing and monitoring servicers and/or the collateral beyond their capabilities and authority.

~ Case Study ~

You are the Trustee for an MBS issue. You have backup servicing responsibilities. You see that there is a dramatic shortfall in the cash flow receipts this month from the servicer report, which is late again.

What do you do?
What are the risks to you?

Answer:

Have in place an agent you can call who can immediately step in to the role of backup servicer for you if needed. Next, you must contact the servicer and determine the reason for both the late reports and the dramatic shortfall in receipts. If the servicer cannot or will not perform its duties, per the Trust documents, you may have to step up and replace the nonperforming servicer. Timing is critical. Notice would then be required to be prepared and sent by you to all interested parties and the bondholders in keeping with the provisions of the indenture and Pooling and Service Agreement (PSA). You should also involve counsel and bring the matter to your Trust Review Committee for consultation as to what action should be taken. If the cash flow shortfall is due not to servicer nonperformance but to delinquencies in the collateral pool, then a trigger event may occur for which you must take action to call bonds or require more collateral.

~ Chapter 10 ~

The Global Trustee

London, England—2006

I am in London visiting the local office at Deutsche Bank, training in basic Corporate Trust concepts. As I pass by a fort built by the Romans some nineteen hundred years ago, it is a humbling experience when compared to the mere two-hundred-year antiquity of buildings in the United States. Here, as in many other parts of the world, there are daily reminders of the long history that easily eclipses anything we have in the United States. I quickly learn that it's not just history and aesthetics that differ from those of the United States, but the rest of the world also looks at Corporate Trust very differently. It is here I learn the invaluable European and global perspective of what a Corporate Trustee is.

The strong regulatory environment surrounding the US securities markets, which arose out of the US experience during the Great Depression, exists to a lesser extent internationally. In the United States, the concept of a Corporate Trustee is well established in law and practice. In Europe and the rest of the world, it is not.

To our people in London, the US Corporate Trust model does not resonate as much as I assumed it would. It becomes apparent I need to shift my perspective and adapt to the European Corporate Trust model. Legally, and culturally, there is a big difference between the two.

For example, when I discuss the fact that most bond issues have a Trustee as an accepted part of the transaction, my London counterparts look at me with puzzled expressions. They inform me that their practice is that a Fiscal Agent or Issuing and Paying Agent performs the primary administrative roles associated with large medium-term notes, commercial paper programmes (the UK spelling of "program"), and Eurobond issues. Even the spelling throws me for a loop. They educate me about how the largely passive Corporate Trust role exists largely in an agency capacity, especially in an Event of Default. When there is a Trustee, the marketplace interprets that as a possible sign of impending trouble. The investors and marketplace might ask, "Why do we need a Trustee?" and "Is a default anticipated?" However, when a Trustee is appointed for a bond issue, the Trustee must act with more discretion. The standard is acting as a reasonable/prudent Trustee both pre-default and post-default. My London colleagues are not in the least concerned about meeting that higher standard of care whereas a US Trustee would be stunned to be under that standard pre-default.

So I learn the valuable lesson that the world is a very different place when it comes to the standard of care for Trustees.

Chapter Objective

The Corporate Trust business extends far beyond US borders. As such, it is important to explore the global aspects of the Corporate Trust business. Wherever there are bonds, there is a need for Corporate Trust services. The services offered, however, take a variety of forms depending on the country. I will describe the various roles and services performed by global Trustees/Fiscal Agents in providing different services to issuers and bondholders throughout the world (although I will focus on the UK model as a convenient point of comparison for reasons discussed later in this chapter). Note that throughout this chapter, I refer to the wide variety of international debt securities generally as "global bonds."

This chapter will focus on:

I.   Corporate Trust Services Utilized in Global Bonds
II. The Roles of Corporate Trustees in the United States and Global Markets
III. How Corporate Trustees Meet the Changing Responsibilities Required by Global Markets

I. Corporate Trust Services Utilized in Global Bonds

While many Trustees in the United States may never become involved with global bonds, this is an area of growth in the Corporate Trust business and deserves ample discussion. As the world financial markets continue to become more integrated through better technology and communication, it will become more likely that issuers, wherever they are located, will want to take advantage of the opportunities presented in and by the global markets. Having access to capital markets anywhere in the world has significant advantages. The cheaper cost of capital in certain markets, due to lower interest rates, is one advantage. Another advantage is access to different investor bases that wish to diversify their investment holdings. The result is lower interest costs for issuers and a fertile source of investors to add liquidity to the bond markets.

What could be better? Corporations have realized the advantage for years of tapping the international bond markets. Now municipalities and other governmental entities are seeking the same advantages. And why not? The global markets are rapidly expanding to welcome all manner of issuers and bond structures to fulfill the dual goals of 1) raising capital cheaply and efficiently to help the world's corporations and governments expand and provide services and 2) offering greater diversity to worldwide investors who wish to take advantage of different investment opportunities to spread their investment risk and enhance their rate of return.

So for all the Corporate Trust professionals who thought this chapter would not be relevant, think again.

A Historical Overview of the Global Bond Market

The global bond market in its modern form can be said to have originated in the early 1900s. This market was based mostly in New York, rather than in London, and included such issues as the Chinese railway bonds denominated in pound sterling (rather than dollars). The true beginning of the global bond market can be said to have begun in the 1950s and early 1960s. The "Eurobond market" began after World War II and featured bonds issued in Europe by both US and European issuers denominated in US dollars. Due to the substantial US dollar trade balance and the power of the US economy in financing the recovery of Europe after the war, US dollars became the currency of the international bond market. As American company subsidiaries and government aid exploded across all parts of the world, the US dollar became the primary currency for business transactions and bonds. The first series of Euro-dollar borrowing originated in London in 1963 by S. B. Warburg & Co. Ltd. for Autostrade, the Italian Motorway Authorities.

The Eurobond market gained further momentum in the 1960s and 1970s with the offering of all types of debt investments to be denominated in US dollars—long-term bonds called Eurobonds, commercial paper, medium-term notes, certificates of deposit, and later structured finance bonds, in addition to project finance bond issues.

The key elements of a Eurobond issue are bonds denominated in US dollars issued in Europe to non-US investors. Because the holders are nonresidents, US regulators, such as the SEC and the Internal Revenue Service (with some limited exceptions), do not have authority over nonresidents or the issuance of the bonds. Today, the term "Eurobond" includes debt securities issued in all parts of the globe and denominated in any number of currencies, including the Euro.

Here is a typical example that illustrates the multinational nature of global bonds today. The issuer/guarantor may be from one country, such as China. The currency will generally be one of the major international currencies, such as the US dollar. The place of issue will depend upon the currency, but in cases where the currency is the US dollar, the place of issue will likely be London. The distributions to both institutional investors and retail investors will occur through a series of banks and central depositories. Each part of this complex transaction includes new roles to be performed by banks engaged in the Corporate Trust business.

Current Services to Be Provided by Global Corporate Trustees

The general services provided by the Corporate Trust provider for global bonds fall into seven distinct categories.

Fiscal Agent: The bank acts as an agent for the issuer and has no fiduciary or discretionary duties. There is no prudent man/person standard of care. The Fiscal Agent can receive reports, monitor compliance items, process payment, and send out notices but is strictly limited in a workout (default) situation. If a workout situation occurs, the bondholders go directly to the issuer to negotiate workout terms and repayment. The Fiscal Agent simply stands by and can make a final distribution as agreed on by the parties. In other words, the Fiscal Agent is a glorified Paying Agent. This is the most common role performed by non-US Corporate Trust businesses. The Trustee role is less common. In fact, there has been a perception outside the United States, especially in Europe, that if the bonds need a Trustee, there may be concern about repayment of the bond obligation to the bondholders. Another way of saying this is that only potentially troubled, less credit-worthy bond issues would go to the trouble and expense of appointing a Trustee, rather than a Fiscal Agent. That perception is now becoming less of a reality, especially for structured finance issues in which a Trustee is commonly appointed.

Trustee: In cases where a Trustee is appointed, the Trustee's conduct is governed by the prudent or reasonable person standard under English law *from the beginning* of the bond issue and not just in post-default situations, as is the case in the United States.

Issuing and Paying Agent (IPA): This is a very common role wherein the bank issues the bonds and serves as Paying Agent. An IPA role is used for all program debt issues and is also commonly used for the following transactions:

- Commercial Paper (CP): Short-term instruments that mature in 270 days or less.

- Medium-term Notes (MTNs): Bonds with maturity of one to twelve years.

- Certificates of Deposit (CDs): Bank obligations of thirty days to five years.

These short- and medium-term debt obligations require recordkeeping, continuous issuance services, and payment duties to the security holders.

Exchange Agent: The Exchange Agent facilitates the exchange of one debt issue for another. This also could involve the exchange of bonds for stock, such as in a merger or even a workout situation.

Listing Agent: Corporate Trust banks can act as intermediaries with certain exchanges to help an issuer list its securities. A common example is the Luxembourg Exchange Listing, with the bank arranging the listing for the issuer.

Classic Global Note (CNG): This is a physical note that represents debt and shows the amount of the issue outstanding. Possession of the CNG is evidence of ownership. Corporate Trust acts as Common Depository, which combines the performance and responsibilities of both the Common Service Provider (CSP) and Common Safekeeper (CSK) roles.

New Global Note (NGN): This note does not show the outstanding issue amount. The records of the International Clearing and Securities Depositories (ICSDs) Euroclear and Clearstream are the prime recordkeepers of the issue. Evidence of debt is achieved through a combination of the records of the ICSDs and the global note. Physical possession of the NGN is therefore not evidence of ownership. Corporate Trust acts as CSP, and where the issue is not potentially eligible, Corporate Trust may also act as CSK.

Other roles performed for safekeeping include:

- **Common Depository (CD):** Corporate Trust serves as a common intermediary between the ICSDs Clearstream and Euroclear and may claim funds on behalf of the depositories.

- **Specialized Depository (SD):** Corporate Trust acts as a custodian to physically hold securities for both positions with the ICSDs Clearstream and Euroclear.

- **Common Service Provider (CSP):** Corporate Trust receives the global note and releases the new issue proceeds to the issuer in addition to maintaining a record of the holdings of the two ICSDs and reconciling the issue outstanding amount with the issuer's Paying Agent. The CSP also identifies and notifies investors about corporate action events (e.g., redemptions) and claims interest and principal sums from the Paying Agent.

- **Common Safekeeper (CSK):** Corporate Trust holds the global note in its vault on behalf of the ICSDs. Where a security is issued in Euros and is identified at the time of issuance as being potentially eligible for use as collateral for the European System of Central Banks monetary operations, then one of the ICSDs will hold the global note as CSK.

The Products the Global Trustee Handles

The following are some of the typical securities products offered in the global capital markets and the services which Corporate Trust professionals can and do offer.

Repacks: The business wherein the bank acts as repackaging agent for issuers that wish to restructure and reissue their debt securities.

Project Finance: A large bond issue used to finance major infrastructure projects in one or more countries. Examples include power plants, water treatment facilities, roads, and dams. The bank acts as construction fund disbursement agent to pay for the building of the project, which also may require Trustee services and depository sources.

Program Debt: Large CP, MTN, or CD programs pursuant to which securities are issued on a continuous, potentially daily, basis. The role performed by the bank is that of IPA, Principal PA, and Registrar.

Escrows: Very similar to escrows in the United States. The bank stands as an agent between two or more parties that need recordkeeping, custodian, or distribution services, usually upon the occurrence of a specific event. Escrows are generally short-term in nature (less than one year), in nature requiring a limited agency role for the bank.

Term Bonds/Eurobonds: Longer-term secured and unsecured debt issued in the global markets by corporations and sovereign entities. The services provided are commonly those of Fiscal Agent, Paying Agent, and Registrar but can include Trustee services as well.

Structured Finance: Similar to transactions seen in the United States involving bonds backed by assets segregated into a Special Purpose Vehicle (SPV) for the sole benefit of the bondholders. Remember that the Trustee standard of care is to act as a prudent/reasonable person from the beginning of the bond issue and not just in a default.

Syndicated Loans: A consortium of banks participate in a syndicate or group to lend funds to a corporation. The bank acts as loan agent for the syndicate. As agent for the syndicate, the bank provides recordkeeping services, monitoring services, and collection services on behalf of the bank syndicate.

II. The Roles of Corporate Trustees in the United States and Global Markets

The overall differences between Corporate Trustees in the United States and those working in global capital markets outside the United States can best be grasped by comparing the following:

- the Trustee structure
- the Fiscal Agent structure

The Trustee Structure

Trustees are appointed to protect the interests of bondholders and act on behalf of bondholders. The difference between the US model and the global model is that the US Trustee is only held to the prudent man/person standard of care post-default. The non-US Trustee is held to the reasonable or prudent person standard from the beginning of the issuance of the bonds through the closing.

There is no legal mandate outside the United States that indicates a Trustee must be appointed for a bond issue. Rather, the decision to appoint a Trustee is made on a case-by–case basis by the lead manager (in the United States, this would be the lead underwriter), issuer, and their lawyers. In the UK, the Trustee Act of 1925, as amended in 2000, describes the role of the Trustee and sets the standard of care but does not mandate the appointment of a Trustee. In contrast, in the United States, the Trust Indenture Act of 1939, as amended by the Trust Indenture Reform Act of 1990, mandates the appointment of a Trustee for all public, corporate bond issues of $10 million or more.

Just as with a US bond issue, the bondholders of a global issue do not have direct control over the initial appointment of the Trustee. The correct legal terminology for a global bond issue for which a Trustee is appointed is to say that the bonds are "constituted by the Trust deed." This terminology reflects the fact that the legal obligations are created between the issuer and the Trustee; the issuer has direct contractual relations with the Trustee, not the individual bondholders. This is similar to the US practice in which the bonds are issued and the Trustee appointed pursuant to a Trust indenture. In the global bond market, the Trust Deed contains the direct obligation of the issuer to pay to the Trustee principal and interest on the bonds and all the other covenants and contractual terms of the issue (just as with a US indenture). The Trust Deed may also grant a security interest in property or collateral as well, if the bonds are secured.

The effect of the Trust Deed is that the issuer has direct contractual relations with the Trustee (and *not* the individual bondholders), while the Trustee also has a duty to act on behalf of the bondholders.

There are differences, however, in the powers granted to the Trustee under the Trust Deed versus the US indenture. Below are some examples of these differences:

- Only the Trustee has power to accelerate the bonds under the Trust Deed. Individual bondholders are not permitted to call a default or accelerate, unlike the US model.
- The Trustee is under no duty to bondholders to accelerate in an Event of Default but is merely given the power to do so. No express restrictions are placed on the Trustee's power to accelerate. This is close to the US model.
- Bondholders are prohibited from taking any action in court to enforce their rights to principal and interest; only the Trustee has a primary right to do so. Bondholders can act if the Trustee fails to bring proceedings within a reasonable time. This

greater restrictiveness on bondholder rights differs from the US model and leaves the global Trustee in a position of having sole power to enforce bondholder rights in a workout, unlike the US model.

- Under the Trust Deed, a number of breaches of the Trust Deed become Events of Default only if the Trustee certifies in writing that such event is "materially prejudicial to the interest of bondholders." Until such certification, no Event of Default is deemed to have occurred. The global Trustee has final and conclusive power to declare an Event of Default for the bondholders. This differs from the US model in which the Trustee does not determine or ascertain Events of Default but must be notified of events that are or could become events of default and may even require an officer's certificate or opinion of counsel before taking any action.

- The Trust Deed also details a number of "terms and conditions" of the bonds; these terms and conditions are entirely within the discretion of the Trustee. For example, the terms and conditions may authorize amendments or changes in security interests on behalf of bondholders, with the Trustee having the power to agree to such courses of action *without* referral to the bondholders. This is different from the US Trustee role in which bondholder consent is required prior to the Trustee entering into any substantive amendment to the terms of the indenture.

As I've illustrated, the UK/global Trustee role gives greater power to the Trustee to act and take the lead with the issuer than the US Trustee role, which usually follows bondholder approval and direction. Yet both Trustee roles involve the same fundamental principal, which is first and foremost to protect the bondholders and to maximize their recovery in an Event of Default. The UK/global Trustee differs in that the issuer interacts solely with the Trustee and *not* the bondholders, who must speak only through the Trustee.

Issuers find this "one-stop shopping"—that is, permitting them to deal with a single, unitary counterparty—to be to their advantage in Events of Default and possible litigation. Bondholders cannot act on their own but most go through the Trustee.

The Fiscal Agent Structure

The major difference between the role of Trustee and the role of a Fiscal Agent is that the Trustee represents the bondholders and the Fiscal Agent represents the issuer, *not* the bondholders. A Trust Deed confers legal rights on the Trustee and gives the Trustee broad discretionary powers to act on behalf of the bondholders. The Fiscal Agent has no such role. The Fiscal Agent is appointed under a Fiscal Agency agreement and is no more than a Principal Paying Agent for the issuer. The Fiscal Agent does not exercise any right of discretion on behalf of bondholders but instead carries out administrative functions and possesses no power to negotiate on behalf of the bondholders. Under the Fiscal Agency structure, each bondholder has a direct legal right to enforce against the issuer. For example, a bondholder can accelerate a bond for failure to pay interest or principal or other Event of Default and can sue the issuer directly for recovery. In addition, the bondholders themselves must monitor issuer compliance with any Trust Deed covenants.

Examples of the administrative functions of the Fiscal Agent include the following:

- Exchanging the global bond for definitive bonds
- Acting as Principal Paying Agent
- Publication of notices that need to be given to bondholders
- Other miscellaneous duties, such as replacing lost or destroyed bonds and selecting the bonds by lot in a redemption

The Closing Process

It is important to examine the differences in the closing process for issuing US and global securities under 1) the US model and 2) the European model.

The US Model: In the United States, the closing process is straightforward. An issuer contacts an investment banker, perhaps upon consultation with a financial advisor, who structures the bond issue and serves as lead underwriter or placement agent. Bond counsel represents the issuer and drafts the documents. The underwriter prepares the prospectus or Offering Statement (OS). The rating agencies may rate the bonds. The bonds are possibly credit-enhanced. The bonds are issued, usually through DTC in book entry form with one global note held by the Trustee. Most bond issues, with the exception of municipal general obligation bonds, have a Trustee appointed to serve as Trustee, Paying Agent, Registrar, and Transfer Agent and to perform other agency roles as required. The process is monitored by the SEC, and if the issue is a public, corporate issue, it is governed by the TIA.

The European Model: In Europe, the closing process involves greater variety than in the US capital markets. When an issuer issues bonds in the Euromarkets, the issuer first contacts a lead manager to arrange the bond issue. Once chosen, the lead manager is appointed by a mandate and written term sheet, which sets out the main terms of the agreement. This mandate is more of a gentleman's agreement than a contractually binding document. For most fixed rate bond issues, the issue is "pre-priced," meaning that all the terms of the issue are fixed at the time of the mandate letter, which condition then allows the lead manager to launch the issue into syndication with all the terms fixed. The alternative is "open pricing" in which the terms are not set until the last minute before the signing of the bond documents. The mandate may also designate the securities issue as either a "bought deal" or a "best endeavors deal." Under a bought deal mandate, the lead manager commits to underwriting the entire issue, while under a best endeavors mandate, the lead manager commits to making his/her best effort to find subscribers.

The lead manager now sends an invitation to potential lenders/managers (e.g., primary investors), generally other investment banks. The investment banks can then accept this invitation and now participate in the syndicate to market bonds.

After launch, and before the signing of the formal legal documents, the lead manager prepares in draft form all legal documents that provide for the marketing of the bonds (such documents could include a prospectus or offering statement) and for the administration of the bonds (such documents could include a Trust Deed or Fiscal Agent Agreement). These draft documents are sent to the participant investment banks for review.

Next, an allotment message is sent by the lead manager, who decides on the allotment of the bonds to each of the participant investment banks. This message is sent one business day following launch.

The next step is for the lead manager to prepare a subscription agreement, which is the contract formalizing the agreement of the syndicate to market its allotment of bonds. This arrangement/process can be contrasted with the US style of underwriting, in which the managers agree to purchase bonds and then resell them to investors. The European system involves the manager finding purchasers of the bonds and taking up any shortfall on a pro rata basis from a defaulting manager. The managers, not the issuer, may then take legal action against the defaulting manager. The team that put the bond issue together is called "the football team."

Now stabilization may occur. Under the Financial Services Act in the UK, the lead manager may "stabilize" or fix the price of the bonds at the beginning of the issue.

Stabilization means that the price is artificially fixed at a level that does not reflect current market conditions. The purpose is to enable the syndicate to more easily market the bonds. The stabilization process does not occur in the United States, where the market sets the price of the bonds.

Listing may also occur. Unlike in the United States, where bonds are not usually listed on an exchange but are traded over the counter, it is common in Europe to list bonds on one or more exchanges to enhance marketability. The lead manager arranges for listing, commonly on either the London or Luxembourg exchanges. Corporate Trust providers may also be employed as "listing agents" to accomplish this task.

The closing will occur as set out in the subscription agreement (signed on the signing date). At closing, proper legal opinions and governing documents will be executed and money will be transferred in exchange for the bonds. The subscription agreement sets the closing date, usually seven days after the signing date.

Defaults

It's important to emphasize one significant difference in the default process within the United States versus outside the United States. In the United States, there exists a well-codified bankruptcy structure, which allows for corporate reorganization (Chapter 11), municipal reorganization (Chapter 9), and liquidation (Chapter 7). Most US bankruptcies involve a reorganization process in which the debtor is protected from its creditors for a time while the debtor formulates a plan of reorganization. The Trustee plays a significant role on behalf of the bondholders during the process, protecting bondholder interests and serving on a creditors' committee, which negotiates a plan of reorganization with the debtor.

By contrast, in the UK, for example, there are several different sets of rules governing bankruptcy, which is more commonly referred to as a "workout." As such, there is no real reorganization period as in the United States. Interested and affected creditors negotiate directly with the debtor to work out and implement a solution. Therefore, in those cases in which a Trustee has been appointed, the Trustee's role is different and more direct, without the intervention of a bankruptcy court as under US law. In the majority of cases, however, there is simply a Fiscal Agent whose role is much more passive to that of a Trustee.

English Regulations Compared to US Regulations

Outside of the United States, the UK has the largest securities market and is therefore worth examining in somewhat more detail. Many global bond issues are issued under English law. This is due to the great constancy of English law and also to its wide and ready acceptance around the globe. English is also the international language of business. As a Trustee, I have traveled in many parts of Europe and Asia and never have had a problem communicating in English.

The Financial Services Act of 1986 (FSA), which provides a framework for investor protection, is the UK equivalent of the US Securities Act of 1933. In the United States, a governmental agency, the SEC, enforces the securities laws and enforces compliance. In the UK, the Self-Regulation Organizations (SROs) enforce the provisions of the FSA, most prominently, the Securities and Futures Association (SFA).

While in the United States most bond issues are not listed on an exchange, the situation is different in the UK and Europe. In London, it is common for a company to issue bonds and list them on the London Stock Exchange (LSE), in addition to meeting several extra requirements under the FSA. One of those requirements is that the issuer produces an Offering Circular (or a prospectus under the FSA), which complies with all the requirements of the London Stock Exchange as set out in the "Yellow Book" (i.e., the book that defines the listing requirements for issues on the LSE). In the United States, the Trust Indenture Act of 1939, as amended by the Trust Indenture Reform Act of 1990, fully describes the roles and responsibilities of the Trustee. In the UK, the Trust and Trustees Act of 1925, as amended in 2000, describes the Trustee standard of care in less detail and the Trustee roles in much broader fashion.

Why did the Eurobond market develop in London and not in New York City? Generally, the answer can be attributed to the prohibitive nature of the US securities laws, which really have no equal in the world. Under the Securities Act of 1933 and the Securities Exchange Act of 1934, the Securities and Exchange Commission (SEC) asserts worldwide jurisdiction over securities issues, which might be offered or sold in the United States or to US citizens. The SEC's requirements may be met by registering with the SEC, but this is expensive, time-consuming, and somewhat distasteful to non-US issuers due to the stringent disclosure requirements not found outside the United States. As a result, it is common to bring Eurobond offerings within an exception to the registration requirements under SEC Rule 144A or Reg S.

The overall impacts on Trustees outside the United States are fewer regulatory requirements, more flexibility, and a different standard of care (i.e., the prudent/reasonable person standard), thereby governing Trustee conduct at all times and not just in an Event of Default.

When I worked for Deutsche Bank, I traveled worldwide as a Corporate Trustee. Through that experience, I have concluded that the future growth for the Corporate Trust business is outside of the United States. Why? Securities are issued in greater volumes overseas. Also, the US securities markets will no longer be the dominant issuance market for Trustees. It is clear that the opportunities for significant growth for the Corporate Trust business will be in the global markets. The Trustees with the vision and commitment to establishing a global presence will be the beneficiaries of this new business potential. There is no doubt in my mind.

III. How Corporate Trustees Meet the Changing Responsibilities Required by Global Markets

The role of the Corporate Trustee is expanding for issues in both the United States and global markets. It is now standard practice throughout the world to have a Trustee appointed for a structured finance issue. While much is already being demanded of Trustees for the types of structured finance issues such as ABSs and MBSs, even more is being demanded of Trustees for the newer types of products in the CDO market. As new, more complex structures emerge, the underwriters, rating agencies, issuers, credit enhancers, bondholders, and regulators will be demanding more from Trustees.

The globalization of the securities markets makes it even more critical for Trustees to develop expertise in more complex transactions involving diverse laws, product structures, currencies, and cultures. Trustees will be required to offer more diversified services for payments, currency conversions, recordkeeping, holding of physical assets, and compliance with increasing regulations as a result of the worldwide economic crisis in 2008. The global Trustee must also establish a physical presence in important financial markets such as London, Hong Kong, Singapore, and other growing markets. The Trustee must have staff members in these locations who speak the language and know the local customs and laws.

Trustees will follow their clients overseas as those clients, issuers, and bondholders seek the best interest rates, cheapest sources of capital, and the most diversified financings and investments. The depositories, Euroclear and Clearstream in Europe and DTCC in the United States, as well as others, continue the trend toward eliminating physical certificates and reduced trading settlement to T+1. Capital will shift between and among various global markets, requiring increased levels of service from Trustees in reporting, monitoring, paying, and safekeeping collateral, among other duties. More proactive Trustees with a worldwide presence, flexible systems, and above all, expert staff will be the winners in the new world capital markets.

Conclusion

The role of the Trustee is certainly different outside the United States with regard to the standard of care. Under English law, the Trustee has discretionary duties as a "reasonable Trustee" from start to finish. Under United States law, the Trustee is an agent pre-default and a "prudent man/person" post-default. Yet under both legal frameworks, the overall role of the Trustee is to perform the responsibilities as stated in the trust documents.

Chapter Summary

- The more common role for the Corporate Trust business outside the United States is to serve as a Fiscal Agent or Issuing and Paying Agent for securities issued globally.

- The Trustee role is becoming much more accepted, especially for secured and structure finance bond issues.

- The Trustee role is a prudent/reasonable discretionary role both pre- and post-default unlike the US Trustee standard of care, which is an agent pre-default and prudent man/person post-default.

- There are two major depositories in Europe—Euroclear and Clearstream.

- The global growth of the securities markets outside the United States will be the growth opportunity for Trustees who establish a presence and commitment globally.

- English law is the most common law governing Trust Deeds and Trust documents overseas.

~ Case Study ~

You are a fiscal agent for a $50 million Eurobond issued by a European subsidiary of a British company. The issuer has defaulted on its payment of principal and interest. What is your role in the workout (default) situation that now unfolds?

      What are your duties to the bondholders?

      How is the role of Fiscal Agent different from that of a Trustee?

Answer:

As Fiscal Agent, you have a passive role regarding a workout situation. The Fiscal Agent will act only upon direction by the bondholders and defaulted issuer. The workout proceeds with the bondholders negotiating directly with the issuer to reach a solution. The Fiscal Agent remains in the background and will make a distribution of funds only as instructed by the parties. The Fiscal Agent has no authority to negotiate or dictate the workout solution on behalf of the bondholders.

If instead of being a Fiscal Agent, you are the Trustee, then the role and responsibilities would be entirely different. The Trustee would take an active role on behalf of the bondholders, who could only negotiate through the Trustee to the issuer.

~ Chapter 11 ~

Operations

Chicago, Illinois—1972

It's my first day on the job as a young twenty-two-year-old Corporate Trust Administrator. My boss has just introduced me to our operations group, the staff members who support our Corporate Trust business. There are over two hundred operations staff in attendance. As I look over the vast office with all these busy workers, my boss says, "Jeff, all these people work for you."

My chest expands, and the feeling of power sweeps over me as I look upon my new empire. It is my first day, and all these people work for me! As the excitement calms and as reality sets in, I have the uneasy thought, "I wonder if they <u>know</u> that they all work for me!"

Thank goodness I understand reality because they really don't work for me. What is more, as I gain experience on the job, I come to quickly realize that the operations people are my peers, not my subordinates. I learn to treat them with the utmost respect, understanding that they have their jobs to do, just like me. Operations staff exist in a very controlled environment, which is tightly regulated and process-oriented. Deadlines are a crucial part of their daily lives. If I want their support, I have to earn it and treat them as well as I treat my own clients—a valuable lesson that has served me well every day throughout my career.

Chapter Objective

It is vitally important for anyone who strives to understand the Corporate Trust business and the role of the Trustee to understand the role operations plays in supporting the business. Without strong and effective operations support, any Corporate Trust business cannot succeed. The main topics I will discuss in this chapter are:

I.   The Importance of Operations

II. Operations Functions and Responsibilities

III. Operations Interaction with Administration

My goal is for the reader to have a true understanding of not only what operations staff do but also the pressures they are under and how a better working relationship can be achieved in concert with administration. The success of the business depends on it.

I. The Importance of Operations

Operations plays a crucial supporting role for the Corporate Trust business. As such, operations is often referred to as the "back office" as compared to administration, which is called the "front office." It is a proven fact that the money, titles, and pay usually go to the front office as the client contracts and revenue-producing side of the business. I will even admit that the front office is the glamour side and that the back office stays in the background.

While the above picture is reality, I need to emphasize that it would be a huge mistake for the bank to under-resource operations. Simply put, without good operations support, there will be no front office *or* clients to produce revenue for the bank. The reason lies in the fact that all the basic processing and recordkeeping functions operations performs should be done as accurately as possible. Payments must be made on time every time. Records kept accurately. Cash and securities processing reconciled daily to the penny. Regulatory requirements met and complied with. Procedures followed to the letter. There is simply no alternative to performing the supporting functions expertly.

I have seen the impact of poor operations support, which results in lost business, tarnished reputations in the market, and losses for the bank. So we need to make sure operations staff have the resources, systems, and attention necessary so they can do their job successfully.

II. Operations Functions and Responsibilities

Operations has the following characteristics distinct from administration:

- Process-driven
- Tightly controlled environment
- Strictly regulated by specific SEC requirements for Transfer Agents
- Detailed procedures for all processes
- Assembly-line structure
- Segregation of duties
- Reconciliation and balancing on a daily basis

The following diagram illustrates the difference between operations and administration:

ADMINISTRATION   OPERATIONS

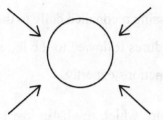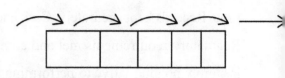

Administration has a more unstructured environment whereby client demands, contract responsibilities, and outside events impact each day. Operations is much more structured with its processes and controls. Just by looking at these two different models, you can see that there are significant differences that can give rise to conflict. Yet the goal of both administration and operations is to provide outstanding service for the bank clients, who do not differentiate between the two areas but expect the correct service from the bank as a whole.

Key Operational Functions

Mindful of the two different environments and the nature of administration and operations, I will now identify the key operational functions.

<u>Payments</u>: The receipt of funds and disbursement for debt service (i.e., principal and interest) or other required distributions. Other disbursements can include the following: redemptions, sinking fund payments, maturities, prepayments, puts, and exchanges. Payments are received and made by check, wire transfers, or ACH and are tightly controlled. Timing is critical, as the funds must be paid on the proper payment date only after "good funds" (i.e., collected funds) have been received.

Recordkeeping: The function whereby operations keeps the books and records on transfers, payments, holders' addresses, and tax information. The key recordkeeping function includes reconciling the authorized versus the issued amount of bonds. The authorized amount is the amount that can be issued. The issued amount is the amount outstanding. This is very simple, but a devastating problem can arise if issued bonds somehow exceed the authorized amount. Such a situation occurred in the mid-1990s with Chase Manhattan Bank's Corporate Trust Operations. The result was very unflattering. A front-page article in the *Wall Street Journal* included a cartoon of someone in a dunce cap adding $1 + 1 = 3$. Needless to say, the reputation risk was enormous, not to mention the potential out-of-balance situation to the tune of $7 billion, which had to be reconciled at a great cost.

Transfers: This aspect of operations represents a diminishing role for operations processing due to the reduction in paper bond certificates in the market today. With most securities originating in book entry form with DTC, there are many fewer physical certificate transfers requiring operations processing. Transfers occur when one bondholder sells his/her bonds to another. Several points need to be made regarding physical transfers, including:

The regulations mandated by the SEC regarding securities transfers require that routine transfers be turned around in seventy-two hours for 90 percent of the transferred items. A routine transfer is defined as a nonlegal item. This means that any transfer requiring legal documentation is considered nonroutine and has no SEC-mandated turnaround time limit. An example of nonroutine transfer is that of one party dying; this requires that a death certificate be provided with the transfer. Another example is that if the certificate is registered in the name of a Trust or corporation, certain legal documents are required, such as a Trustee certificate or a corporate resolution, to make the transfer. It is the job of operations to know the various legal requirements that affect different types of transfers before executing the transfer. Any deficiencies must be rejected back to the parties. Various types of transfers include:

- Joint tenants with rights of survivorship
- Tenants in entirety
- Tenants in common
- Street name
- Minors
- Trusts
- Corporate owners

A summary of the SEC Transfer Agent Rules is included in Exhibit E.

Medallion Program (STAMP): This program includes a surety bond insurance coverage established by the Securities Transfer Association for the purpose of eliminating the need for signature cards to verify transfer party signatures. As long as a medallion stamp appears on the security or bond power, the Transfer Agent can rely on it as an authentic proper signature without further responsibility to verify the signature. If the signature turns out to be fraudulent, then under the medallion program, the insurance will cover any liability of the Transfer Agent.

CUSIP Number: The nine-digit identification number identifying the security issue. An ISIN is a twelve-digit certification number for international securities.

Stop Payments: The Transfer Agent must place a stop payment on bonds reported lost or stolen. This is required under SEC Rule 17 Ad 17, which mandates that the Transfer Agent must report a lost or stolen certificate to the Securities Information Center (SIC®) within twenty-four hours of being notified of the lost or stolen security. A special form is used for the reporting. The way I remember this requirement is to say, if I lost my bond, I would feel sick as if I have the twenty-four-hour flu.

Authentication: If physical bonds or a global bond form are present, then they must be signed by the Trustee in order to be considered negotiable.

Endorsement: When a bondholder wishes to sell his/her security that is in physical form, then the bondholder must sign the bond or bond power to effect a transfer. The signature must exactly match the registration on the bond.

Escheat: This is the formal term that refers to unclaimed funds, uncashed checks, or unpresented funds that remain uncollected by their owners. Past a certain time, which is dictated by the requirement of each state, the funds/securities are escheated (i.e., paid to the state). As supported by the US Supreme Court, the following rule stands:

bonds/securities are escheated to the state of last known address of record of the owner. So if the bondholder's last known address is Texas, then Texas has claim. If there is no last known address of record, then the funds/securities are claimed by the state of legal incorporation of the issuer of the bonds. Of all the operational duties, escheat is one of the most crucial because the states are very proactive in claiming unclaimed funds, and as a result, a number of lawsuits have arisen over such monies. The advice I give is "when in doubt, pay it out." You should not sit on escheat-eligible funds, and under no circumstances should you take them into your income. It would be a guaranteed lawsuit, as has occurred against Bank of America in 1995. I saw the disastrous results of that action, which contributed to Bank of America's decision to sell the Corporate Trust business. On a somewhat humorous note, I would comment that the Bank of America case involves a former Bank of America operations employee who "blew the whistle" on the bank for taking the funds into income. Under the state whistleblowers statute, he was protected from litigation and received a percentage compensation of the recovery, which amounted to millions of dollars. The moral of the story is to treat all operations staff with care and respect.

Tax Reporting: Operations is responsible for reporting tax information to the bondholders and the IRS. Brief descriptions of the tax reporting forms are:

- **1099 INT**: Interest for both taxable and nontaxable bonds. The reason for reporting on tax-exempt bonds is the prospect of the bondholder complying with the alternative minimum tax.
- **1099 DIV**: Dividend reporting.

- **1090 B**: Principal reporting. Also includes the requirement to report cost basis to the holder.

- **1099 OID:** Original Issue Discount. This form is to report the accrued interest on a deep-discount or zero-coupon bond even though no funds were paid as the interest is paid at maturity.

- **28 Percent Backup Withholding**: The IRS requirement for the Paying Agent to withhold 28 percent of any payments if the bondholder fails to provide a certified Taxpayer Identification Number (TIN) or Social Security number (SSN). The withholding is to occur only after operations receives a "B" notice of no TIN on file and a "C" notice instructing operations to withhold. Both notices come from the IRS. In between notices, operations is required to attempt to contact the bondholder to obtain the TIN. Tax reporting to the IRS and to the bondholder is to be sent by January 31 annually. Extensions can be granted by the IRS but not without good reason. Failure to meet the January 31 deadline will result in significant fines.

SEC Reporting Requirements: The SEC-registered Transfer Agents need to file the following reports with the SEC:

- **TA-1**: New Transfer Agent and any changes in Transfer Agent status. This form is only required to be filed once by the Transfer Agent and not for each new issue.

- **TA-2:** Annual report detailing a number of items as required by the SEC on reconciliations, outstanding payments, etc.

- **T-1:** The required registration form to be sent to the SEC by the Trustee for every new TIA issue certifying the Trustee is qualified to act.

- **T-2:** Registration form filed for Co-Trustees.

- **T-6:** Foreign Trustee Registration.

Other Operations Functions:

- Fee billing
- Debt services billing
- Redemption processing: This can include a number of tasks, such as selecting the bonds to be redeemed, preparing a notice to bondholders, and either mailing the notice or publishing it as required by the Trust documents.
- Specialized reporting
- Holding inventory of bonds in the vault
- Record setup for original issuance instructions for new bond issues
- Processing tenders or exchanges

Interaction with DTC

Next, I will briefly describe operations interaction with the Depository Trust Company (DTC), which is a subsidiary of the Depository Trust Clearing Corporation (DTCC). Since the overwhelming number of security issues are held in book entry at DTC, the largest depository in the world, operations has significant contact with them. Following are the basics.

Closings: Most operations units are "FAST agents" with DTC, meaning they have an account at DTC for securities movement. As a FAST agent for a bond issue, operations will interact with DTC to facilitate the bond closing, which will involve one global note being established to evidence the issuance of the bonds. The global note is held in the vault in operations. At the closing, operations will execute a FRAC instruction to DTC as explained by the following:

Fast Reject and Confirmation Form (FRAC): This is the action taken by the Trustee as a FAST Agent to confirm the position of the underwriter holding the securities to be issued at the closing. In the industry, this is referred to as fracking the position of the underwriter. This verifies the bonds in the underwriter's account at DTC. The underwriter is now authorized to move bonds from its account to other underwriters/banks and eventually to the beneficial owners who are the bondholders as purchasers of the bonds.

A second action that can be performed by operations is called a DWAC, which is described as follows:

Deposit Withdrawal at Custodian (DWAC): When executed, the DWAC moves the security position from the custodian's account to another account as occurs when a holder sells his/her bond, moving the bond position from one broker/custodian to another

Payments: In order to be disbursed that day, funds must be received by DTC no later than 3:00 p.m. Eastern Standard Time. Failure to meet that deadline has serious consequences. DTC no longer allocates funds for delinquent payments. As such, DTC will then post a notice on its electronic notice system (LENS) explaining that "no funds are available for XX issue." Obviously, this is a serious development, which can be interpreted as a default by the marketplace.

List of Bondholders: A participants list can be requested from DTC; this lists the first level of participant holders for a bond issue. The list will not disclose the beneficial owners of the bonds and therefore is of limited value.

Claw Back: DTC can be asked to return funds within twenty-four hours of payment upon request from the Paying Agent. This is rarely used but does exist as an alternative for the Paying Agent if an error in payment occurs.

Swing Letter: This is a form required to be sent to DTC ten days prior to position changes of one Trustee/Paying Agent changing or swinging to a new Trustee/Paying Agent on a bond issue. This is common for a successor Trustee situation. The swing letter is also now required for the SEC rule 17Ad-16 for establishing the Trustee/Paying Agent position with DTC for all new issues. Controversy surrounding this requirement for swing letters to be originated by Trustees on new issues raises the question of whether such letters are redundant and unnecessary since adequate notification to DTC already exists for new issuance of bonds. However, the current SEC position for Trustees is to provide such swing letters on all new issues.

III. Operations Interaction with Administration

The key to a healthy relationship between operations and administration is *mutual respect* for the other's position. Here I'll describe the two different worlds again:

Administration: Client-focused, multitasked with legal and market pressures. The front-end part of the business. A revenue producer (i.e., profit center).

Operations: A support-focused, process-oriented, strictly controlled environment with adherence to specific procedures and subject to SEC oversight. An expense to the business (i.e., cost center).

Herein lies the problem. The attention, resources, and glamour go to administration. The pressure to constantly become more efficient and cut costs falls on operations. In many cases, the inherent conflict of administration and operations is made worse by the fact that the two divisions do not report to the same manager. It is commonplace for operations to report to an entirely different management structure separate from administration. When that occurs, it is even more difficult for the two to come together and function as one.

Some suggestions for improving the operations/administration relationship include the following:

- Improve communications. Hold periodic frequent meetings to air issues and reach a consensus.

- Keep written minutes. Track ongoing issues to resolution.

- Educate both operations and administration as to how each operates, their focuses, responsibilities, and most of all what they need to do their job successfully.

- Immediately discuss and resolve problem issues in a cooperative no-fault environment to focus on the problems, not people.

- Avoid "exception processing" issues, where operations is surprised by a new requirement. Communicate any new requirements early. Ask for feedback before committing.

- Cross-train by having operations staff sit with administrators and vice versa. Have operations staff attend select client calls and attend closings to more freely understand the process.

- Celebrate successes together.

- Praise each other when things do go right instead of always criticizing what doesn't.

- Have operations and administration report as close to the same manager as possible.

- Understand that operations needs information as early as possible and then be sure to deliver it. If it's not possible to provide the needed information soon enough, explain why.

In the end, there is simply no substitute for an effective working relationship between operations and administration. The success of the business depends on it.

Conclusion

Operations is a vital part of the Trustee business and absolutely critical to the successful service delivery to the parties of a bond financing. Proper resources must be allocated to operations both in terms of people and systems in order for the business to perform the required responsibilities of the financing.

Chapter Summary

- Operations staff provide the processing support for the business and need the proper resources to do their job effectively.
- Administration as the front office must consider the needs of operations for timely, accurate information at all times.
- Important operations functions include payments, recordkeeping, transfer agent duties, tax form preparation, and reconciliation duties.
- The key to an effective relationship between operations and administration is open, honest communication in a no-fault environment.

~ Case Study ~

You have just received a new piece of business. It involves a bond issue for which payments can be made in cash or gold to bondholders. Operations must be involved, but you're unsure how to approach them.

What should your course of action be?

Answer:

You call a meeting with operations. In the meeting, you ask for, not demand, their suggestions to learn how to make payments in gold. It has not been done before, so you approach operations saying that this is a new process and that you need their help to figure out how to execute it. You trigger enthusiasm for working on something new and play to their expertise in reaching a solution. It works. Together, you and operations create a process whereby receipts are given. The bondholders can then redeem the receipts at the gold window.

I actually did what I just described above years ago for an issue called Refinement Gold Bonds. I could never have succeeded without the help of operations, and this experience helped me see the true value in treating them as equal partners. So can you.

~ Chapter 12 ~

Relationship Management

Boston, Massachusetts—1990

I am on a cold call with a new customer I have never met. I am attempting to be named Trustee for an escrow relationship for the deposit of funds from a company providing accounting, custody, and operational services for mutual funds. This would be a significant revenue generator for our bank. Several other competitors are bidding on the business, so my presentation must be spot-on.

I am the last one to present. I am well prepared and detailed regarding our capabilities, highlighting what we could do to meet the customer's needs and communicating our relationship management philosophy. At the conclusion of my presentation and after probing for what the customer ultimately wanted, I say these fateful words, "We want your business."

I am pleasantly surprised when I am awarded the business right then and there. I am even more surprised when my new customer tells me the reason. They do believe I can meet their needs. The deciding factor was that I actually <u>asked</u> for the business. Apparently, none of my competitors actually asked for the business, let alone with the sincerity I did.

The relationship blossoms into a very profitable account for us, producing strong six-figure revenue flow for years.

Thus, always ask for the business like you mean it. You may be pleasantly surprised at the result.

Chapter Objective

I have included this chapter on relationship management because I strongly believe it is of crucial importance, and possibly the hidden secret, to the success of any Corporate Trust business. In this chapter, I will discuss:

I.   The Importance of Developing Strong Customer Relationships

II.   Developing Strong Customer Relationships through a Structured Calling Program

III. The Dos and Don'ts of Relationship Management

I. The Importance of Developing Strong Customer Relationships

I believe that the underlying key to the success of any Corporate Trust business is developing and maintaining strong, ongoing professional relationships with customers. Having a solid relationship from the start makes it easier to serve the customers' needs and also makes it harder for them to leave. Keeping their business and obtaining new business is the objective. Enhancing cross-selling opportunities is also a goal to increase the bank's services to the customer. Since Corporate Trust provides long-term customer service, Trustees are well positioned to establish productive, ongoing relationships that produce customer loyalty.

The best way to establish strong customer relationships is to meet the customers face to face, preferably in their place of business. To do that, the Corporate Trust business must establish customer calling as a high priority. Frontline administrators should be incentivized to visit their customers and should be given the time, training, and budget to do so.

Here are some common obstacles to establishing a customer calling program:

- No budget dollars
- Not enough time as administrators are too busy
- Lack of training on how to make a successful customer call

However, the greatest roadblock I have encountered personally is the administrator's fear of the word "sales." Indeed, administrators were hired primarily to administer accounts, move money, execute investments, manage tickler duties, and read documents—to name a few of their duties. Most likely, they were not hired for their "sales ability."

The reality is that everyone is really selling simply by interacting with customers and doing their job. To be an effective relationship manager, you only have to be yourself and talk to people as you would in any face-to-face meeting. The customers are people just like you with business needs and pressures. Your job is to help make their jobs easier by effectively administering their accounts and being aware of their need to know about their accounts. So take the fear out of the word "sales" because you are developing relationships and, in doing so, enhancing your prospects of securing more business.

Once again, the objectives of relationship management are as follows:

- Keep existing business to grow revenue.
- Make more money.
- Combat predatory pricing.
- Develop the skills of your staff in building customer relationships and loyalty.

- Uncover new product/service opportunities by understanding customer needs.

The job of developing customer relationships should not be the job of the sales force alone. The administrative staff who are responsible for the day-to-day activity of customer accounts should also take on this task. These are the most effective people to develop ongoing relationships as they are most knowledgeable about the accounts and are the ones customers most want to see and connect with.

Where to start? Establish a business culture that puts the customer first and foremost. Constant, ongoing communication is needed with customers to stay connected and aware of their needs. To be effective, it is important to develop a strong rapport with customers so they believe you have their best interests at heart. You need to identify what customers want and need. You need to build trust. Trust is critical. It takes years to develop and only minutes to destroy.

II. Developing Strong Customer Relationships through a Structured Calling Program

The best way to develop strong customer relationships is to establish a customer calling program. The criteria should be to identify your most important customers in terms of revenue, new business prospects, and market presence. These are the customers you want to schedule first. If time and opportunity present themselves, the second-level customers can be seen. The goal is to use your time and focus on the top-tier customers since they have the most impact on your business.

Once customers are identified, a calling schedule by quarter should be established. The ideal call involves visiting customers at their place of work. You should see your main contact person first and foremost. Introductions to upper-level managers, CFOs, and treasurers are desired as well because they will be decision-makers. But the main influence will come from the day-to-day staff you interact with.

The Basics of a Customer Call

First comes the preparation. Do your homework by learning about your customer. Review their latest financial report. Google their website. Know what business you currently do with them from a bank perspective (e.g., lending, cash management, or other Trust services). Finally, review your Trustee account and know what you do for them.

Second, prepare an agenda, in writing, to present to them. The agenda should contain topics such as the following:

- Status of their account
- Any new services you can provide
- Any concerns or problems you want to address
- Current news about your bank
- Any information on the markets, general interest rates, or developments that may be of interest

It is always appropriate to bring any reference material you have. However, unless you are actually presenting the material, it should be used as a leave-behind for the customer to review after your call. Do not hand them the materials unless you want them to read them now. Your goal is to engage them in a dialogue to uncover their needs.

Third, be sure you have the exact address and entry information to reach their office. Always have a contact phone number in case of delay. Always arrive a few minutes early so you can gather your thoughts. I prefer taking a cab versus renting a car if possible to avoid the extra time and stress of driving myself, parking, etc.

Fourth, dress professionally. Carry a pad to take notes. It is always good practice to write down any points of emphasis, new business leads, concerns, and follow-up items. This shows the customer you will follow through. I always am suspect when a waiter in a restaurant does not write down my order. The same applies to a customer call.

Fifth, be prepared, relaxed, and confident. Remember, you are establishing a relationship with another person. You can do this. Treat it as an enjoyable experience whereby you will learn something about your customer and the business. It should be fun.

Sixth, the actual face-to-face meeting should progress in this manner:

1. **The Greeting**: Engage with a smile and firm handshake. Exchange business cards. Comment on the office or surroundings. If you see a golf trophy, for example, do not hesitate to ask about golf. Personal recognition will establish common rapport, which is your goal.

2. **The Body of the Call**: Thank them for their time. Introduce any other parties to the call. Present the agenda. Don't rush, but be mindful of their time being important. Get down to business. Probe and ask open-ended questions. Listen more than you talk. Try to develop empathy for the client and view them from their perspective.

3. **The Closing of the Call**: Summarize any follow-up items you have written down. Set any deadlines for when the follow-up is needed by the customer. Observe body language and comments so as not to overstay your welcome. Thank them for their time.

4. **Post-closing**: Summarize the call in a short call report and circulate to any other bank product areas dealing with the customer. The call report should also be shared

with management and sales. Follow-up items should be addressed and completed. If the deadline promised cannot be met, then call the customer to inform them and set a new deadline.

Common Fears in Customer Calling

There are several concerns common to anyone making a customer call. These concerns may include the items listed below.

The Surprise Question: Something you did not anticipate or prepare for. *Solution:* Don't panic. Answer as best you can. Don't try to pretend you know the answer when you don't. It is okay to say, "I do not know, but I will get back to you."

The Angry Customer: A situation may occur in which a customer is angry or emotional. *Solution:* First attempt to understand the source of their discontent by asking questions. Stay calm and unemotional. Do not raise your voice or argue. You may agree to disagree in the end, but you must project an air of calmness while listening with sympathy to the customer's position. Usually, the anger will subside, and you can reach a compromise.

The Problem Situation: Dealing with a problem can be difficult, especially if it is your fault. *Solution:* Take responsibility for the error or problem and apologize. Next, probe for the facts causing the problem. Then propose a solution or promise to research the issue to bring a successful resolution. You can turn a customer problem into a trust-building event if you acknowledge the issue and bring prompt action to reach a successful result.

304

Key Questions to Ask

In my Corporate Trust calls, I have used the following questions to identify opportunities from customers:

1. What financing needs do you foresee in the next one to three years?
2. When do you anticipate going to the debt market?
3. What information or assistance can I bring to you?
4. What can I do to help you?

These open-ended questions will help you reach the customer's needs and develop a stronger relationship.

III. The Dos and Don'ts of Relationship Management

I have several suggested items for anyone who wants to be a successful relationship builder on a customer call.

The Dos

- Do smile.
- Do ask questions.
- Do listen more than you talk.
- Do observe the office and surroundings and notice personal items in order to establish a common interest.
- Do be conversational and relaxed.
- Do take notes.

- Do pay for lunch (if they let you).

- Do follow up to meet their expectations.

- Do send a thank you note or email.

- Do put the customer first and foremost.

- Do create a written call report.

The Don'ts:

- Don't talk more than you listen.

- Don't argue or raise your voice.

- Don't bad-mouth the competition.

- Don't be late or overstay your welcome.

- Don't forget to inform other bank areas, sales, and management of the call both before and after.

- Don't act arrogant or condescending.

- Don't fail to follow up on any customer requests.

Other Customer Contact Situations

When calling on a customer at their office is not possible, there are several alternative ways to develop the relationship.

Telephone Calls: Next to face-to-face calling at the customer's office, I favor personal communication by phone because you are able to convey information and probe for customer needs in a more personal, interactive way. Be sure to keep your tone of voice steady. Be positive and pleasant but professional. Also, be mindful of the time spent so as to not stay on the phone too long.

Email: In today's world of technology, emails certainly have become a common communication vehicle. They are less effective for developing more personal relationships as the face-to-face meeting or phone call. However, they are a source of communication. Be careful with emails as they can be misinterpreted. They also create written communication that is discoverable in litigation. On the other hand, sometimes having a paper trail to refer back to can be very helpful in business.

Customer Events and Conferences: This is a good way to develop relationships as a means to meet multiple customers in one setting. Do remember it is acceptable to talk about business issues even at sporting events or concerts. Remember, you are representing the bank and must conduct yourself professionally at all times, even if the customer does not. Be open, conversational, and informative at these events.

The End Result

I firmly believe that the key to success for a Corporate Trust business is to develop strong customer relationships. To do so requires frontline administrators and staff to make the effort to see their customers and meet their needs. Face-to-face calling is the best way to achieve that goal, produce customer loyalty, and bring more business to the bank.

Conclusion

It is of critical importance for Trustees to strive to develop strong customer relationships. The best way to accomplish this is to have face-to-face meetings with the customers to get to know them as people. The relationships you build will make all the difference in responding to customer needs and keeping the business you have.

Chapter Summary

- Relationship management is everyone's responsibility and the most effective way to achieve customer loyalty and obtain new business.
- The face-to-face customer call is the most effective way to develop strong personal customer relationships.
- The key elements of a customer call are: 1) the preparation, 2) the greeting, 3) the body of the call, 4) the conclusion, and 5) the follow-up.
- There are a number of dos and don'ts in customer calling that need to be considered in conducting a successful call.

~ Case Study ~

You are conducting a customer call with one of your most important customers. The customer asks you a question you do not know the answer to. The question is, "Can your bank provide FX (foreign exchange) trading and currency conversions for me?"

How should you respond?

Answer:

You do not know if the bank can provide FX services. The first thing you must do is answer," I do not know, but I will find out for you and get back to you with the answer." Do not try to pretend you know something about FX trading when you don't. Try to ask several questions to obtain more information about what the customer needs. Ask when the customer needs a response.

When returning to the bank, find the business unit that may provide FX services, then arrange a phone call with the FX representative and your customer. You should be on that call to introduce the parties and participate so you will know firsthand if the call is successful in meeting the customer's needs. You will also learn something.

If the bank cannot provide the service, then promptly report that to your customer with your apologies, but try to suggest another source. Remember, you are trying to help your customer meet their needs.

~ Chapter 13 ~

Management of Corporate Trust

Bangalore, India—2007

I am in Bangalore, India, training the Deutsche Bank staff who will be providing our bank's operations support for the Corporate Trust European business. They will also prepare our US fee bills and our modeling and analytics support for the MBS business. It is my ninth trip to Bangalore. There has been a massive turnover in the staff here; this requires me to return frequently to train the new hires. The management decision to outsource our operations from London to Bangalore was made initially to save money in staffing expense, due to a highly reduced salary structure in Bangalore. It is also the trendy thing to do since so many businesses are turning to outsourcing. I participated firsthand in the outsourcing initiative, and I can say it has not turned out as expected. While we initially saved on costs, that differential quickly dissipated due to errors, communication issues, time zone issues, and processing problems. Cultural differences have also been a factor. The real issue, however, is the turnover.

This particular managerial decision to outsource our operations had a significant impact on our Corporate Trust business. Many difficulties could have been avoided with careful analysis of the pros and cons to the outsourcing decision. The impact on our service quality cost us some business as well.

Witnessing the implications of outsourcing firsthand, I conclude that management decisions must be made with due care and a full understanding of the business impact. In today's markets, there simply is no room for error.

Chapter Objective

Management of the Corporate Trust business presents unique challenges. Those challenges arise from the very nature of the business, which is faced with:

- Evolving security structures
- Increased regulation and compliance oversight
- Lack of understanding of the business both by internal and external parties
- Increasing litigation risks
- Ongoing competitive pricing pressures
- Difficulty in producing revenue

Yet there are also solutions to the challenges facing the business. This chapter will provide suggestions for:

I.   Successfully Managing the Corporate Trust Business
II.   Addressing Management Challenges and Developing an Action Plan

I. Successfully Managing the Corporate Trust Business

In order to successfully manage the Corporate Trust business, there are several key issues to focus on. These issues are highlighted below.

Business Basics

Any manager must familiarize him/herself with how the business really works in reality, not theory. Here are the basic concepts to internalize:

- The unique relationship of the Trustee must be understood. The Trustee works for the issuer but is ultimately responsible to the bondholders.

- The Trustee's role dramatically changes from pre-default to post-default. The Trustee changes from an agency role with little or no discretion to one of a prudent man/person standard of care requiring greater discretion and proactive conduct. This is not a fiduciary standard as in other Trust businesses. To explain this more clearly, the Trustee's responsibility shifts from taking direction from the issuer and following the strict duties described in the indenture to proactively pursuing the claims of the bondholders in an Event of Default. This truly unique transformation is unlike any other bank service.

- The Trustee role is one of long-term service, which may last for ten, twenty, or thirty years over the life of the bond issue.

- The Trustee fees represent annuity revenue over a long period of time for the bank.

- The Trustee fees appear insignificant compared to the size of the bond issue caused by pricing competition and issuer perceptions of the passive role of the Trustee pre-default. However, fund balance credits and investment fees can enhance those fees.

- Traditionally, no bank capital is required to be set aside for the business. However, the implementation of the LCR (Liquidity Coverage Ratio) under Basel III banking accords will have an impact on Corporate Trust businesses, which now may require bank capital. Also, it may be required that cash balances be collateralized as per Reg 9 and state requirements. There are costs associated with both requirements.

- The business does not require large staffing resources, especially in operations, due to the impact of DTC in reducing physical transfers and debt service payments to bondholders.

- Due to the nature of the business as a long-term relationship (with the possible exception of escrows), the issuers can form close relationships with their Trustees. This presents opportunities for cross-selling other bank services. Corporate Trust can be a doorway into these customers.

313

- The business is "sticky." By this, I mean it does not move readily. This is due to the legal requirements for moving the business and the cost.

- The Trustee services are needed for the securities markets to properly function. Issuers want a Trustee to provide the needed services such as processing debt service payments, facilitating transfers, making investments, processing redemptions, sending out tax forms, and interacting with DTC, to name a few. The bondholders want Trustees as the professional third party to pursue their claims in an Event of Default as well as to monitor specific covenants of the issuer. There is no other party to provide all these services other than the Trustee.

- An assumption of high-quality service is an expectation for the business. The standard is that all payments, transfers, and processing duties are done correctly. Errors are simply not expected of the Trustee, meaning a delivery of high service quality to the customers, resulting in satisfied customers of the bank.

- Corporate Trust can be an asset gatherer for the bank, meaning that customers may invest in bank money market and investment vehicles.

II. Addressing Management Challenges and Developing an Action Plan

Now that the basics are understood, I will outline what I consider key challenges managers face and suggestions on how to meet them. These include:

- **Regulatory and Compliance Pressures:** The increasing demands placed upon the business from the heightened regulatory and compliance environment require an extraordinary time and resource commitment. This pressure can impact the business by reducing focus of the staff on customer service and revenue generation, not to mention my greatest fear: the resulting inattention to the thinking details of the business (e.g., reviewing documents, addressing interpretation issues that arise in the financing, and resolving customer requests), which are key to properly managing risk. To meet these challenges, the manager must first have a dedicated risk-management resource (at least one, perhaps more) to take up this responsibility. Second, the manager must strike a balance between doing everything asked and pushing back where needed if the compliance request does more harm than good or does not increase controls at all. By this, I mean the manager must be sure that the cost in time, resources, and ability to comply does not outweigh the benefits. The manager should also gather support from compliance and senior management for making a business case where needed to achieve a compromise.

- **Advocate for the Business:** The Corporate Trust manager must be an active advocate for the business. This means making presentations to senior management and other areas of the bank at every opportunity. Educating everyone who will listen and promoting the business are both critical steps to gaining support. The manager must also take every opportunity to recognize other areas of the bank for their referral of business. I would attend staff meetings of the commercial lenders and public finance staff who brought us business and then formally highlight the win for the bank. I also sent congratulatory messages to managers of the staff who helped us win business. It works.

- **Sales:** I have found the best way to generate revenue is to have a dedicated sales force for Corporate Trust. Full-time new business salespersons are a must if you want to grow your business. Sharing sales resources is not effective due to the need to fully understand the business and not lose needed focus. It is difficult to attract new clients in Corporate Trust, as the business is "sticky," meaning it does not move readily. For that reason, I strongly encourage the administrators to engage in active relationship management calls with their customers. This is an effective way to build customer loyalty. It also keeps your core business, as over 80 percent of Corporate Trust revenues come from repeat customers. To keep them, you must pay attention to their needs. The administrators who have the day-to-day contact are the best resource in achieving that goal.

- **New Product Development:** It is important to develop new products and seek new sources of revenue. A resource to identify new products is a real bonus for any Corporate Trust business, whether that person is part-time or full-time. This person can devote the time to research and promote new product opportunities. New product criteria should also be developed to add structure to the process. The structure analysis should include revenue potential, risk analysis, market projections, and cost to provide the needed service.

- **Risk Management:** It goes without saying that a crucial part of any manager's job in Corporate Trust is to effectively manage risk. Considering the increasing burden that new regulations and compliance pressures are placing on the business, a dedicated risk resource is needed. This resource can focus on the important areas of Bank Secrecy Act and Anti-money Laundering (BSA/AML) and Office of Foreign Asset Control (OFAC) compliance, procedure writing, compliance testing, tickler review, performing secondary account setup reviews, and being the point person for audits/regulatory examinations. Failure to have adequate risk resources will consume the management of Corporate Trust and take key staff time and attention. This will lead to a dangerous lack of attention to successfully running the business.

316

What the Manager Needs in Order to Manage Risk

To successfully manage risk, the Corporate Trust manager must also have the following:

- **Account Acceptance Committee:** This committee is needed to review and approve new business.

- **Review Committee:** This committee should meet at least monthly to review defaulted and troubled accounts to direct appropriate actions.

- **Watch List:** This is a list of at-risk accounts, defaulted accounts, and delinquent ticklers past ninety days for the Review Committee to monitor. Minutes should be kept for the above committees but only reflect short positive statements of action that avoid speculation and assumptions. Remember, all documentation can be discovered in litigation.

- **Legal Resource:** Any Corporate Trust business must have access to legal advice on legal issues that arise in the business. I have found that a dedicated legal resource in the business reporting to the Corporate Trust Manager is the most effective way to obtain the ongoing legal review and input needed. This should be supplemented by available outside counsel for opinions and bankruptcy assistance. Both internal and external counsel can also assist in document review for new issues, which is a good risk control practice. A dedicated legal counsel resource for Corporate Trust is one of the most important pieces of a successfully managed Corporate Trust business.

- **Administration:** The basic administration of the accounts requires dedicated, responsible, detail-oriented staff. It is vital that there are enough administrators to effectively cover the variety of administrative duties. Overburdened administrators will make mistakes because they lack the time to pay proper attention to the details of the accounts. It is also important for administrators to be able to think about why they are doing something in order to determine what is needed to properly analyze the best course of action. It all starts with the frontline administrators to provide the needed customer service and risk management on a day-in, day-out basis. The account administrators and any support staff should also be trained with an ongoing training program. A Certified Corporate Trust Specialist (CCTS) designation from the Institute of Certified Bankers (ICB) is also helpful as a professional designation of a level of expertise. The administrators should also be encouraged and trained to be strong relationship managers to be able to call on customers.

- **Structure of the Business:** There are a number of structures for the Corporate Trust business. The traditional structure was for administrators (Vice President and Trust Officer levels) to have complete responsibility for all aspects of administering an account from document review to closing and all ongoing compliance, from cash movement through maturity. They were supported by assistants and grouped in teams. Many of the administrators were lawyers. The Corporate Trust structure has evolved to encompass a *middle-office* structure with more specialization. This structure has the following characteristics:
  - *Relationship Manager*: Primary client contact and responsibility for calling on existing customers.
  - *Account Control:* Account setup with compliance monitoring, investing, and most tickler duties.

- *Cash Processing:* Responsibility for all debt service, cash flow processing.
- *Operations*: All DTC contact, payments to bondholders, fee billing, recordkeeping, and tax form processing.
- *The Middle Office*: Account control and cash processing, which may be combined.

A centralized team of people (formerly assistant level) would serve all accounts in various locations. The relationship managers can be local. One further trend is for operations to become part of Trust Operations to take advantage of operational economies of scale (e.g., payments, recordkeeping, and tax form processing).

There has always been a controversy as to who should be the point of contact person for the customer. Should it be the account administrator (often referred to as the relationship manager) or someone else in sales, middle office, or management? I would recommend the customers be educated and given a choice of using the relationship manager as their single point of contact or offering several additional contacts in the middle office. The middle office contacts would be familiar with the customers' accounts and be able to resolve questions more efficiently than going through the relationship manager, who then has to contact the middle office for the answers. This delay can be frustrating to customers.

In addition to the above structure, the successful Corporate Trust business should have separate dedicated sales staff, risk staff, legal resources, and product managers. With the proper resources and structure, the business has the greatest chance of success. Corporate Trust is a self-contained business and should be treated as such.

Training

Training is my favorite topic and one I have based my career on. There simply is no substitute for well-trained people. To achieve this, the Corporate Trust Business Manager must develop and implement an ongoing training program specifically for the Trust business. It should be comprised of these elements:

- One-hour classes on specific core Trustee responsibilities, procedures, and policies.
- Orientation training class on the introductory overview of the business plus appointment of a mentor to answer questions as the new hire learns the business.
- Establishment of a Corporate Trust curriculum of classes for Corporate Trust I, II, and III, leading to the CCTS certification designation. This can be achieved by developing an in-house training program, hiring outside training consultants, or having employees attend the Cannon Financial Institute Corporate Trust Schools.
- Having legal counsel deliver specific training on document review, for example. They will usually do this for free.
- Bank generic training on soft skills classes such as team building, leadership, BSA/AML compliance, and sales.
- Systems training by the vendor or internal systems technicians or someone on your staff.

I prefer classroom training in person for maximum interaction and learning results. Online training classes are popular with many organizations, and they do have a place; however, they should not be the only avenues for training. Online courses and webinars can be impersonal and provide for a more restricted discussion/feedback environment. They can also be expensive to produce. However, it is beneficial that there are a variety of methods to deliver training available, and a manager can choose the right method for his/her particular business.

Regardless of the training method used, the one constant is that the training should be ongoing, scheduled, and delivered by training professionals whenever possible. While subject matter experts can be effective, they should be trained in delivery techniques. Written handouts, checklists, and materials should be provided. What should be avoided at all costs is the training session where the presenter just reads off the PowerPoint slides, thus putting everyone to sleep. Delivering effective, thought-provoking training is a unique skill that few possess, especially with a highly technical topic like Corporate Trust. I have always found that mixing in personal stories and real-life examples makes a big difference in the learning success of class participants. I feel you can never do too much training for the business. Corporate Trust staff should be constantly upgrading their knowledge and skills to meet the ever-changing demands of the market.

Revenue Generation

There are a number of revenue-generating ideas for the manager of the Corporate Trust business to consider. Product diversity is the key to growing the business, especially as market changes occur, thus causing certain products to underperform or disappear (e.g., Variable Rate Demand Bonds and BAB bonds). Flexibility is important with an opportunistic approach to new securities developments. One example I have seen was the explosion of collateralized mortgage obligations in the 1980s and '90s. In this case, a bank named Texas Commerce became the overnight market leader in Corporate Trust because it saw the opportunity in being a CMO Trustee and seized the moment.

Revenue-generating Ideas to Consider

- **Escrows:** Do as many escrows as possible and look for all types from your bankers and law firms.

- **Custody:** Look to hold assets, mortgages, and other documents in safekeeping.

- **Municipal Leases:** Consider this specific type of financing, which can be very rewarding for holding funds to invest.

- **Corporate Bankers and Public Finance Bankers:** Be sure to target internal bank resources for referral business. Include your real estate and leasing areas.

- **Successor Trustee/Default Business:** Develop a business with default administration expertise to take on resignations due to conflicts of interest for accounts proceeding into default or in default.

- **Target Your Sales Force:** Focus your sales force on uncovering new customers primarily, and leave existing customer relationships as the focus of the administrators/relationship managers.

- **Be Visible:** Go to conferences, host events, and speak at gatherings (both internal and external to the bank) to maximize exposure.

- **Look for Acquisitions:** Grow your business by acquiring another book of business. You must determine what would fit with your strategic direction in terms of products, only acquiring a business that is within the existing footprint of the bank or looking to develop business that is currently outside your current product offerings. It is also a way to bring experienced staff into your business with a different perspective on the business compared with your organization.

- **Go Global**: Look to expand to international markets. While the resources needed to expand beyond the United States can be a hindrance, I can attest to the fact that there are significant opportunities globally for the Corporate Trust business. In my many travels around the world, especially in Asia, I have seen a substantial amount of Corporate Trust business as the global securities markets expand. However, you must be in the right places with the right capabilities (e.g., London and Hong Kong).

- **Directorships:** Establish a director business in tax-advantaged locations. This service involves serving as a director for various trust relationships as a board member. The director holds meetings, keeps minutes, abides by the bylaws and governing documents of the Trusts, and makes decisions on behalf of the Trusts. The Trusts can be Special Purpose Vehicles (SPVs) holding title to assets such as aircraft or ships. The Trusts can be onshore or offshore in tax-neutral or tax-advantaged locations (i.e., Cayman Islands; Dublin, Ireland; Channel Islands; Mauritius; or Delaware in the United States). I have trained in all these locations plus more and can attest to the strong revenue opportunities this business presents.

- **Reporting/Recordkeeping:** Be open to providing customers with specialized reporting and recordkeeping services. Include valuation services. One example is serving as Disclosure Agent for issuers that want a third party to pass along the reporting information required to comply with SEC rule 15c2-12 (Secondary Market Disclosure).

- **Charge for Extraordinary Services**: Create a list of services for which you charge a fee and which are considered outside your standard administrative fee quote. Examples are: supplemental indentures, consents, investments, construction fund withdrawals, optional redemptions, puts, and special reporting.

- **Fee Increases**: Initiate periodic fee increases. I strongly recommend you initiate periodic fee increases. I know what you are thinking, "My customers will never accept a fee increase." I can tell you from personal experience that they will if you present it the right way. First of all, you must convey the fact that your costs go up as in any business and that you must be able to cover those costs in order to continue to provide the service quality your customers have come to expect. I have had success by increasing fees in certain categories, such as out-of-pocket expenses. You should also be aware of competitive pressures and make sure that your original fee quotes specifically provided that you can increase your fees. It not only can be done, but it must be done because to expect to have your business locked into a fee arrangement for twenty to thirty years without an increase is insane.

- **Operations**: Provide private label services from your operations group to other banks. I have seen this work in several banks I have worked for. In effect, you turn your operations cost center into a profit center by providing recordkeeping, transfer services, and paying capabilities to other Corporate Trust providers.

- **Credit for Cash Balances:** Receive credit for cash balances. Make sure you receive revenue credit from the bank for your uninvested cash balances. The bank uses those balances, so make sure Corporate Trust receives the credit and not someone else.

- **Credit for Investing in Proprietary Money Market Funds:** Receive credit for investing in a bank-sponsored money market fund. Corporate Trust should receive a revenue credit for investing in a bank's proprietary money market fund complex. Whether that is called a 12b-1 fee or is part of a management fee, you should receive that credit just as is the case if you use money market funds outside the bank. The funds would not be invested in banks funds without Corporate Trust, so credit should be given where credit is due.

- **Incentives for Bank Referrals:** Offer cash incentives to other areas of the bank for bringing new business to Corporate Trust. A controversial practice is for the bank department that refers a piece of business to receive shadow credit either above the line or below the line (direct versus indirect) in their budget for a percentage of the fee revenue generated. Many banks frown on this practice. However, it is an effective means of gaining attention for Corporate Trust business. In one case, I was able to make cash awards to the person responsible for referring business. I can assure you that cold, hard cash gets people's attention, as does the revenue credit to the budget.

- **Watch Indirect Expenses:** Pay careful attention to the indirect expenses charges to your business. Challenge unfair allocations. You will generally see indirect expenses allocated based upon headcount or number of accounts, so be watchful.

Conclusion

In today's highly competitive market, the successful Corporate Trust Manager must wear many hats. Being a strong advocate for the business and obtaining the proper resources are vital. Be a cheerleader for the business, both internally and externally. Have the proper strategic direction in supporting the bank's goals. Be opportunistic, constantly searching for new revenue sources. Success is yours for the taking.

Chapter Summary

The manager should remember these key attributes of the Trust business:

- Annuity revenue
- Fee-based revenue
- Funds-balance generator
- Asset gatherer
- Long-term relationship product providing cross-selling opportunities
- Needed service for the securities markets required by both issuers and investors
- High-quality service
- Attractive profit margins

~ Case Study ~

You are the manager of the Corporate Trust business. A commercial officer of the bank brings you a new business opportunity. It is a municipal industrial development revenue bond issue of $10 million to build a tire recycling plant in the town of Pleasantville, a small picturesque town in the middle of your state. You are under pressure to take the deal both from the commercial officer and your manager to help a new start-up company as a bank client and generate revenue needed to make your budget.

What should you do? Should you accept the business or not?

Answer:

Your first duty is to do due diligence on the transaction to understand what the financing is to accomplish. You want to ask yourself how you could get into trouble with this business. In other words, what are the real risks of your assuming the Trusteeship on behalf of the bank? A little research discloses some disturbing facts. The town is partially opposed to the plant for environmental reasons as there will be a large smokestack in their fair community. Demonstrations have occurred, attracting national press coverage. There are environmental risks if you have to foreclose on the plant. This would be the result of the sponsor company filing for bankruptcy protection. The Trustee would be responsible for taking over the property and safeguarding it on behalf of the bondholders. The company is new with an untried process for burning the tires to produce electricity. The electricity will be sold to residents. Unfortunately, the cost of the electricity is above market rates. The state has agreed to subsidize the difference so the electricity can be sold. In your experience, you have seen such subsidies/government guarantees revoked.

Your conclusion: Too great a risk. You decline the business. It goes to one of your competitors.

This is an actual situation I faced as a manager. One year later, the worst scenario occurred. The company sponsor went into default by filing for Chapter 11 bankruptcy protection. The Trustee had to foreclose on the facility and try to manage it and sell it for much less than the original cost of $10 million. The state revoked its subsidy guarantee as well, making any sale of the electricity impractical. To make matters worse, the investor brought litigation against the parties to the financing, including the Trustee. All in all, a bad ending for the Trustee and for everyone involved. I would like to end the story there, but there is one more item to report. I changed jobs. I now worked for the bank Trustee who had taken this business. So I never really got away from it.

~ Chapter 14 ~

The Future of Corporate Trust

Windsor, Colorado—Present Day

If a bank CEO approached me today, asking if he/she should start a Corporate Trust business, I would answer, "Yes." Why? There is a future in this business.

Corporate Trust is a unique specialty business requiring expertise. It can be a strong relationship builder in which the bank can become a long-term service provider for corporate and municipal clients. The business traditionally has had high profit margins. While reduced since the 2008 economic crisis with the low-interest-rate environment, it still produces attractive profit margins in the 15 to 30 percent range. Rising interest rates and a stronger economy will improve those margins as more debt is issued.

The Corporate Trust business produces fee-based revenue over the long term of twenty to thirty years or more. It provides an annuity stream of revenue for the bank year after year. The business also can support bank investment products such as money market funds. The business also provides cash balances, which can be helpful for a bank in support of its lending business.

In short, I would answer, "Yes. Start a Corporate Trust business," given you can deliver the expertise, commitment, market presence, and proper resources necessary to do the business right.

Chapter Objective

No book on Corporate Trust in my opinion would be complete without answering the question: "Does the Corporate Trust business have a future?" As you can see from my opening vignette, the answer is "yes, absolutely." In order to paint a realistic picture, however, I will add some caution to my reasoning due to the increasingly difficult challenges facing Corporate Trust today and in the future.

> I.   Why Corporate Trust Has a Future
> II. The Challenges Facing Corporate Trust

There are a surprising number of positive attributes to the Corporate Trust business. Let's find out what they are.

I. Why Corporate Trust Has a Future

There is a *need* for the role of the Trustee as well as for the agent duties performed by the Corporate Trust business. There simply is no other provider of these particular services for the issuers of debt or the investors who buy it. The Paying Agent, recordkeeping, and Transfer Agent services are the basics of the business. There are a variety of other services including investing, cash flow processing, monitoring issuer compliance, interacting with DTC, holding physical assets/collateral (or holding title to such assets), reporting information, and many more services. The reality is that no one else can deliver these services together.

The issuers receive these services. The investors in the bonds receive the protection of a Trustee in a default. Once again, no other provider can deliver this protection to consolidate and pursue the claims of the investors in a bankruptcy/default than the Trustee.

330

The Corporate Trust business provides the services to the issuers and protections for investors found in no other business all in one provider. The additional services offered such as escrow agent, custodian, and information provider add to the need for the business. The proper functioning of the securities markets depends on these needed services provided by Corporate Trust. Debt is more efficiently issued and serviced because of Corporate Trust. Let's not forget all the operations services provided that support Corporate Trust, including tax form processing, securities transfers, payments of principal and interest, escheatment of unclaimed funds, and recordkeeping. All are necessary for the smooth functioning of the securities markets at what has been a very reasonable cost.

Federal Law Supports Corporate Trust

The Trust Indenture Act of 1939, as amended by the Trust Indenture Reform Act of 1990, strongly supports the formal role of the Trustee. It enshrines the standards of conduct for Trustees in Corporate Trust as an important service for the proper functioning of the securities markets. That law stands today as a verification of the need for the role of the Trustee in the Corporate Trust business for the debt markets. It has served its purpose well for all these years since the Great Depression without requiring taxpayer or regulatory intervention.

Recall my earlier story of my testimony in the mid-1990s to a congressional committee on the Trust Indenture Act and its reason for existence. Congress continued its support for the law and the concepts it established for Corporate Trust. My further testimony to the SEC also affirmed that agency's support for the role of the Trustee. When I asked the commissioners if the SEC wanted to step in to provide the services of a Trustee, I was told "no." My conclusion is that the role of the Trustee and the services of the

Corporate Trust business have stood the test of time, accomplishing what was envisioned for the securities markets.

Annuity Revenue and Other Financial Benefits

The Corporate Trust business produces an annuity revenue stream over a long period of time (twenty to thirty years for many clients). Profit margins are healthy. The number of staff needed to provide the services is relatively small, thereby keeping expenses down. The annuity revenue is also largely fee-based revenue as well; this is attractive to the bank. Balances are also provided to the bank. Support for other bank services such as proprietary money market funds is an added bonus. These attributes of Corporate Trust are all benefits to the bank.

Additional Reasons for Providing Corporate Trust Services

The following topics represent the reasons why the bank should provide Corporate Trust services:

- **Service Quality:** The service quality for Corporate Trust is required to be high. Corporate Trust rises to this challenge; this results in satisfied clients for the bank.

- **Variety of Services:** The current Corporate Trust business must look to deliver a diverse set of services beyond the basic Trustee/Paying Agent products. The securities markets are creating new products that require more Corporate Trust involvement and specialization, for example, providing special reporting and monitoring services. The evolution of new products and services will provide new sources of revenue for the business going forward.

- **<u>Use of Bank Capital</u>:** Traditionally, Corporate Trust has not required the use of bank capital as the lending area has. This benefit is now eroding due to the Basel III accords, which require banks to reserve more capital against "deposits," including uncollateralized uninvested funds held in trust accounts. Yet the offset to this is the overall value and benefit to the bank of Corporate Trust for supporting proprietary bank investment products, providing balances, and producing fee-based revenue.

II. The Challenges Facing Corporate Trust

While there are many benefits to being in the business of Corporate Trust, there are also some challenges. While meeting these challenges will not be easy, I constantly witness Corporate Trust providers rising to the task in order to successfully meet these challenges. The high quality of the many Corporate Trust professionals I have met over the years leaves no doubt in my mind of the future success of the business. Some of the more significant challenges are as follows.

Revenue Production

The low-interest-rate environment resulting from the 2008 economic crisis has diminished several important revenue sources for the business, namely money market returns and the resulting reduction in fees earned by Corporate Trust. Also, there is a reduced value of cash balances for the bank as banks cut back on lending and as they therefore do not need access to such balances from Corporate Trust. Bond volume has also declined, as issuers found it more difficult to access the debt markets due to market fears. Also, issuers were working to reduce their overall debt to strengthen their balance sheets. Fewer bond issues meant lower fee revenue for Corporate Trust. To meet these revenue challenges, the business has moved to diversify its service offerings to find new sources of revenue. A strengthening economy will also cause securities markets to improve as issuers find a more favorable reception for their debt issues. Bond financing will continue to be needed as infrastructure needs grow and corporations need to raise capital to expand their business. Also, the rebirth of structured finance bond issues is making a comeback and will provide new opportunities for revenue to Corporate Trust.

Regulatory and Compliance Pressures

There is a perceived need for the securities markets to be more controlled due to the 2008 economic crisis and the Dodd-Frank banking reform legislation. This contributes to more regulatory/compliance pressures on Corporate Trust and banks. These pressures will increase the cost of doing business. It will also require more resources for the business to meet the growing regulatory/compliance demands especially in the BSA/AML, investment, and funds movement areas of the business. Corporate Trust businesses are establishing the proper procedures and are meeting these challenges. I also see not only an increase in the number of procedures but also in the testing of those procedures, as well as added requirements that take time and attention. This will detract from efforts to focus on developing the business and providing ongoing attention to administering the business. It does present a greater burden on the smaller providers that do not have the staffing or systems resources of their larger competitors. Yet the smaller regional providers do not have the regulatory focus of the larger banks or larger business models to control. I feel there is room for both large bank providers and smaller regional providers in this business. Smaller providers do not have the large cost structure to support. They have a future if they continue to provide superior, local service as compared to the larger, more distant banks.

Investor and Issuer Demands for More Service

There is a recognized effort on the part of institutional investors to demand higher levels of service from Corporate Trust providers. Issuers as well are now demanding more from Trustees. Unfortunately, both parties have not yet been willing to pay more for the increased service demands. Largely centered on the mortgage-backed securities bond financings, institutional investors are pushing Trustees to take a much more active oversight role in monitoring servicers and resolving collateral deficiency issues for troubled securitizations. These institutional investors are even lobbying for the Trustees to assume a fiduciary standard of care. The rating agencies and regulators are also taking notice of the increasing clamor for Trustees to do more. As I have explained before, Trustees are not fiduciaries, but rather they are agents pre-default and prudent men/persons post-default, which plays a lesser role than does a fiduciary. Trustees have no authority to act as fiduciaries in the governing documents, nor are they compensated as such.

However, if such a standard is applied to Trustees, then it must be clearly defined and authorized in the governing Trust documents. The Trustee's compensation must also be dramatically increased to cover the increased costs of resources, legal expertise, and legal liability a fiduciary standard imposes. I also would predict that the Trust Indenture Act would need to be amended to reflect this new fiduciary standard of care.

The Corporate Trust business has always risen to meet the new demands of the securities markets. Such was the case with the creation of the structured finance securitization market. Corporate Trust can do so again but only with the needed compensation and resources the new securities market structures and increased demands on the business require.

Senior Bank Management Understanding and Perception of Corporate Trust

The increasing need for the banks to drive revenue and control risk are critical factors the Corporate Trust business cannot ignore. Corporate Trust managers must be persistent in educating bank management of the benefits of Corporate Trust as well as meeting the increasing control requirements mandated. This task is not an easy one—and it is one that requires ongoing attention. However, it can and must be done for the business to survive.

Resources Needed for People and Systems

There is no more important component of a successful Corporate Trust business than well-trained, experienced people. The business must also have a sufficient number of staff. I have experienced the dangers of under-resourcing the business myself, both as an administrator and as a manager in my career. Even the best person cannot perform appropriately if overburdened and overwhelmed. That is when shortcuts are taken and mistakes occur. Judgment becomes impaired because there is no time to think through an issue. In the Corporate Trust business, the mistakes can have large dollar signs attached to them, such as million-dollar overdrafts, to name just one potential mistake. To be successful, the business simply must have the proper human resources, training, and support it needs to do the job right.

Proper systems are also required, especially in the advanced technology world we live in today. The variety of bond structures and unique features of the services required of Trustees makes system support an ongoing challenge to keep up with the needed automation required. The danger of resorting to too many Excel spreadsheets to fill the gap presents control issues for the business. There is no easy system answer for Corporate Trust, which is why multiple systems are employed. The key is connecting these systems. In all my years in this business, I am still waiting for that one magical system that will cover all aspects of our business and enable us to input data just one time instead of multiple times. I believe I will be waiting for the next forty-two years of my career for that to occur. Thus, we need to do our best with what we have.

Yet the greatest system in the world will not be able to interpret an indenture, solve a client's problems, or anticipate a default. Only people can do that. Well-trained, responsible, dedicated people who enjoy what they do. Those who believe they are doing important work both for the bank and their clients. Those who believe, as I do, that they are contributing to the successful functioning of the securities markets by facilitating the financing of infrastructure building, housing for our citizens, and supporting the growth of corporations to provide needed goods and services. That is what Corporate Trust is all about to me and to the many professionals I have come to know in this fascinating business.

Conclusion

I have been a Corporate Trust professional for my entire business career spanning forty-two years and counting. I have seen the business prosper. I have seen the business consolidate, just as banking has consolidated. I have seen new products, security structures, and services come and go. I have experienced the pressures on the business from litigation and increasing regulations. I have also travelled domestically and internationally, meeting countless numbers of Corporate Trust professionals.

Based on my forty-plus years in the industry, I conclude that the Corporate Trust business will survive the current-day pressures and continue to be a valuable service for the securities markets both in the United States and around the globe. There is light at the end of the tunnel, and it is not a train. It is the light of opportunity. So to all Corporate Trust professionals, I advise you to continue to serve the business with the passion, integrity, and dedication you have always shown.

I wish all Trustees success as we work together to continue this challenging and always changing business of Corporate Trust—a true partner in finance.

Chapter Summary

The need for Trustees will continue as long as bonds are issued. The role of the Trustee will continue to be an important part of bond financings with the Trustee providing critical service both pre-default and post-default. The issuers will continue to need the processing and monitoring services provided by Trustees to facilitate the workings of the bond financings. The bondholders will continue to rely on the protection provided by

Trustees in a default in order to maximize their recovery. As the securities markets continue to evolve, so will the Corporate Trust business and the services provided by Trustees.

~ Case Study ~

If I were asked by my two daughters, Kristen and Denise, "Dad, should I seek a job in the Corporate Trust business?" a few questions would arise. Could they have a meaningful career? Could they expand their skills and make a meaningful contribution? Would they be challenged with interesting work?

What would I say to my daughters?

Answer:

The answer is "Yes." I would further add the following: If you want a career in an interesting, ever-changing business in the financial services industry, Corporate Trust is a good place to be. Be prepared to be constantly learning new aspects of the business and learning new lessons. You will be working with some of the nicest, most sincere, most responsible people you will ever meet. You will enjoy the experience. You will come away with valuable knowledge and experience that will benefit you for the rest of your life. So go for it, but be prepared to never be truly comfortable that you know it all because you never will. That is why I love the business with such passion. It is ever-evolving and interesting. It will challenge you every day. You will continue to learn every day, which is a fascinating prospect.

~ Exhibit A ~

Trust Indenture Act of 1939: Summary of Key Sections

Section 310: Eligibility and qualifications of Trustees—requires $150,000 in capital and surplus and Corporate Trust powers. Section 310(b)(1-10) lists the ten conflicts of interest a Trustee must address in an Event of Default to either resign or cure the conflict within ninety days.

Section 311: Preferential collection of claims against the obligor in keeping with the bankruptcy code ninety-day preference period.

Section 312: Provisions regarding reporting by obligor of bondholder lists and ability of bondholders to access information. Establishes the requirement that it takes three or more bondholders to request a list of all bondholders of the issue.

Section 313: Reporting obligations of the Trustee in providing an annual Trustee's Report to bondholders, the SEC, and any exchange the bonds are listed on but only if there is a material change in the position of the Trustee regarding the conflicts of interest in Section 310(b)(1-10).

Section 314: Reporting obligations of the obligor, including requirements for certificates, financial reports, and opinions for compliance with the indenture and of fair value. Requires any annual, quarterly, or material event reports, which the obligor must send to the SEC, to also be sent to the Trustee. Requires an annual officers' certificate of no default

340

be provided to the Trustee. Also requires an annual recording opinion be provided to the Trustee if the bonds are secured by the mortgage or pledge of property.

Section 315: Provisions relating to the responsibilities, duties, and standards of care for the Trustee pre-default and post-default. Specifically, Section 315(c) established the prudent man standard of care post-default. The section also states the requirement for the Trustee to give bondholders notice of defaults (Events of Default) within ninety days after occurrence but notes that the Trustee may withhold such notice if the Trustee determines it is in the best interests of the bondholders.

Section 316: Details the circumstances and limitations on bondholder directions and waivers to the Trustee. Authorized bondholders of not less than a majority of principal amount of the bonds to direct the trustee as to remedies. Also authorizes bondholders of not less than 75 percent of principal amount of the bonds to postpone any interest payment for a period not less than three years from its due date. Authorizes Trustees to establish a record date for purposed of Trustee actions for obtaining bondholder consents or other actions.

Section 317: Details certain powers of the Trustee with respect to collection of claims in a default and Paying Agent duties. Also establishes the authority for the Trustee to file proofs of claim in a bankruptcy.

~ Exhibit B ~

Corporate Trust: A Brief Description

Definition

Corporate Trust is a service provided usually by a bank to issuers of bonds. Those issuers can be a municipality (i.e., city, county, state, or governmental entity) or corporation that issues bonds to build or buy something. The bank acts as a Trustee to provide a variety of services required by the bond documents on behalf of the issuer. The Trustee is paid a fee by the issuer to provide these services. The Trustee acts as an agent for the issuer but changes its role to prudent man/person acting on behalf of the bondholders if the issuer defaults in its obligations to the bondholders.

How It Works

The Trustee provides services of paying the bondholders (Paying Agent) from funds received from the issuer or assets of the Trust; keeping records of the bondholders and amount of bonds outstanding (Registrar); and transferring bonds (Transfer Agent) resulting from bondholders selling their bonds. Among other responsibilities, the Trustee also monitors the provisions of the Trust documents such as receiving reports and certificates, investing funds at direction from the issuer, and making other disbursements of fund, such as construction funds monies, as directed. The Trustee does not have discretion pre-default but must exist within the four corners of the Trust documents as strictly prescribed. Post-default, the Trustee has a discretionary standard of care to act on behalf of the bondholders to maximize their recovery. This is not a fiduciary standard of care but below it in terms of discretion to act.

Whom the Trustee Works For

The Trustee works for the issuer pre-default and for the bondholders post-default. If asked the question as to whom the Trustee's ultimate boss is, the answer is the bondholders.

Other Corporate Trust Services

Corporate Trust can act not only as a Trustee for bond issues but also in a variety of other roles. One of those roles is serving as Escrow Agent for two or more parties that enter into a short-term agreement whereby the Escrow Agent holds assets or provides services on behalf of the parties. Another common service is that of a Custodian where the bank is holding assets in safekeeping. There is a long list of other specialty services that can be found in Corporate Trust, including recordkeeping, funds movement, and reporting services. So Corporate Trust is a business that has many potential parts.

~ **Exhibit C** ~

How to Successfully Manage Risk in Corporate Trust: Best Practices

There are several suggested best practices Trustees can incorporate to more effectively manage risks. The following list is by no means all-inclusive, but it is a good place to start:

- Do what you are supposed to do under the documents.

- Read and understand the documents—doing one without the other is useless.

- Hire good legal counsel to assist you in reviewing documents and in interpreting the documents during the life of the issue.

- Get opinions in writing.

- Hire experienced bankruptcy counsel for all bankruptcy situations, preferably counsel you know and who knows about the role of the Trustee (i.e., experience with Trustees).

- Get good systems and proper training in them.

- Perform a periodic account load study to analyze the account workload of administration so that adjustments can be made.

- Have teams of administrators, operations, and support staff cross-trained so that others can step in when absences or turnover occur.

- Hire a "swing administrator" to work as a resource to fill in for absences or to provide support for new business.

- Perform a "secondary review" of the account setup by an independent party to try to catch any missed ticklers or errors in the record setup within ninety days of the account setup.

- Draw a picture of a waterfall or flow of funds to more completely understand it, verify it with lead counsel, and provide an easy record for anyone else to use in your absence.

- When in doubt, tickle it.

- If the documents do not specifically require you to receive something such as insurance evidence, then do not accept it if provided but instead return it with a letter stating you are not required to receive it. Do not put it in your files.

- If receiving financial reports, place language in the documents that you do not have to review the reports other than to simply verify they are what is required to be furnished to you. If you do decide to read them, then I suggest you conduct a review by identifying 1) net income, 2) the accountant's opinion, and 3) the balance sheet items of current assets minus current liabilities, which will tell you if the issuer is solvent. Document this as a procedure for all to follow. This is called Jeff's eight-minute review because it only takes eight minutes to complete. At the end, it will tell you 1) if the issuer made or lost money last year, 2) if the accountants found any discrepancies, and 3) if the issuer is solvent, meaning it has enough assets to pay for its liabilities over the next one-year period. I have conducted this review of financial reports and found it useful in being aware of the general financial condition of the issuer. It helped me anticipate financial difficulties (i.e., potential default). I know that this concept is a hard sell to Trustees for a number of reasons:
    1. No time (eight minutes?).
    2. No training (anyone can do this).
    3. Not required by the indenture provisions but useful information that can help Trustees to anticipate a default; this information can aid the Trustee to better protect the bondholders.

- For insurance covenants, try not to receive any evidence. If you do receive evidence, try to limit it to just a brief opinion by an insurance professional stating that all insurance is in effect. This will help you control your risks of not understanding the insurance requirement if you are supplied complex insurance certificates and policies. Insurance requirements are one of my greatest concerns for Trustees. I have done extensive research into the different types of insurance and discussed the indenture insurance provisions with insurance experts. My experience resulted in my realization that it is very difficult to properly understand and monitor insurance covenants due to the complexity of ever-changing industry practices. Cancellations, vague language, unclear provisions, and difficult terminology all make insurance compliance a difficult issue for Trustees to follow. My resulting fear is that the insurance evidence provided proves inadequate and that a loss occurs for which disgruntled bondholders sue the Trustee, alleging that the Trustee should have known about the deficiency.

- For investments, always ask for written direction. Include your proprietary funds in the permitted investment language. Establish a standing instruction direction that will allow you to invest funds if you cannot reach anyone.

- Provide three investment choices to the issuer for any investment.

- Do a practice run for any new letter of credit prior to first drawdown to make sure you know precisely how the draw process works.

- Always question any collateral substitution if it does not certify that the collateral replacing the existing collateral is of equal or greater value.

- Include precise language clearly stating how the Trustee should calculate any valuation of funds.

- Eliminate invoices from construction fund requisition requests as a requirement under the indenture.

- Never release funds, collateral, or assets without direction. If any question exists at all in your mind, seek advice of counsel before acting. Do the same for any request for waiving or amending the Trust documents.

- If environmental risks are a potential for any bond issue with real property, include language in the trust documents to allow you to seek expert opinions/reports such as a Phase I or Phase II environmental report or expert opinion as to the environmental status of the property prior to taking any foreclosure action by the Trustee. If desirable due to the nature of the property (e.g., a chemical plant), the Trustee can require an annual opinion as to the environmental status of the property. Also include in the trust documents the indemnity provision for the Trustee to seek indemnity from bondholders if the Trustee needs to take foreclosure action on the property.

- For any account for which you may be designated backup servicer, have a written list of potential servicers whom you can call and who can step in on your behalf immediately. Try to include in the Trust documents a provision to have any backup servicer fees paid out of the cash flows or by bondholders if the Trustee assumes the role of backup servicer.

- Establish a new product individual who will have the time and ability to process new product ideas.

- Understand the strategy of the bank and focus your Corporate Trust strategy to support it.

- If errors occur, promptly notify your client and keep your client informed of your damage control efforts. It is better for you to relate any service quality issues than for the client to discover them itself or hear it from your competitors. Do the same thing with your management. Never hide problems; the cover-up will always catch up with you.

- Include in the definition of written instructions electronic transitions (e.g., via email).
- Institute a call-back procedure for nonrepetitive wire transfers.

Products and Bond Issue Descriptions for Municipal Bonds

Municipal Bond Subcategories of General Obligation and Revenue Bonds

Healthcare: Revenue bonds used for hospitals, assisted living facilities, elderly care facilities, or other medical care facilities.

Transportation: Bonds used to finance airports, bridges, tunnels, toll roads, and transit systems.

Utility: Revenue bonds used to finance gas, water, sewer, and electric power systems.

Pollution Control: Revenue bonds used to finance a private firm's efforts to control pollution.

Municipal Notes: Short-term interest-bearing bonds used to assist in financing a project or help a municipality manage its cash flow. Examples include the following:

- **Tax Anticipation Notes (TANs):** Issued to finance municipal current operations in anticipation of future tax receipts from real estate taxes. Usually General Obligation (GO) bonds.
- **Revenue Anticipation Notes (RANs):** Issued for the same purpose as TANs except that the anticipated revenues come from sources other than general tax receipts, such as federal and state subsides. Usually GO bonds.
  - **Bond Anticipation Notes (BANs):** Issued in expectation of receiving funds (grants) from the federal government.

- **Construction Loan Notes (CLNs):** Issued to provide funds for construction of a project that will eventually be funded by a bond issue.

Tax-free Money Market Instruments: Tax-exempt commercial paper and variable rate demand bonds. A variable rate demand bond will adjust its interest rate at specified intervals and may allow the bondholder to sell its bonds on the date the new rate is established.

Certificates of Participation (COPs): Notes issued to finance the leasing of a municipal facility.

Tax Increment Financings (TIFs): Bonds or notes backed by the specific tax revenues in a specified geographic area until the bonds or notes are paid off. All tax revenues from that area only go to paying the bonds/notes.

~ Exhibit E ~

SEC Transfer Agent Rules

- 17Ac2-1: Apply to be a Transfer Agent (TA) (one-time filing) or change form TA-1
- 17Ac2-2: Annual Report from - form TA-2
- 17Ac3-1: Withdraw TA-W
- 17Ad-1: Definitions: SCL (Shipment Control List)
- 17Ad-2: Turnaround—90 percent routine within seventy-two hours
- 17Ad-3: Penalties
- 17Ad-4: Exempt TA—Less than five hundred transfers in a six-month period
- 17Ad-5: Written inquiries response times
- 17Ad-6: Recordkeeping requirements—daily receipts, monthly logs
- 17Ad-7: Record retention requirements
- 17Ad-8: Security Position Listings (SPLs)
- 17Ad-9: Definitions; master files; control book
- 17Ad-10: Posting requirements and buy-ins in sixty days
- 17Ad-11: Reports required monthly and quarterly to be sent to regulators
- 17Ad-12: Funds and securities in safekeeping
- 17Ad-13: Annual Account Report on internal controls
- 17Ad-14: Tender Agents and specially designated accounts
- 17Ad-15: Signature Guarantee—Medallion Stamp Program
- 17Ad-16: Swing Letter—swing the position from one TA to another

- 17Ad-17: Lost/stolen securities--perform two database searches to try to identify the bondholder's address
- 17Ad-18: Y2K
- 17Ad-19: Cancelled certificates disposition
- 17Ad-20: Stock ownership
- 17Ad-21T: Y2K
- 17F-1: Reporting lost/stolen securities on form X-17F1-A within twenty-four hours reported to Securities Information Center (SIC) if criminal conduct suspected. The form can be submitted within forty-eight hours if no criminal conduct is suspected.
- 17F-2: Fingerprinting requirement for all employees

~ Exhibit F ~

Types of Asset-backed Securities

- Credit cards
- Auto loans
- Home equity loans
- Student loans
- Manufactured housing
- Small business loans
- Franchise loans
- Equipment leases
- Boat loans
- Trade receivables
- Healthcare receivables
- Insurance premiums
- Future flow receivables (e.g., James Brown royalties; David Bowie royalties)
- Taxi medallions
- Tax lien receivables
- Annuity contracts
- 12b-1 fees
- Nonperforming credit cards
- Computer leases
- CLOs
- CBOs
- CDOs

EXHIBIT G
TYPICAL ASSET-BACKED
BOND ISSUE

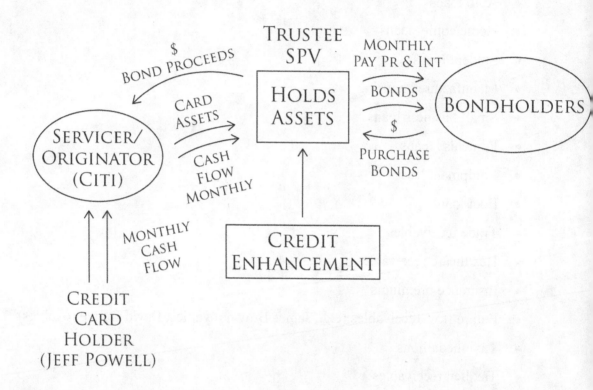

CPSIA information can be obtained
at www.ICGtesting.com
Printed in the USA
FSHW021729101219
64691FS